Orlando

S U N S H I N E   S O N A T A

URBAN
TAPESTRY
SERIES
TOWERY
PUBLISHING, INC.

Orlando

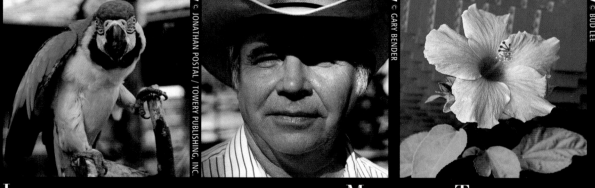

INTRODUCTION BY MIKE THOMAS

SUNSHINE SONATA

ART DIRECTION BY ENRIQUE ESPINOSA

© BUD LEE

Table of Contents

I AM NOT FROM DISNEY WORLD.

BY MIKE THOMAS

NOR AM I FROM SEAWORLD, PAINT BALL WORLD, BELZ FACTORY OUTLET MALL WORLD, OR HUBCAP WORLD.

I AM FROM REAL CITY WORLD, ALSO KNOWN AS ORLANDO, A PLACE WHERE PEOPLE DON'T WEAR BERMUDA SHORTS WITH DARK SOCKS AND SNEAKERS.

ORLANDO IS FAR REMOVED FROM THE FANTASY WORLDS THAT HAVE PUT US ON THE INTERNATIONAL MAP.

ON A GOOD DAY, I DON'T GET WITHIN 20 MILES OF A SIX-FOOT MOUSE.

OR, AS WE CALL HIM, THE MOUSE. ☞

Friends and relatives sometimes tell me, "It must be great to live in the vacation capital of the world."

They think that every weekend we locals pile in the minivan, put on our happy faces, and head off for a fun-filled day with Mickey, King Kong, and Shamu.

Here is what we actually do on weekends. We sleep in. We go to the mall. We yell at Little League umpires. We honk our horns at tourists who slow down to gawk at Universal Studios' giant ET billboard on Interstate 4. And most of all, we endlessly mow the grass and trim the shrubs because vegetation in Florida grows nonstop except for a three-day period in February.

By the way, our hedges are not shaped like topiary animals.

Here in our real city, we have real crime and real traffic jams, and we even get an occasional whiff of real air pollution.

This is all because we are growing real fast.

In addition to those common urban woes, we also have real lakes in our real neighborhoods, real oak trees in front of our houses, and real red bricks on many of our streets.

The thing we have the most of is change. A building from the 1940s is historic and one from the 1920s qualifies for pyramid status. We change so fast that residents who moved here last year talk about the good old days.

What changes most is the people. Orlando is the easy-come, easy-go city.

Every week, about 1,000 new residents move into the region. To make room for them, about 900 leave. On top of that, some 820,000 tourists show up during that same week. Sometimes I feel like I'm living in the world's biggest train station.

So we have somewhat of an identity crisis. We don't have any real institutions such as a Wrigley Field. We don't have a regional food like Philly's cheese steaks or New York's bagels. We don't have a song like San ☛

Francisco does. We're in the South, but we're not really The South. There are more New Jersey accents here than southern accents. We have a college, the University of Central Florida, but its football team can't compete in popularity with state powerhouses like Florida State, the University of Florida, and the University of Miami. We have a love-hate relationship with our tourists. We love their money, but it also has turned us into a service-oriented economy dangerously dependent on it.

Orlando is a confused adolescent on the verge of puberty. It is trying to mature from tourism boomtown to established city. We have cultural diversity with growing numbers of Latinos and Asians, and now we would like more culture and more economic diversity.

If we succeed, then this truly will be a place that offers the best of both worlds.

The hub of Central Florida is Orange County. The word Orange is a bit misleading: You'd have better luck finding a snowstorm around here than an orange grove.

Urban encroachment uprooted the groves long ago. Most of the remaining trees can be found in backyards. That's where mine is. I begin every winter morning by walking out to my tree, usually in bare feet, and snatching a dozen oranges to make fresh juice.

Try doing that in Ohio.

The demise of citrus in the area is part of the general demise of agriculture. Just as much of the Midwest has lost its bedrock base of manufacturing and mining, we have lost the citrus, vegetable, and cattle farms that got us started back in the 1800s. Our "cracker" cowboys—so called because of the crack of their whips—may not have been as famous as their western counterparts, but they worked vast ranches and drove herds of cattle through Florida's treacherous swamps. The big difference between them and their western counterparts was that they were too busy shooting water moccasins and alligators to become folklore by shooting each other.

Farmers used the area's plentiful water supply to grow acres of citrus trees. Vegetable fields were tilled in the rich, mucky soil underlying the ☞

swamps. Back then, not many people came here for a vacation. It was miserably hot and humid. The land was wet and flood prone. There were at least two dozen mosquitoes per square inch of skin. And, of course, there was the fear of Indians.

And if all that wasn't bad enough, there was no ocean—and no ocean breeze—in landlocked Orlando. What was the point of going to Florida if you couldn't surf?

Four events put Orlando on the map.

The invention of DDT helped control the mosquitoes. Unfortunately, it also helped control the bald eagles and pelicans.

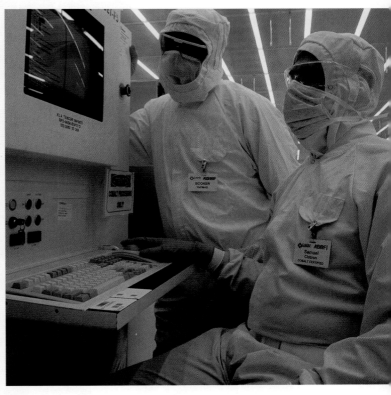

The invention of air-conditioning helped control the heat and humidity.

The third event was the launch of *Sputnik*, which led to the development of Cape Canaveral in neighboring Brevard County. This is where men took off for the moon as they now take off for the space station. In Orlando, you can walk out in your front yard to watch the shuttle going up. More than once, I've been jolted from my bed by a sonic boom from a shuttle coming back down. The space center attracted high-tech industries like the Martin Company, which eventually became Lockheed Martin. In time, Orlando developed an economy based on old-world agriculture and cutting-edge aerospace technology.

The fourth event occurred in the 1960s when a man from California began looking for the right location to expand his empire. He needed several things. He needed lots and lots of cheap land. He needed a highway to bring people to his land. He needed politicians who would give him free rein. He found it all in the backwoods and swamps of Central Florida, about 20 miles to the south and west of Orlando, a place where the deer, cattle, and alligators roamed.

The man sent his emissaries to begin secretly buying land from the old cattle barons. By the time he was done, he had purchased 27,000 acres in ☛

50 discreet sales. He had paid $180 an acre. Rumors were rampant of a huge, new industry moving to town.

On October 21, 1965, the *Orlando Sentinel* broke the story with this headline: "Is Our 'Mystery Industry' Disney?"

And yes, the mystery man was Walt Disney.

Almost immediately, the gold rush began. Between 1960 and 1980, Orange County's population grew by 80 percent. Developers and tourism businesses bought up huge chunks of neighboring Osceola County, a quiet rural place that had held on to its cattle ranching roots. The main thoroughfare through the county, U.S. Highway 192, eventually was lined with endless rows of motels, tourist shops, and huge, blinking marquees advertising everything from LIVE SHARKS INSIDE!!! to 3 MICKEY T-SHIRTS $9.99!!!

Further north, Orange County developed its own tourism corridor on International Drive, which is anchored by the Orange County Convention Center. The complex covers 4 million square feet, and has an exhibition center so big you could display the Sears Tower if you could lie it on its side and get it through the doors. Plans are under way to add another million square feet of exhibition space.

The convention center brings in almost 1 million visitors every year, arriving with their coveted expense accounts.

Once a sideshow to Disney, the International Drive area has become a competitor. The two are always trying to outdo each other, adding new attractions, new twists, new discounts for locals. Between the two areas, there are seven major theme parks—the Magic Kingdom, Disney/MGM Studios, Epcot, the Animal Kingdom, SeaWorld, Universal Studios, and Islands of Adventure. There also are four water parks, a dozen lesser attractions, an endless number of chic shopping districts, more outlet malls than there are hot days in summer, three major nighttime venues, and, lest I forget, one Cirque du Soleil. ☛

And beyond these two locations, you can find roadside attractions such as the ever popular Gatorland Zoo with its famous jumping alligators. Ecotourism is growing, with visitors buying tickets for adventures such as airboat tours on the St. Johns River, where, thankfully, the alligators don't jump. The bass are so big in Lake Tohopekaliga and Lake Kissimmee that you don't have to lie about them. A local guide from Kissimmee will be happy to take you out in search of some trophies.

But all this tourism growth has its downside. A comprehensive assessment of life in Orange County by community leaders came out in 2000. In a nutshell, it said: Too much Mouse. Not enough Bill Gates.

Despite efforts to diversify the economy, we are dependent on tourism. Service jobs now make up almost half the total employment in Orange County. Two of the four largest employers in Central Florida are Disney and Universal, with a combined full- and part-time workforce of about 67,000 employees. The poverty rate is high, urban sprawl is a continuing problem, and the roads are becoming increasingly clogged. The infrastructure, in short, just hasn't been able to keep pace with the growth in relatively low-paying service sector jobs.

And if all that isn't bad enough, in a great psychological blow to our region, we lost Shaq to the Los Angeles Lakers. But you know what? We got Grant Hill and Tracy McGrady, and once again are ready to take on the NBA.

While our other problems may not be so easily solved, we are headed in the right direction.

As of late, downtown Orlando was the place to go if you wanted a tattoo or, perhaps, a pierced navel.

Downtown once bustled with thousands of tourists, attracted to an entertainment district known as Church Street Station. This fed customers to a variety of nearby clubs and restaurants. Downtown also became a hotbed of late-night partying, with teens flocking in on weekends for rave dances. ☛

I would ride my bike down Orange Avenue early Sunday and watch kids stumbling out of the clubs like vampires trying to beat the sunrise home.

But competing nighttime venues at the theme parks stole the tourists, and a crackdown on rave clubs got rid of the kids.

Now, downtown is poised for its next metamorphosis.

Three new office towers joined the Orlando skyline in 2000, adding about 1 million square feet of space. Plans are on the board for five more towers. New hotels have gone up, including a Courtyard by Marriott, an Embassy Suites, and a 14-story hotel called the Westin Grand Bohemian.

These additions follow a revival in downtown residential neighborhoods that has been ongoing for several years. New residents have found beauty in old homes, restoring them to their 1940s glory. These homes sit on brick streets shaded by towering oak trees. Values have skyrocketed. Once neglected and decaying, the Thornton Park neighborhood has become the trendiest in Orlando. Nearby College Park, with its small bungalows and sense of community, has been a hot commodity on the real estate market for 20 years.

People want to be downtown. About 1,000 upscale apartments are rising to accommodate the demand. It's this influx of residential development that is spurring plans for a major overhaul of downtown's nightlife. There now is enough discretionary income surrounding downtown to attract more sophisticated restaurants, retail, and entertainment.

Plans include a small convention center, a theater district, a performing arts center, a shopping district, a multiscreen movie complex, and a new arena for the Orlando Magic. The price tag for all this is in the $1 billion range.

The forecast among the experts is that Orlando soon will have the hottest downtown in Florida, bolstered by a strong business base during the day, plenty of amenities for evenings and weekends, and surrounding neighborhoods that are established and growing in value. ☛

A few miles away, Orlando is about to undergo more major change. When the military began closing bases several years ago, one of the casualties was the Orlando Naval Training Center. This opened up a huge chunk of land for development near the center of the city. Plans call for putting some 1,900 homes and condominiums, 1,300 apartments, 350,000 square feet of shops, and 215 acres of parks on the 1,100-acre site.

To the north, the cities of Winter Park and Maitland are determined to maintain their neighborly atmosphere in the midst of the booming growth around them.

Winter Park is best known for its chic shops on Park Avenue and its quiet neighborhoods nestled amid a chain of lakes where the area's most expensive real estate can be found. Maitland is a divided city. On one side are its quiet neighborhoods, teeming with children. It's a place for those who want a family atmosphere, as well as a short commute to Orlando. But it also is home to the bustling Maitland Business Center, a complex that rivals downtown Orlando. The Orlando Magic recently moved its headquarters there, along with an upscale health club in a complex called RDV Sports.

These are the core cities of Central Florida, and it is around them that growth is exploding. New subdivisions sprout like kudzu in surrounding Seminole, Lake, and Osceola counties. Escalating prices near Orlando are pushing residents farther and farther out, bargain shopping for homes that will give them twice the square footage for the buck.

Area politicians have been dealing with growth management, although not very successfully, since Disney arrived. On one side are powerful developers and builders, pushing for ever more growth, and on the other are proponents of the environment and quality of life, who believe we are growing too fast.

But we have done some things right. Various government programs have bought up thousands of acres of land, preserving beautiful rivers such as the Wekiwa and the Econ, and ensuring great swaths of greenspace for ☛

the next generation. We are building a network of bike trails throughout Central Florida. We have almost finished with an expressway that circles the region, although many complain about the tolls.

We have a cultural arts park with a science center, two art museums, and a theater complex.

A new regional history center opened in September, part of the newly diverse downtown. The annual Orlando International Fringe Festival attracts actors from Europe and Canada, and brings thousands to downtown for theatrical productions.

Most important, however, we are beginning to diversify the economy. Central Florida now has a $10 billion, high-tech industry. We have almost 4,800 companies in defense, aerospace, Internet, E-commerce, wireless communications, simulators, lasers, and microchips. Orlando's problem, however, is people still think of it more as The Mouse town than as a high-tech town.

To help change this perception, we are about to spend $17.5 million on an image makeover. Most of the money will come from private companies such as SunBank and Lockheed Martin. The idea is to market the area and recruit more companies, with the eventual goal being to bring in approximately 18,000 jobs with some $1.35 billion in payroll.

Orlando already has the name recognition. And once the downtown revival gets under way, we'll have the types of amenities that the sophisticated workforce in the new economy demands. All we need to do is tweak how the eyes of the world perceive us, and this should become one of the hottest cities in America.

And then, there will be no shortage of pride when we say that we are from the real and kicking city of Orlando. ✳

THOROUGHLY MODERN oasis, Orlando offers all the opportunities and activity of any sizable metropolis. The city's urban skyline blends with the area's lush natural environment, lending Orlando a personality all its own.

O R L A N D O

THE YEAR 1992 WAS A MEMOR-
able one for Orlando politics.
The city elected its first
female mayor, Glenda E. Hood
(LEFT), who was reelected in 1996
and 2000. That same year, Orlando
also opened its new City Hall
(OPPOSITE), a neo-classical building
featuring a 120-foot copper dome
and two art galleries, as well as
commercial and municipal offices.

CENTRAL FLORIDA IS HOME TO more than 1,200 named lakes, many of them within Orlando's city limits. With Centennial Fountain at its center, Lake Eola (OPPOSITE AND PAGES 30 AND 31) shimmers in the heart of downtown, encouraging families, couples, and workers from the nearby business district to enjoy a moment in the sun.

W ATERFOWL BOTH LIVE AND inanimate flock to Lake Eola. While swans float across the gentle waves and waddle around on shore, paddleboats shaped like the signature aquatic bird carry sightseers around the lake on scenic tours.

36

W ITH MANY VERDANT PARKS, historic fountains, and tree-lined avenues, Orlando and its surrounds are a walker's paradise (PAGES 34-37). The city's sidewalks bustle with people, whether they're shopping, seeing the sights, or simply enjoying one of the area's famously sunny days.

Not merely a tourism capital, Orlando also serves as a hub for government in Central Florida. Built in 1995, the 23-story Orange County Courthouse (ABOVE) on North Orange Avenue houses the Ninth Judicial Circuit Court of Florida. Nearby City Hall (OPPOSITE) oversees the maintenance and management of the bustling metropolis (PAGES 40 AND 41).

STREET SMARTS: SINCE ITS official founding in the mid-1800s, Orlando has enjoyed more than a century and a half of progress and expansion. Long the center of civic and commercial activity, the downtown area is experiencing a renaissance that is restoring its previous grandeur.

ENTRAL FLORIDA'S RICH SOIL, temperate climate, and ample sunshine make the region perfect for growing citrus fruits and vegetables, and for decades, Orlando relied on agriculture to cultivate its economy. While tourism has supplanted farming as the area's primary source of income, Orange County still maintains nearly 1 million citrus trees—covering some 9,000 acres—which help Florida provide approximately 25 percent of the world's citrus crop.

ORLANDO

I N ADDITION TO CITRUS FRUITS, Orange County's more than 800 farms produce a cornucopia of other crops, including strawberries, watermelons, green peppers, and sugar cane.

ORLANDO

I F YOU MISS THE FARMER'S Market—held each Saturday on West Church Street—you'll be out of order and in a pickle. Displayed at the market and throughout the region, Florida's produce—along with the accompanying packaging and advertisements—add color to an already vibrant landscape (PAGES 50-55).

ORLANDO

ALTHOUGH THEY'RE USUALLY about the size of a baseball, oranges have an enormous sphere of influence in Central Florida, reflected at the city's many theme parks. Shaped like its namesake merchandise, Orange World (OPPOSITE TOP) in Kissimmee sells all things citrus related from its popular half-dome building.

ORLANDO

E VEN AFTER THE SUN'S GONE down, the Globe in Heritage Park is still serving breakfast sunny-side up. The 24-hour café, which moved to its current location in 2000, offers the morning meal at any hour, along with a good cuppa joe and a hip, spacious atmosphere perfect for perusing the paper.

ORLANDO

FINE EATERIES LIKE THE HARD Rock Café and Carlos 'n Charlie's dot the avenues throughout Orlando, serving up menus as diverse as the city's population. Cooking Tex-Mex fare with true flair, local favorite Amigo's (LEFT) began as a single restaurant in 1989 and has grown into a successful regional chain.

IN THE SHADOW OF THE SUNTRUST Center, Church Street Station (BOTTOM) is Orlando's hot spot for nightlife, and features a number of bustling restaurants and bars, including the Irish-themed Mulvaney's (OPPOSITE). On nearby Orange Avenue, One Eyed Jack's serves up hot—as in spicy—entrees and draws cold beer for a slew of patrons.

NO 1950S RETRO DINER IS complete without burgers, fries, shakes, and a lot of neon lights for atmosphere. Supplying those in full measure are Mel's Drive-In (TOP), located at Universal Studios, and—for those who don't want to brave the theme-park crowds—the Cadillac Diner (OPPOSITE), situated in the Old Town district of Kissimmee.

Taking advantage of Orlando's proximity to the ocean, most upscale restaurants fill their menus with fish, shrimp, mussels, and lobster, among other delicacies. Known for its extensive wine list and elegant atmosphere, Sergio's serves sophisticated Italian and seafood fare created by Executive Chef Fred Nater (LEFT).

SINGING FOR THEIR SUPPER: After hearing classical music performed by the Bach Festival Choir and Orchestra, conducted by John V. Sinclair (ABOVE), concertgoers can finish the evening with a meal of classic Italian cuisine at Christini's Ristorante Italiano, where Chris Christini (OPPOSITE) oversees all aspects of dining—from the food to the service to the welcoming atmosphere.

Take a bow: Beginning as a small chamber music group in 1991, the Orlando Philharmonic Orchestra today is one of Central Florida's premier cultural organizations, with more than 80 musicians performing some 95 shows each year. As music director since 1995, internationally renowned Hal France (LEFT) has conducted the group to its finest successes.

RLANDO'S VIBRANT ART SCENE produces an abundance of compelling works in various media. Rima Jabbar (TOP) renders figure studies in oil paintings, and elegant nudes sculpted by Helaine Schneider (OPPOSITE) grace public and private collections throughout the country. A former art instructor at Seminole Community College, local favorite Grady Kimsey (BOTTOM) reveals his quirky imagination in unique, whimsical sculptures.

SUNSHINE SONATA

HAS JUST
LEFT THE
BUILDING

VIVA ORLANDO! IN CENTRAL Florida, Elvis is still the King, inspiring several tributes by area artists. Each year, the Best Western Hotel becomes Heartbreak Hotel as hundreds of fans attend Elvis Fest, a celebration sponsored by the local Big-E fan club, the Elvis Presley Continentals.

ORLANDO'S MANY FLEA markets reel in shoppers looking for brightly painted, handmade crafts or old, often-kitschy-sometimes-classy relics of fashions past. If they don't get a nibble there, locals know that the Great American Trading Co. will hook them up. Operated by Ludi Long (OPPOSITE), the business provides one-of-a-kind items to collectors, decorators, restaurants, and motion picture productions.

Downtown Orlando radiates with rich colors, which have been intensified by the ongoing arts boom the city is experiencing. Several new galleries have opened to complement and compete with established public galleries like the Maitland Art Center (TOP), a mainstay since the late 1930s.

CENTRAL FLORIDA'S PERFORM-
ing arts organizations fill
a lot of audience seats
throughout the year. Both the
Mount Dora Theatre Company– under the leadership of Director
Terrance Shank (OPPOSITE)—and
the Mad Cow Theatre Company
(ABOVE) have garnered applause for
their adventurous productions.

ORLANDO'S MARK TWO DINner Theatre mixes fine dining with high drama, leaving its audiences hungry for more. Established in 1958, the Orlando Opera Company—now following the vision of Director Richard Swedberg (OPPOSITE)—presents popular operas along with lesser-known works at the Dr. Phillips Center for Performing Arts.

© JAMES LEMASS

© JONATHAN POSTAL / TOWERY PUBLISHING, INC.

KIDS AND ADULTS ALIKE CAN scare up a lot of good times at Orlando's theme parks. But the annual Shakespeare Festival, organized by the University of Central Florida, has made a tradition of tingling its audiences' spines with creepy productions like 2000's *The Woman in Black* (OPPOSITE).

ORLANDO

THERE GOOOZE THE NEIGH-borhood: Nickelodeon produces a slew of messy television game shows at Orlando's Universal Studios. An afternoon favorite among children, the interactive *Slimetime Live!* (ABOVE) douses its contestants in a spew of green slime, while *Figure It Out*, hosted by Olympic champion swimmer Summer Sanders (OPPO-SITE), showcases contestants' bizarre talents.

T HANKS IN PART TO A NUMBER of local production studios, Orlando has become a hot spot for teen talent like Phillip Van Dyke (ABOVE, FOREGROUND), star of Nickelodeon's *Noah Knows Best*. Lisa Maile Image, Modeling & Acting—under the direction of Lisa Maile herself (OPPOSITE, ON RIGHT)—helps its clients strike just the right pose—whether they're on the runway, in front of the camera, or delivering business presentations.

BOY BAND LAND: THE BIRTH-place of such teen sensa-tions as the Backstreet Boys and N'Sync—as well as up-and-comers like the Latin-flavored

C Note (ABOVE)—Orlando has become a mecca for the teen pop phenomenon. The man behind the music, former airline president

Lou Pearlman (OPPOSITE) created, produced, and marketed most of these groups from his local Trans Continental Studios.

ORLANDO

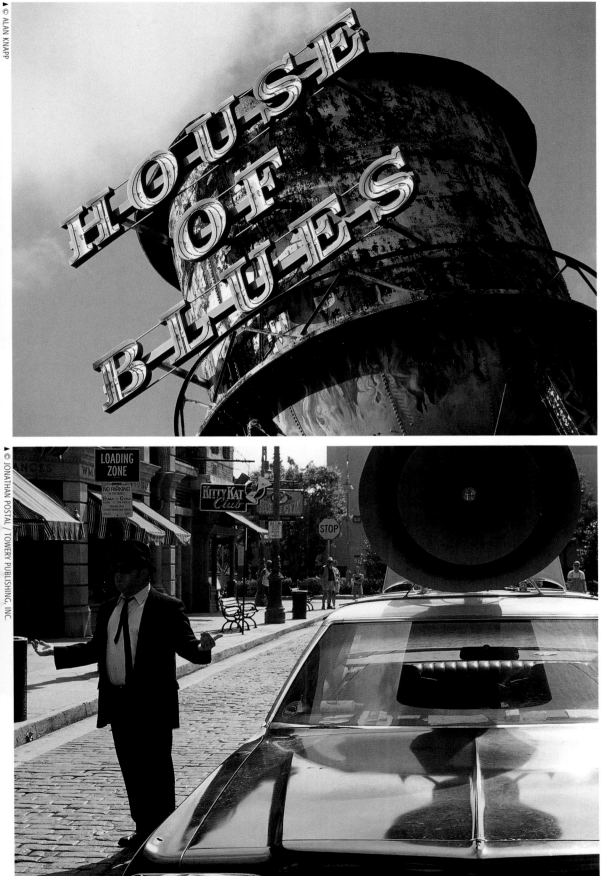

Sitting in the heart of Disney territory, the House of Blues (top) hosts national acts as well as a weekly Orlando Rocks! night, which gives local artists a chance to turn up the stage. Sam Rivers (opposite) certainly has sax appeal. A veteran jazz musician, he plays several shows around town and across the country. With mikes in hand, both Michael Andrews (page 98) and Scott Anez (page 99) charm their audiences, albeit in completely different realms: Andrews fronts the local retro group Svingerhead, while Anez hosts AM 580 WDBO's *Inside Magic* basketball talk show.

ORLANDO

H OP ON THE BUS, GUS: ORLANdo residents get around downtown in style aboard the brightly painted Lymmo shuttles. Such innovative programs not only have decreased traffic congestion and air pollution in the city, but also have earned Orlando's transit agency, Lynx, a ranking as one of the best in the country, according to the American Public Transit Authority.

As Central Florida's high-profile theme parks grow in number, so do the totals for incoming tourists. Each year, more than 40 million visitors purchase tickets to Disney World, Universal Studios, Splendid China, and Epcot Center, among many others.

DON'T SKIRT THE ISSUE: In 1880, South Florida Railroad brought the first train to Orlando, and during the decade that followed, the city's population more than doubled. Today, with many residents coming and going, trains remain a popular travel option, hauling countless carloads of passengers each year. The Orlando Train Station (PAGES 108 AND 109), built in 1926, has gained landmark status and was renovated in 1990.

Each year, millions of moms and dads bring the kids to Orlando on vacations, but the area's emphasis on family extends beyond its theme parks and attractions. Ever since the first settlers arrived more than 150 years ago, Orlando has cherished its strong ties between kith and kin.

ORLANDO

OLDING TIGHTLY TO ITS heritage, Central Florida's African-American population honors its heroes in numerous ways. Thousands gather each year to celebrate Martin Luther King Jr. Day, while nearby Eatonville—the oldest incorporated black community in the United States—honors one of the country's finest writers with the Zora Neale Hurston National Museum of Fine Arts, which operates under Executive Director N.Y. Nathiri (OPPOSITE).

RED, WHITE, AND BLUE ABOUND throughout Central Florida, evidence of the population's strong political fervor. While some citizens divide their loyalties along party lines—as seen immediately following the 2000 presidential election—others opt for more individual forms of patriotic expression.

ORLANDO

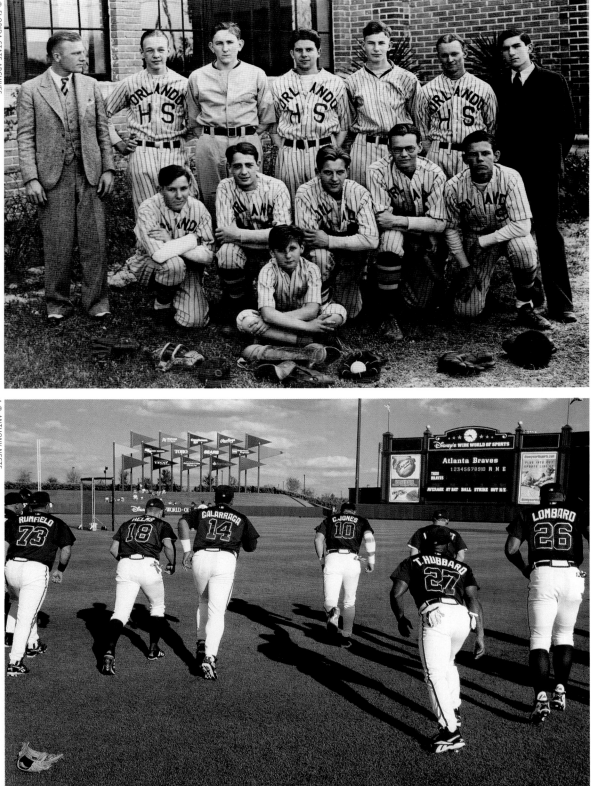

BASEBALL HAS LONG BEEN AN important part of life in Central Florida, from the early days before professional teams took the field to today's preseason Grapefruit League. Orlando greets the Atlanta Braves (BOTTOM)—who hold their spring training at Disney's Wide World of Sports Baseball Stadium—with several weeks of sunny weather and packs of cheering fans. Professional basketball continues to score its own home runs—or slam dunks, as the case may be—with local crowds as well. The WNBA's Orlando Miracle, featuring 2001 All-Star Guard Nykesha Sales (OPPOSITE), averaged more than 7,000 fans per game in 2000.

ORLANDO

S EATING SOME 70,000 FANS, the Florida Citrus Bowl, constructed in 1936, is a locus for sports in the region. In addition to football events— including University of Central Florida Knights games—the stadium has also hosted World Cup and Olympic soccer matches.

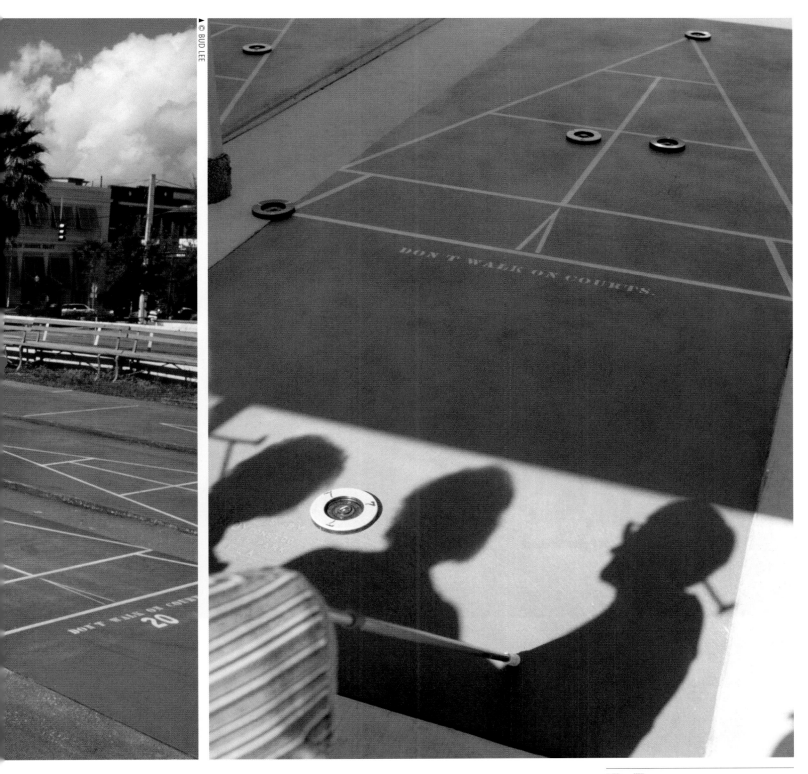

DON'T WALK ON COURTS.

N OT CONTENT TO JUST LET THE days glide by, many area residents—regardless of age—take advantage of Orlando's sunny afternoons by cuing up a game of shuffleboard.

BUILDING THE PERFECT BODY requires a lot of sweat and strain, not to mention quite a few visits to local fitness centers. At the Orange Avenue Gym—which opened in 1950 and is Orlando's oldest health club—locals pump old-fashioned barbells and lift weights in search of a physique that never goes out of style.

ORLANDO

PROVING THEIR PEDAL METTLE: Thanks to perfect weather and safe streets, cycling remains a popular pastime throughout Central Florida. Each fall, the Mount Dora Bicycle Festival (TOP)—the largest such gathering in the state—steers some 1,300 cyclists to the small town just north of Orlando, where they traverse the scenic trails around Lake County and compete in races like Homer's Doughnut Run. The event shifts the local economy into high gear, bringing in more than $500,000 and booking up local inns and bed-and-breakfasts.

RACING FANS WILL FIND thrills both big and small in the Orlando area. Race Rock restaurant (ABOVE) exhibits a large collection of motor sports memorabilia, as well as a menu featuring fast food. Locals cheer for NASCAR racer Keith Roggen (OPPOSITE), a Winter Haven native whose career has been on fire since he was named Ledger Driver of the Year in 2000.

THE BEAT GOES ON: During the late 1950s, when *On the Road* inspired readers to hit the highways, its author, Jack Kerouac, lived with his mother in a small house on Clouser Street in Orlando's College Park district. Here, in just 11 days, he wrote his follow-up book, *The Dharma Bums*. To commemorate his literary legacy as a leader of the Beat Generation, the Kerouac Project of Orlando sponsors writers in residence—like poet Emily Sayers (LEFT)—who live in the house rent-free and devote their time to creating masterpieces of their own.

W ITH VERY DIFFERENT approaches to journalism, Jeff Truesdell (ABOVE) and Kathleen M. Waltz (OPPOSITE) make sure the local beat is well covered. Truesdell helms the city's alternative newspaper, the *Orlando Weekly*, which provides a thorough, often dissenting examination of regional goings-on. Since June 2000, Waltz has led the *Orlando Sentinel* in its mission to provide comprehensive world news with a strong local emphasis.

Having quietly acquired some 28,000 acres southwest of Orlando over several years, Walt Disney (OPPOSITE, ON LEFT)—the man who built a multimillion-dollar empire on creations such as Mickey Mouse—along with his brother Roy (OPPOSITE, ON RIGHT), put in motion what was to become Disney World. Opened in 1971—five years after Walt Disney died—the theme park attracted more than 10 million tourists during its first year of operation, not only making news but also forever changing the landscape of Orlando.

S ince its inception, Disney World has always looked to the future. Opened to great fanfare in 1982, Epcot (above)—whose name is an acronym of Experimental Prototype Community of Tomorrow—showcases the latest in science and technology, while Disney's Tomorrowland (opposite), which features the popular Space Mountain ride, offers a version of the future as it might have been seen during the 1940s and 1950s.

136

ROM Splendid China (TOP)
to Disney-MGM Studios
(OPPOSITE AND BOTTOM LEFT)
to the basketball-themed restaurant NBA City (BOTTOM RIGHT),
Orlando offers many attractions
on a grand scale.

ORLANDO

THERE'S A FUNGUS AMONG US: Orlando's warm, moist lawns present the perfect platform for the ubiquitous mushroom. Not confined to ground level, its familiar umbrella shape also works well in more practical settings.

MANY OF THE BUILDINGS along International Drive turn traditional architecture on its head. Topped with an inverted pyramid, Guinness World Records Experience (ABOVE) show-cases record-breaking accomplishments by people across the globe, while the interactive science exhibits at WonderWorks (OPPOSITE) capture the playful spirit of the site's upside-down exterior.

ORLANDO AT LARGE: DWARFING all visitors, gargantuan likenesses of children's toys act as eye-catching billboards for popular retail centers like FAO Schwarz (OPPOSITE).

ORLANDO

ORLANDO'S HOTELS AND THEME parks offer many ways to beat the heat on a warm afternoon. Guests at Disney's All Star Sports Hotel (ABOVE) can enjoy a dip in the pool or a sip from the towering Coca-Cola cup. Visitors to Seuss Landing (OPPOSITE) will find a bit of shade under The Cat in the Hat's hat.

© BUD LEE

IN ORLANDO, APPEARANCES CAN often be deceiving. What seems to be a deserted New York City street is actually Disney-MGM Studios' New York backlot street (OPPOSITE). In preparation for the real thing, Disney erected a residential facade (ABOVE) to herald the founding of Celebration, its 4,900-acre planned community in Osceola County. Today, Celebration contains top-notch retail, medical, and education facilities, as well as more than 1,000 homes—all of which are three-dimensional.

ORLANDO

OPENED IN 1993, THE 76-ACRE Florida Splendid China offers visitors a view of Chinese architecture, culture, and history in miniature. Along with models of ancient temples and landmarks, the park includes the popular Terra Cotta Warriors (BOTTOM), to-scale figurines of the more than 8,000 statues unearthed in 1974 near the city of Xi'an.

Y OU'VE GOT TO HAND IT TO Splendid China: The park's intricate, colorful statues and dragons—including the Guanyin 1,000 Hands and Eyes Buddha (TOP)—capture visitors' imaginations. The country's culture is also on display at Epcot's China World Showcase, which features traditional dances and performances in ornate buildings like the Hall of Prayer for Good Harvest (OPPOSITE).

ORLANDO

OFFERING AN EXTENSIVE VIEW of the world, Orlando has erected myriad replicas of historic landmarks from around the globe, including the streets of Germany (ABOVE) and the Doge's Palace in Venice (OPPOSITE RIGHT)—both at Epcot—as well as Splendid China's half-mile replica of the Great Wall (OPPOSITE LEFT). Compared to the quaint woods around the region, the fantastic forests at Seuss Landing are positively otherworldly (PAGES 154 AND 155).

Dense with lush foliage and scenic swamps, Central Florida's numerous state parks have been attracting vacationing families long before the theme parks came to town. Today, they continue to entice boatloads of visitors looking for picturesque spots for hiking, fishing, camping, and just lounging around.

ROMANCE BLOOMS IN ORLANDO, where lovers reveal their affection with stolen kisses. For a more permanent show of amour, many sweethearts erect their own small monuments in Florida's green fields, while others make their mark directly on nature.

W ITH AN ECSTATIC KISS, a comfortable embrace, or an intimate hand in hand, couples in every stage of their relationships find Central Florida a perfect backdrop for togetherness.

Orlando's own Eden, the Harry P. Leu Gardens cover more than 50 acres near Lake Rowena with myriad flowers and plants, as well as a network of scenic trails. Donated to the city by local businessman Leu and his wife, the popular gardens— overseen by Executive Director Robert E. Bowden (OPPOSITE)— boast one of the largest rose conservatories in the Southeast. In addition, the 1906 Leu House Museum (ABOVE) contains exhibits on life at the turn of the century.

ORLANDO

I T'S A JUNGLE OUT THERE: At Silver Springs (ABOVE), glass-bottom boats ferry visitors along lush riverways to view Florida's above- and underwater wildlife. Diners in the Rainforest Café (OPPOSITE), located at Disney's Animal Kingdom, can learn about endangered ecosystems and walk through aquariums filled with exotic fish while eating a bowl of the restaurant's famous Rasta Pasta.

ORLANDO RARELY GETS A white Christmas, but its holidays are still very colorful, thanks in part to Cypress Gardens' annual Gardens of Light show. Truly brightening the season, more than 5 million lights depicting holiday and fairy-tale scenes bring in thousands of visitors during the winter season.

168

Cypress Gardens, which opened in January 1936, is the area's oldest attraction and remains a popular draw for visitors looking for an exotic get-away. The resort features an extensive botanical garden with some 8,000 plants from more than 75 countries, plus a stretch of sandy beach and a world-famous aquatic sports show that has earned it the nickname Water Ski Capital of the World.

THE EYES HAVE IT: CENTRAL Florida's wildlife includes an ark's worth of different creatures inhabiting the woods and wetlands throughout the region—as well as unlikely places around town (PAGES 170-173).

CENTRAL FLORIDA'S FLORA and fauna share a number of similarities. With their hot-pink feathers and down-turned bills, the flamingos at SeaWorld have become popular crowd-pleasers. The graceful petals and exotic colors of birds-of-paradise enliven gardens and greenhouses throughout Orlando.

DOGGONE IT: WHETHER AS family mascot, artistic motif, or slipper fetcher, man's best friend has found a good home in Orlando.

ORLANDO

© IAN WILSON JORDAN / GEOIMAGERY

© BEN VAN HOOK

© JONATHAN POSTAL / TOWERY PUBLISHING, INC.

Disney's 500-acre Animal Kingdom (TOP AND BOTTOM LEFT) showcases more than 1,000 animals from all over the world, while Discovery Cove (OPPOSITE) gives curious kids an up-close look at dolphins, fish, tropical birds, and creatures like Lucky the two-toed sloth. Shoppers at Pointe Orlando (BOTTOM RIGHT), a retail and entertainment complex, may be surprised to see brightly plumaged parrots parading through the courtyards.

SUNSHINE SONATA

179

L OOKING FOR A WHALE OF A good time? At SeaWorld, the killer whales at Shamu Stadium (ABOVE) and the dolphins in the Key West at SeaWorld attrac- tion (OPPOSITE) perform for schools of visitors several times a day. Underwater windows allow views of the aquatic mammals as they rest up for the next big show.

Tourists can enjoy a peaceful afternoon at Universal Studios, dining on seafood at Lombard's Landing (OPPOSITE) or just watching the seagulls. Each evening, the cove comes alive for the Dynamite Nights Stuntacular revue, featuring death-defying, 60-foot jumps into the water.

IN ORLANDO, ALLIGATORS ARE A main attraction for both tourists and scientists. The popular Gatorland not only allows visitors to feed the thousands of reptiles in its main pit (LEFT), but also conducts aquacultural research with the University of Florida. At Epcot, the Land pavilion (OPPOSITE) educates guests on Florida's natural resources, as well as on the scientific advantages of alligator farming.

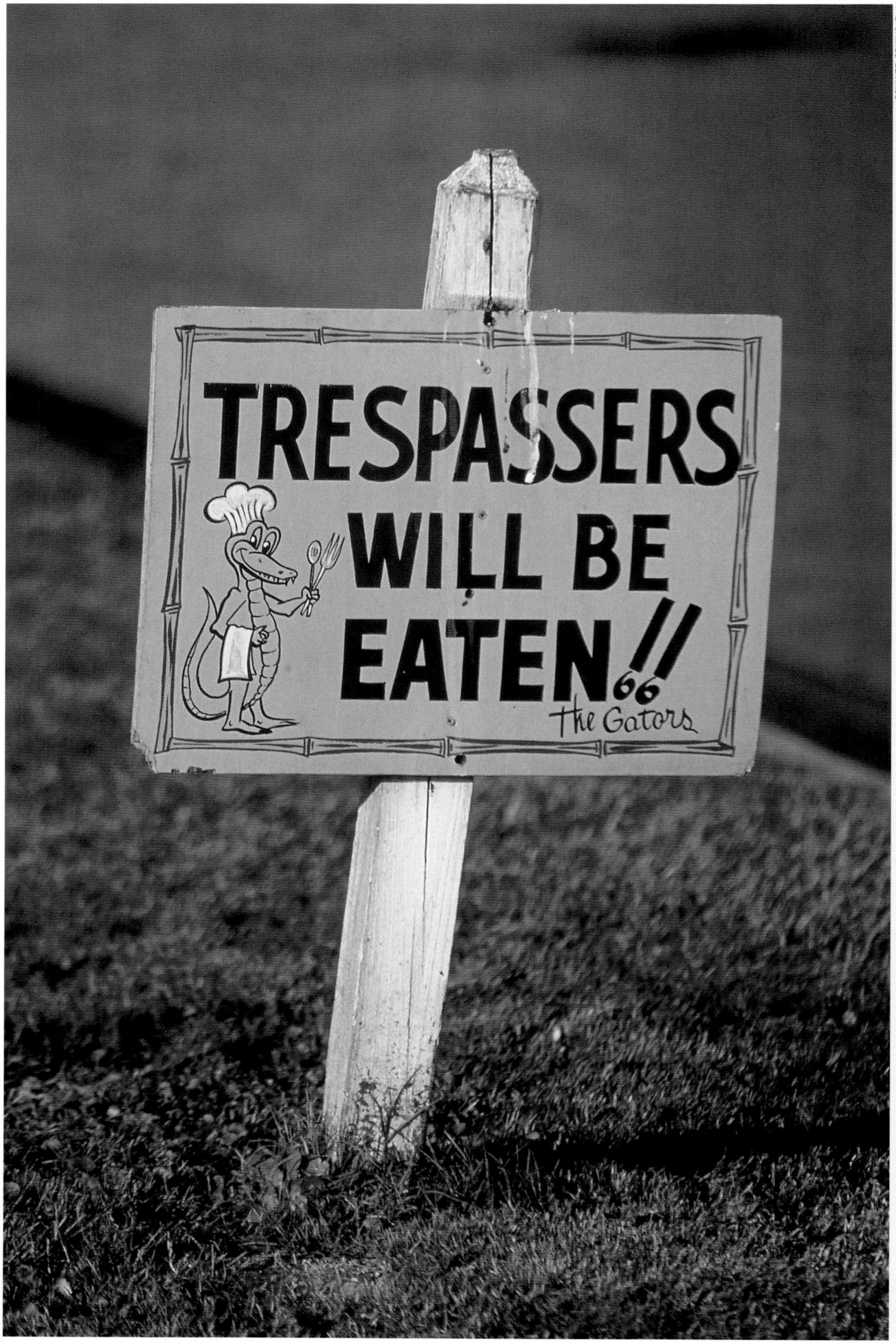
TRESPASSERS
WILL BE
EATEN!!
The Gators

STEERING CLEAR OF ALLIGATORS is always a good safety precaution, but it's especially wise in Orlando, where the beasts inhabit lakes, ponds, and, occasionally, swimming pools. The 20-foot jaw at Gatorland (BOTTOM) isn't threatening, but inviting: Millions of tourists have passed through the famous entrance since it first bared its teeth in 1962.

OPEN UP AND SAY AHHH: Many people hear about some of Orlando's best activities—including the LEGO Imagination Center (TOP RIGHT), the Jungleland Zoo (BOTTOM RIGHT), and the Orlando Science Center (OPPOSITE)—not from advertisements or tour guides, but through word of mouth.

REALIZING THAT CENTRAL Florida's natural resources are truly invaluable, many area activists are taking a stand against pollution and overdevelopment. President of Friends of Lake Apopka Jim Thomas (OPPOSITE) has spearheaded a campaign to revitalize the lake—once a popular resort site located near Winter Haven—as a sports-fishing haven.

CENTRAL FLORIDA'S LAKES and ponds teem with large schools of bass, which lure avid fisherman to angle for a good spot on shore and cast a reel at day's first light.

ORLANDO

ATER, WATER EVERYWHERE: Whether for active sports like kayaking and windsurfing or for a lazy day spent floating on an inner tube, Central Florida's vast collection of crystal-blue lakes and waterways offers locals many opportunities to enjoy the great outdoors.

F OR BETTER OR FOR WORSE, bustling growth and rapid development have profoundly altered the topography of Central Florida. Before Walt Disney bought the land around Bay Lake, it was wet with marshes and swamps (OPPOSITE). Today, those once-empty acres are the site of Disney's Magic Kingdom and Seven Seas Lagoon (ABOVE).

THRILL SEEKERS MAKE A BIG splash at Wet 'n Wild (TOP AND BOTTOM), Orlando's largest and most popular water park. At Disney's Fantasyland, visitors stay on dry land but get to meet many creatures of the deep, including King Triton (OPPOSITE) from *The Little Mermaid*.

ORLANDO'S PERPETUALLY sunny weather and cool, clear water tempt some locals to shed both their clothes and their responsibilities in order to enjoy a quick dip in the pool.

THE GULLS KNOW WHERE the buoys are: Flocks of seagulls, terns, and other aquatic fowl are common sights above many of Central Florida's beaches, as the birds scavenge for insects, mollusks, and small crustaceans in the shallow waters.

WHILE MANY LOCALS CHOOSE to catch some rays, others prefer to grab a board and catch a wave. Hoping to ride the crests coming in from the Atlantic Ocean, surfers from around the region flock to Florida's east-coast beaches, including Vero Beach and Canaveral Beach—both only a short drive from Orlando.

S WIMSUIT FASHIONS MAY HAVE changed in the last century, but Central Florida's pristine beaches and sun-drenched days have been consistently attracting vacationers to the region since the 1880s. Today, many people still find the area to be a quiet, peaceful escape from the daily grind (PAGES 210-213).

O R L A N D O

YOU NEVER KNOW WHAT YOU'LL find in the sand, but be careful: Not all buried treasure is real. At DinoLand USA in Disney's Animal Kingdom, children can unearth a giant mammoth skeleton at the Boneyard (ABOVE). Near the pier at Cocoa Beach, a 10-foot tiki head (OPPOSITE) stands not as a reminder of an ancient civilization, but as an advertisement for the Mai Tiki Gallery, which sells tiki poles and masks.

Don't Be Afraid OF TOMORROW
God IS ALREADY THERE
HE IS THE SAME TODAY & TOMORROW

ne,
ou.

A NYONE LOOKING FOR A SIGN from above might just find it in Orlando. The city is blessed with an active religious community, whose spiritual com- mitment manifests itself in many churches and synagogues, as well as a theme park, the Holy Land Experience, which opened in 2001.

H OLDING THEIR BELIEFS VERY dear, Father Paul Henry (LEFT) at St. John Vianney Catholic Church and Rabbi Rick Sherwin (OPPOSITE) at Temple Israel offer spiritual guidance to their parishioners and congregants.

OUT OF THE BLUE: ORLANDO'S faithful take their individual missions very seriously. Orange County Sheriff's Department chaplain Ken Odom (LEFT) teaches Bible classes to inmates at the Orange County Jail. Dr. Daniel J. Tyler (OPPOSITE), pastor of the New Vision Community Church in Zellwood, also serves as the president of the International Seminary, an interdenominational Bible college in Plymouth.

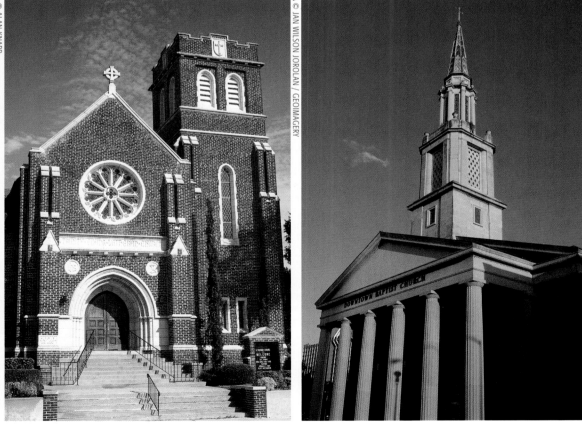

CENTRAL FLORIDA'S RELIGIOUS architecture proves as varied as the beliefs of its different congregations. Throughout the region, many houses of worship—including St. Luke's Episcopal Church (TOP), Trinity Evangelical Lutheran Church (BOTTOM LEFT), Downtown Baptist Church (BOTTOM RIGHT), and Catholic Church of Saint Luke (OPPOSITE)—offer a spectrum of denominations and building styles.

Schools of design: Built in 1920, the Delaney School (ABOVE) is one of the oldest public education buildings in the city; today, it houses the Beardall Senior Center. One of Orlando's finest examples of Mediterranean Revival architecture, the Cherokee School (OPPOSITE), erected in 1926, still holds classes for emotionally troubled and learning-disabled children in kindergarten through fifth grade.

HOME SWEET HOME: Decorative details on quaint houses add a little color to the residential comfort of Orlando's historic neighborhoods. Evidence of the city's preservation efforts, the Dr. Phillips House (TOP), built in 1893 in the Southern Victorian style, has been restored to its original lavishness. It is now home to a restaurant—Louis' Downtown—and a guest house.

MAINTAINING HIGH EDUCA-
tional standards and
boasting exacting aca-
demic programs, Orlando's colleges and universities—including
the University of Central Florida
(OPPOSITE, TOP LEFT), Valencia
Community College (OPPOSITE, TOP
RIGHT), the North Orlando Campus
of Florida Metropolitan University
(OPPOSITE, BOTTOM RIGHT), and
Rollins College (ABOVE AND OPPO-
SITE, BOTTOM LEFT)—help their
students to commence successful
professional careers.

HISTORY HAS BEEN MADE several times over at Cape Canaveral, just east of Orlando. In 1961, NASA launched the first American in space, Alan Shepard, aboard the Mercury-Redstone (OPPOSITE). Five years later, (ABOVE, FROM LEFT) David Randolph Scott and Neil Armstrong boarded the *Gemini 8* to perform the first space docking of two orbiting craft.

236

NAMED AFTER FORMER President John F. Kennedy, the Kennedy Space Center Visitor Complex (OPPOSITE) documents the history and technology of NASA's space program and offers tours around Cape Canaveral. Nearby, the Astronaut Hall of Fame displays artifacts and memorabilia from several space missions, and the adjacent Space Camp trains future astronauts with realistic simulations (BOTTOM).

ORLANDO

B **IS FOR BOMBER: FORMED IN** 1977, Valiant Air Command maintains a fleet of some 350 vintage aircrafts, many of which are on display at the War-bird Museum (ABOVE). Located in Titusville, the facility sponsors aviation exhibits as well as occasional air shows. In Polk City, Fantasy of Flight (OPPOSITE) boasts one of the largest private collections of old and rare aircraft. Holding daily air shows, the attraction was featured in the local independent film *Florida City*, as well as in the television show, *Sheena, Queen of the Jungle*.

From the decades-old tradition of Fourth of July parades (PAGES 240 AND 241) to reenactments of battles past, Central Florida has a long history of honoring its long history.

Throughout the region, gatherings like Mount Dora's annual Battle of Townsend's Plantation and Civil War Festival help preserve the area's legacy for present and future generations.

Civil War reenactors in Central Florida show a supreme respect for the past, whether portraying Confederate infantrymen or Union commanders. With an intense attention to detail, historians emphasize authenticity of dress and equipment, frequently wearing handmade uniforms and using historical weapons in battle.

C OWBOYS STILL RIDE THE RANGE in Central Florida, wrangling a lot of attention at professional and amateur rodeos throughout the area. Kissimmee's Silver Spurs Arena hosts several livestock-roping contests throughout the year, and cowboys- and cowgirls-in-training lasso prizes by competing through the Florida High School Rodeo Association.

CENTRAL FLORIDA GIVES ITS residents many opportunities to go for a spin, whether at Cypress Gardens (OPPOSITE) or at the Volusia County Fair (ABOVE), a popular annual event since 1923.

In Kissimmee, revelers can get a remarkable view of the city and its surrounds from atop the 60-foot Century Ferris Wheel at Old Town, a four-block dining and entertainment complex (PAGES 250 AND 251).

As dusk descends on Orlando, the ever brilliant sunset brings out the intense colors of the city and its natural setting, creating a true sunshine sonata.

WELCOME TO FLORIDA

1927 ORANGE COUNTY COURTHOUSE

AMERICAN ALLIGATOR

65 E. Central Blvd

HISTORY CENTER

NOW OPEN

PROFILES IN EXCELLENCE

A LOOK AT THE CORPORATIONS, BUSINESSES, PROFESSIONAL GROUPS, AND COMMUNITY SERVICE ORGANIZATIONS THAT HAVE MADE THIS BOOK POSSIBLE. THEIR STORIES—OFFERING AN INFORMAL CHRONICLE OF THE LOCAL BUSINESS COMMUNITY—ARE ARRANGED ACCORDING TO THE DATE THEY WERE ESTABLISHED IN THE ORLANDO AREA.

ADVANTOR CORPORATION * ALBERTSON'S INC. * AMERICAN PAVING CONTRACTORS, INC. * ANSON-STONER, INC. * BARNIE'S COFFEE & TEA COMPANY * THE BRANDON COMPANY * BEERS CONSTRUCTION COMPANY * CAMPUS CRUSADE FOR CHRIST * CANAVERAL PORT AUTHORITY * CENTEX ROONEY CONSTRUCTION COMPANY * CENTRAL FLORIDA NEWS 13 * CENTRAL FLORIDA YMCA * CENTURY III * CHAMPIONSGATE * CHEP * CHRISTOPHER WREN CONSTRUCTION, INC. * CITRUS CLUB * COLONIAL BANK * CORRECT CRAFT, INC. * DARDEN RESTAURANTS * DATAMAX CORPORATION * DEMETREE BUILDERS * FIDELITY TITLE AND GUARANTY COMPANY / FIRST AMERICAN TITLE * FIRST UNION CORPORATION * FISERV CBS WORLDWIDE * FISHER, RUSHMER, WERRENRATH, DICKSON, TALLEY & DUNLAP, P.A. * FLORIDA EXTRUDERS INTERNATIONAL, INC. * FLORIDA HOSPITAL * FOUR POINTS BY SHERATON ORLANDO DOWNTOWN * GREATER ORLANDO AVIATION AUTHORITY * HUGHES SUPPLY, INC. * INFINITY OUTDOOR, INC. * KISSIMMEE-ST. CLOUD CONVENTION & VISITORS BUREAU * KNIGHT IMAGES * LAKE HIGHLAND PREPARATORY SCHOOL * LEISURE BAY INDUSTRIES, INC. / RECREATIONAL FACTORY WAREHOUSE * LOCKHEED MARTIN CORPORATION * MASSEY CADILLAC * MASSEY SERVICES, INC. * MIDLAND INFORMATION SYSTEMS, INC. * MORRIS ARCHITECTS * NEMOURS CHILDREN'S CLINIC * ORLANDO MAGAZINE * ORLANDO REGIONAL CHAMBER OF COMMERCE * ORLANDO REGIONAL HEALTHCARE * ORLANDO SANFORD INTERNATIONAL AIRPORT * ORLANDO SENTINEL COMMUNICATIONS * ORLANDO UTILITIES COMMISSION * ORLANDO/ORANGE COUNTY CONVENTION & VISITORS BUREAU, INC. * PATTERSON/BACH COMMUNICATIONS, INC. * PAYSYS INTERNATIONAL, INC. * PBS&J * PHOENIX INTERNATIONAL * THE PIZZUTI COMPANIES * PROGRESSIVE COMMUNICATIONS INTERNATIONAL * PUSH * QUE PASA! HISPANIC MAGAZINE/MAGELLAN MEDIA CORPORATION * RADISSON PLAZA HOTEL * RISSMAN, WEISBERG, BARRETT, HURT, DONAHUE & McLAIN, P.A. * SAWTEK, INC. * SPACE COAST OFFICE OF TOURISM * SPRINT * SUNTRUST * THOMAS W. RUFF & COMPANY * TRINITY PREPARATORY SCHOOL * TUPPERWARE INTERNATIONAL * UNIVERSAL ORLANDO RESORT * UNIVERSITY OF CENTRAL FLORIDA * WALT DISNEY WORLD RESORT * WESH NEWSCHANNEL 2 * WKMG-TV * YESAWICH, PEPPERDINE & BROWN * ZOM *

1876–1959

THE LARGEST MULTIMEDIA COMPANY IN CENTRAL FLORIDA, ORLANDO SENTINEL COMMUNICATIONS IS A news and information force driven by a Pulitzer Prize-winning newspaper, award-winning magazines, interactive Internet services, key advertising publications, and the area's only 24-hour, all-news local cable channel. ⚜ With a history that dates back to 1876, Orlando Sentinel Communications now reaches more than 1 million Central Florida residents. Through the years, its mission has always been clear: To be a leader in the community by stimulating debate and influencing positive change while serving as the area's most valued information source.

"There's a powerful connection between our company and the community, and it becomes stronger every year," says Kathleen M. Waltz, president, publisher, and chief executive officer. "Everything we do is for and about our community. Whether in print, on-line, or on the air, we provide information that Central Florida residents can use immediately to help make their day-to-day lives easier."

A subsidiary of Tribune Company, Orlando Sentinel Communications has transformed over the years to reflect a rapidly growing and changing Central Florida. To reach the area's thriving Hispanic population, the company has expanded coverage locally with its weekly *¡Impacto!* newspaper feature and added a San Juan bureau, becoming the only stateside paper with a full-time Puerto Rico pres-

TODAY, THE *Orlando Sentinel* RANKS 35TH NATIONALLY IN DAILY CIRCULATION AMONG LOCAL MARKET DAILIES, REACHING NEARLY 800,000 METRO ORLANDO READERS ON SUNDAYS AND MORE THAN 500,000 ON WEEKDAYS.

ence. Several Tribune Company newspapers also joined together to open the first news bureau in Havana, Cuba since the 1960s.

In 2000, the *Orlando Sentinel* took a huge step to reach out and connect with the community by completely redesigning the newspaper, cover to cover, with more graphics; a front-page Quick Read for busy residents; new, color-coded sections; and more news of interest to a diverse population.

In a partnership with Time Warner Communications, the company has pioneered the region's first 24-hour, all-news cable channel, Central Florida News 13, which reaches more than 550,000 area viewers. Coverage and commentary by *Orlando Sentinel* reporters and columnists have become popular News 13 broadcast features around the clock.

Orlandosentinel.com—the company's growing on-line newspaper component, produced by Tribune Interactive/Orlando and the *Orlando Sentinel*—features up-to-the-minute news, entertainment, weather, and sports coverage

relevant to Central Florida. The company's Go2orlando.com is a travel-oriented Web site targeting global travelers planning an Orlando-area vacation. And *Sentinel Classifieds* has national affiliations with apartments.com, CareerBuilder.com, cars.com, and newhomenetwork.com.

ONE-STOP ADVERTISING

To give advertisers a broad forum, the company offers a full range of publications, including *O!Arts, Orlando Sentinel Apartment Marketplace, New Homes, Job Xtra, Auto Finder Guide to New and Used Vehicles, Sentinel Value$ Shopping Guide, Coupon Catalogue, Hot Properties Real Estate Guide*, and *TargetCards* single-sheet ads.

Advertisers reach Central Florida consumers through a variety of *Orlando Sentinel* ad services. "There are so many ways for marketers to tell their story through the Sentinel," says Bill Steiger, vice president and director of advertising. "We can take their message to every home and business in Central Florida."

Advertisers can target specific zip codes or the entire market reached by the *Orlando Sentinel*. Niche services, such as Sentinel Direct (direct marketing) and on-line services, offer proven and new advertising opportunities. Powerful classified databases allow on-line viewers to narrow their search for goods and services by price, geography, and product specification.

A HISTORY OF INTEGRITY

The roots of Orlando Sentinel Communications run deep in the community. On June 6, 1876, the *Orange County Reporter* was first published as the company's founding newspaper. Over the next century, the paper grew and merged with other local papers, taking the *Orlando Sentinel* name in 1982. Today, the *Orlando Sentinel* ranks 35th nationally in daily circulation among local market dailies, reaching nearly 800,000 metro Orlando readers on Sundays and more than 500,000 on weekdays. The *Orlando Sentinel* is one of 11 Tribune Company dailies—including the *Los Angeles Times*, the *Chicago Tribune*, and *Newsday*—known for award-winning journalism, multimedia reporting, and technological innovation.

Newsroom innovations such as the multimedia desk have earned the *Orlando Sentinel* industrywide attention. Situated in the heart of the paper's newsroom, the multimedia desk is where decisions are made on content use across multiple platforms: newspaper, on-line, cable TV—even radio through the *Sentinel*'s local content-sharing agreement with several radio stations.

As the newspaper has grown in size and status, so too has the scope of its news coverage, investigative reporting, and commentary. In 2000, John C. Bersia of the *Sentinel*'s editorial board won the newspaper's third Pulitzer Prize for "Fleeced in Florida," his yearlong series advocating the regulatory reform of cash-advance businesses.

The company strives to be not only a community watchdog, but a philanthropic leader as well. Since 1995, the firm's employees have volunteered more than 20,000 hours of time in the community. Through *Orlando Sentinel* advertising support, corporate contributions, and the generosity of Orlando Sentinel Communications employees, more than $2 million goes to community groups each year. The *Orlando Sentinel* Family Fund—which includes communitywide contributions for the yearly Sentinel Santa programs—provides more than $2.5 million each year to Central Florida's nonprofit organizations to improve the lives of children, families, the elderly, and those who suffer from disabilities, hunger, homelessness, and illiteracy.

"People come to Central Florida and, at once, sense the community spirit," Waltz says. "We live in a growing, vibrant market, and the *Sentinel* is growing right along with it—providing the most comprehensive portfolio of news, advertising, and other information important to Central Florida residents."

WITH A HISTORY THAT DATES BACK TO 1876, ORLANDO SENTINEL COMMUNICATIONS NOW REACHES MORE THAN 1 MILLION CENTRAL FLORIDA RESIDENTS.

FOR MORE THAN A CENTURY, FIDELITY TITLE AND GUARANTY COMPANY HAS PLAYED A MAJOR ROLE IN the emerging Orlando real estate landscape. As one of Orlando's pioneer companies, Fidelity Title and Guaranty Company first opened its doors in 1883 as Orange County Abstract. For much of the 120 years since then, Fidelity was under the ownership and leadership of the former mayor of Orlando, William Beardall—one of Orlando's favorite citizens—and his family. ⚜ Fidelity continued to prosper, expand, and innovate, and in 1986, the company was purchased by local investors Harris Turner, Carl Bauchle, and Larry P. Deal.

In 1994, Fidelity again expanded to become part of the First American Title Insurance family. First American, one of the oldest title insurance companies in the world, welcomed the opportunity to expand its presence in Central Florida with the significant acquisition of Fidelity. First American, too, has an illustrious history, beginning in 1889 in Orange County, California. Today, First American Title operates a network of offices and agents throughout the world and is considered a leader in title technology.

Committed to the concept of local service and support, First American/Fidelity continues to service the residential and commercial real estate market in Central Florida by being a leader in title automation, plant facilities, and closing services. With offices throughout Central Florida, the company is one of the largest title insurance firms in the Orlando area. Its title plant is one of the area's largest and most complete, with records for Orange and Seminole counties dating back to the days when Orange County was known as Mosquito County. Despite tremendous growth, service remains personalized and customer focused.

SOLID COMMUNITY SUPPORT

Community involvement has been important to First American/Fidelity since the days when Beardall was at the helm. Today, organizations like the Central Florida Blood Bank, American Heart Association, Habitat for Humanity, United Way of Central Florida, and the local PBS station benefit from hours of community service by First American/Fidelity employees. Students from area high schools and the University of Central Florida get firsthand experience in the company's offices.

With a goal to set the standard for the title insurance industry in Central Florida over the next 100 years, First American/Fidelity continues to work diligently to serve the real estate industry, and to be a leader in automation and technology without losing its historical commitment to local service. Deal says, "After more than 100 years, we are looking forward to the next century of service."

SINCE 1883, FIDELITY TITLE AND GUARANTY COMPANY/FIRST AMERICAN TITLE HAS PLAYED A MAJOR ROLE IN BOTH THE REAL ESTATE MARKETS AND THE COMMUNITIES OF CENTRAL FLORIDA.

IN 1918, A GROUP OF ORLANDO RESIDENTS AND PHYSICIANS RECOGNIZED THE NEED TO IMPROVE COMMUNITY HEALTH care services. Under the name of the Orange County Hospital Association, the group invested its time and money, collected donations, purchased land, and hired a team to build the 50-bed Orange General Hospital, one of the first modern health care facilities serving Central Florida. ❧ The association built more than a hospital. It established the foundation for what would become the city's premier health care network—Orlando Regional Healthcare. Today, the 1,870-bed, community-owned, not-for-profit organization serves more than 2 million Central Florida residents and 6,000 visitors annually. As Central Florida's only Level I trauma center

and statutory teaching hospital system, Orlando Regional is renowned for excellence in surgery, cardiac care, trauma and emergency medicine, cancer care, and pediatrics.

The downtown building that once housed Orange General Hospital now operates as Orlando Regional Medical Center, one of nine hospitals and numerous health care services united under the Orlando Regional Healthcare umbrella.

HEALTH CARE THROUGH TEAMWORK

Orlando Regional Healthcare has been consistently voted one of the country's top 100 hospital systems by HCIA Mercer, as well as one of the top family-friendly companies in the area by *Central Florida Family* magazine. The more than 8,000 Central Florida employees of Orlando Regional Healthcare make up a team that is committed to serving the community with a focus on excellence.

Prominent among the organization's facilities is Arnold Palmer Hospital for Children & Women, one of only six such facilities in the nation. More than 8,000 babies are born each year at Arnold Palmer Hospital, and more than 1,000 babies receive neonatal intensive care. Another high-profile facility is M.D. Anderson Cancer Center Orlando, which provides state-of-the-art cancer care in a program jointly sponsored by Orlando Regional Healthcare and M.D. Anderson Cancer Center in Houston. The center features a highly regarded team approach to providing diagnostics, treatment planning, and delivery for each patient.

Other major Orlando Regional Healthcare facilities include Orlando Regional Medical Center, specializing in trauma, emergency

care, cardiology, orthopedics, neuroscience, diabetes care, and critical care; Orlando Regional Lucerne Hospital; Orlando Regional Sand Lake Hospital; Orlando Regional South Seminole Hospital; Orlando Regional St. Cloud Hospital; South Lake Hospital; and Leesburg Regional Medical Center. Also part of the network are the Orlando Regional Healthcare Foundation, benefiting community health care programs, and the Hubbard House, which offers affordable and convenient living accommodations for families of patients.

A MISSION TO SERVE

Orlando Regional Healthcare's mission statement promises a commitment to "improve the health and quality of life of the

individuals and communities we serve." Orlando Regional Healthcare has earned a reputation as a health care system that looks beyond profits, reinvests its services and funds back into Central Florida, and embraces a mission of long-term service to all members of the community. Orlando Regional Healthcare continues its mission through advanced science research and by expansion of services through new facilities and partnership programs.

"Since 1918, Orlando Regional Healthcare has grown hand in hand with Greater Orlando," says President and CEO John Hillenmeyer. "In this age of high-tech hospitals, our goal remains to provide patients and families with individualized care and treatment. We plan to continue this tradition for generations to come."

IN 1918, THE ORANGE COUNTY HOSPITAL ASSOCIATION INVESTED ITS TIME AND MONEY, COLLECTED DONATIONS, PURCHASED LAND, AND HIRED A TEAM TO BUILD THE 50-BED ORANGE GENERAL HOSPITAL, ONE OF THE FIRST MODERN HEALTH CARE FACILITIES SERVING CENTRAL FLORIDA.

TODAY, ORLANDO REGIONAL HEALTHCARE IS A 1,870-BED, COMMUNITY OWNED, NOT-FOR-PROFIT ORGANIZATION SERVING MORE THAN 2 MILLION CENTRAL FLORIDA RESIDENTS.

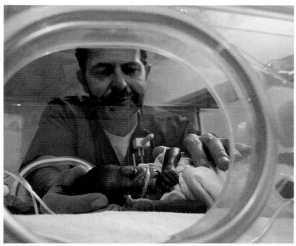

ORLANDO IS WIDELY REGARDED AS A LEADER IN HEALTH CARE, AND FLORIDA HOSPITAL STANDS AT the forefront of patient care, professional education, and medical research. A Central Florida Christian health care system, Florida Hospital is known internationally for its programs in cardiology, oncology, neurosurgery, orthopedic surgery, organ transplantation, and limb replacement. Other specialty areas include emergency medicine, obstetrics, outpatient services, pediatrics, psychiatry, rehabilitation and sports medicine, diabetes, and women's medicine. ❦ Florida Hospital is one of the largest private not-for-profit hospitals

in the state. Founded in 1908, the 1,772-bed acute health care system serves Central Florida and much of the Southeast, the Caribbean, and South America. It is the largest of the health care facilities that make up the Adventist Health System, Florida Hospital's parent company, which is operated by the Seventh-day Adventist Church.

The Florida Hospital system includes seven hospitals and more than a dozen Centra Care Walk-In Medical Centers, and several out-patient diagnostic centers. Each year,

the system's some 12,000 employees, 1,800 medical staff members, and 1,000 volunteers touch the lives of more than 1 million people—including approximately 74,000 admissions and 196,000 emergency cases. Its tradition of continued quality health care has earned Florida Hospital statewide, national, and international recognition—including the National Healthcare Forum Quality Award, National Research Corporation Quality Leader Award, and Governor's Sterling Award for Quality. *U.S. News & World Report*

also named Florida Hospital as one of America's Best Hospitals in 1999 and 2000.

FLORIDA HOSPITAL FOUNDATION

Through the years, Florida Hospital has remained true to its founding mission, one that reflects its ongoing commitment to deliver high-quality service and to show concern for patients' emotional and spiritual needs as well as their physical conditions. As a not-for-profit institution, Florida Hospital operates the Florida Hospital Foundation to help support the hospital's various programs and maintain its standard of excellence in care.

The foundation allows members of the community to help improve the quality of health care through a variety of programs. From establishing a permanent endowment—one that pays a percentage of interest every year to a specified center or program—to simply acting as a hospital volunteer, Florida Hospital Foundation has a way for people to participate. Tribute gifts, deferred gifts, and annual gifts as well as special events—aside from simply being potential tax deductions—are also ways citizens can touch the lives of those in need.

Aside from typical phone donations and fund-raisers, Florida Hospital Foundation also utilizes the Internet, offering citizens the chance to donate time and money through its Web site at www.foundation.floridahospital.com.

CARDIOLOGY SPECIALISTS

Cardiology has long been a Florida Hospital specialty. Since its beginning more than 25 years ago, the Florida Heart Institute has emerged as a leader in advanced cardiac care,

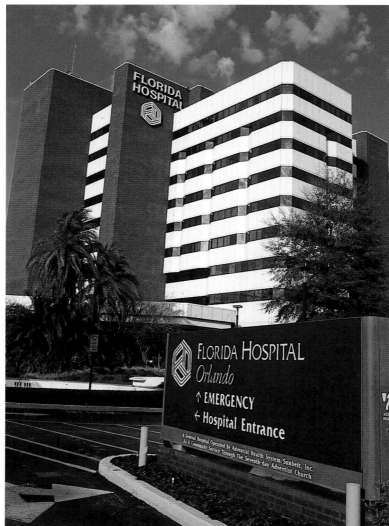

FLORIDA HOSPITAL IS ONE OF THE LARGEST PRIVATE NOT-FOR-PROFIT HOSPITALS IN THE STATE. FOUNDED IN 1908, THE 1,772-BED ACUTE HEALTH CARE SYSTEM SERVES CENTRAL FLORIDA AND MUCH OF THE SOUTHEAST, THE CARIBBEAN, AND SOUTH AMERICA.

SPENCER FREEMAN

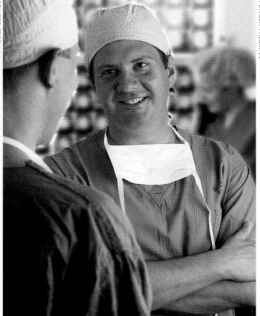

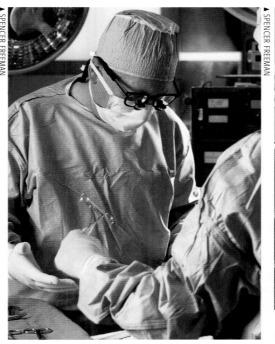

ranking as the largest cardiac center in the state and among the top five nationwide for open-heart surgery. The institute's staff includes cardiovascular surgeons, cardiologists, and hundreds of highly skilled nurses, technicians and other health care professionals.

To serve the needs of patients with peripheral vascular disease, Florida Hospital's renowned cardiology program offers sophisticated tools for providing diagnostic invasive and surgical services for peripheral procedures, including diagnostic, arterial, venous, simple, complex, atherectomy, therapeutic, and laser.

Since 1990, Florida Hospital has participated in numerous nationally and internationally recognized cardiac research studies and clinical testing for a variety of specialized drug treatments, medical devices, and procedural studies. In addition, the Florida Heart Institute offers patients the latest technological advances in cardiac services and programs such as rehabilitation, catheterization, angioplasty, open-heart and bypass surgeries, valve replacement, therapeutic cardiology, pacemaker implantation, and monitoring.

A LEADER IN CANCER TREATMENT

The Walt Disney Memorial Cancer Institute (WDMCI) at Florida Hospital is one of the nation's leading cancer treatment centers and the largest basic cancer research facility in the state. It is staffed by a broad-based group of oncologists, surgeons, radiologists, hematologists, psychologists, nurses, therapists, technicians, and researchers covering a variety of cancer treatments. The integrated network of medical staff treats some 3,500 newly diagnosed cancer patients annually with programs that include comprehensive, state-of-the-art diagnostic treatment, research, education, and support services.

WDMCI offers patients the latest in available cancer treatments: in- and outpatient surgery, biological therapy, surgery and radiation therapy combinations, chemotherapy, and innovative research programs. The institute also offers cancer-specific patient care through several award-winning programs, such as the Gynecologic Oncology Center, which provides specialized care for patients with precancer and cancer of the reproductive organs; the Ovarian Cancer Screening Program, with state-of-the-art diagnostic services for women who are at high risk of ovarian cancer; and the Hematology/Oncology Center for Children and Adolescents, which offers the most advanced technology and expertise available for diagnosing and treating a variety of inherited and acquired blood disorders, including sickle cell disease, hemophilia, and leukemia.

Affiliations with leading cancer centers allow WDMCI to offer the most advanced treatment protocols to patients in Central Florida. The institute's collaboration with Duke Comprehensive Cancer Center produced Central Florida's first bone marrow transplant (BMT) program, which includes the inpatient Bone Transplant Unit, the outpatient Bone Marrow Transplant Center, the Stem Cell Processing Laboratory, and a facility for stem cell biology research.

Florida Hospital's newest cancer treatment center, the Gamma Knife Center, comprises a multidisciplinary group of neurosurgeons, radiation oncologists, physicists, and nurses. Powerful and precise, gamma knife radiosurgery treatment uses a single dose of precisely directed radiation without an incision. This noninvasive outpatient procedure is offering new hope for patients with brain tumors, vascular malformations, and functional disorders.

THE FLORIDA HOSPITAL NEUROSCIENCE INSTITUTE

The Florida Hospital Neuroscience Institute, one of the most comprehensive such institutes in the Southeast, is the first Central Florida facility to offer interventional neuroradiology services, which use a minimally invasive approach to treat vascular diseases of the central nervous system. The technology allows physicians to treat previously untreatable diseases or those that would have required surgery. The institute's goals are to help discover neurological problems—such as strokes, brain tumors,

PRESIDENT DON JERNIGAN TOOK OVER THE LEADERSHIP OF FLORIDA HOSPITAL IN 2000.

Alzheimer's disease, Parkinson's disease, and others—in their earliest stages, begin treatment as quickly as possible, and help patients experience an improved quality of life.

The institute's treatment services include the Gamma Knife Center, Stroke Management and Rehabilitation Team (SMART) unit, Sleep Disorder Center, Neuro Critical Care, and Brain and Spinal Cord Injury Outpatient Rehabilitation Center. The SMART unit, which is a dedicated stroke unit, treats more stroke patients than any other Florida facility. And every year, more than 2,972 neurosurgeries are performed at the institute, making it the second-largest facility in Florida for neurological procedures performed.

FLORIDA CHILDREN'S HOSPITAL

Florida Hospital physicians performed Central Florida's first pediatric surgery in 1908, laying a stepping-stone for today's comprehensive children's health care services. Today, pediatric bone marrow transplants and renal transplants are just some of the specialized services offered only at Florida Children's Hospital. The hospital's integrated care network, which includes the Children's Emergency Center and the Level I Pediatric Intensive Care and Level III Neonatal Intensive Care units, provides children with nonthreatening care and innovative services. In 2000 alone, Florida Hospital delivered more than 8,000 babies, gave

emergency treatment to approximately 12,000 youngsters, and took care of more than 28,000 children in its walk-in centers.

NEW ADVANCES IN DIABETES CARE

Since its inception, the Florida Hospital Diabetes Center has been a leader in diabetes education, training, outreach, and clinical care. The self-management program promotes early detection and treatment of diabetes, and teaches patients the skills needed to manage the disorder. Accredited by the American Diabetes Association, the program operates within national standards for diabetes education.

The Diabetes Center serves more than 15,000 people each year, offering a health care team approach to diabetes management. The center's registered nurses, registered dietitians, and behavioral counselors are nationally certified diabetes educators. The Diabetes Center's ongoing support groups help answer questions about the disease in a monthly support group setting. In addition to treatment and education programs, the center provides a specialized exercise program with personal training by exercise physiologists.

In addition, the center's ongoing research with the University of Florida and the National Institutes of Health promises future breakthroughs in the treatment and prevention of diabetes.

WOMEN'S CENTER

Florida Hospital is acclaimed nationally for its women's medicine programs, and is the only hospital in the state that has been recognized by *Self* magazine as one of America's top 10 hospitals for women. The hospital offers full-service obstetric and gynecologic care on both an inpatient and an outpatient basis to women of all ages.

The center's breast screening and education program provides breast

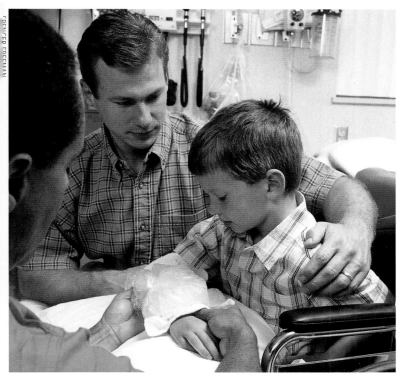

SPENCER FREEMAN

FLORIDA HOSPITAL CELEBRATION HEALTH

A continuously innovative, comprehensive health campus, Florida Hospital Celebration Health is a 265,000-square-foot health care facility that includes inpatient and outpatient medical services, physician offices, emergency services, fitness rehabilitation, and other health care programs for Central Florida residents, tourists, and international patients. The facility includes a state-of-the-art surgery center, a world-class diagnostic center, rehabilitation and sports medicine programs, health activities and a fitness center, primary care services, specialty physicians, a dental clinic, and a pharmacy.

In addition, Florida Hospital Celebration Health serves as a hub for community health activities. The new facility features a 60,000-square-foot fitness center, along with a basketball and volleyball gym, a swimming pool, a therapy pool, a cardiovascular fitness area, an integrated rehabilitation center, spa services, weight and strength training, and health education services.

In this new era of medical progress, Florida Hospital has made great strides and continues to earn awards for being a health care leader. Generous support keeps Florida Hospital on the leading edge of technology, providing the equipment and research needed for doctors and scientists to make important discoveries for a healthier tomorrow.

THE DEDICATED CHILDREN'S EMERGENCY CENTER IS JUST ONE OF THE WAYS FLORIDA CHILDREN'S HOSPITAL IS TAKING CARE OF THE LITTLEST PATIENTS.

FLORIDA HOSPITAL CELEBRATION HEALTH IS A 265,000-SQUARE-FOOT HEALTH CARE FACILITY THAT INCLUDES INPATIENT AND OUTPATIENT MEDICAL SERVICES, PHYSICIAN OFFICES, EMERGENCY SERVICES, FITNESS REHABILITATION, AND OTHER HEALTH CARE PROGRAMS FOR CENTRAL FLORIDA RESIDENTS, TOURISTS, AND INTERNATIONAL PATIENTS.

diagnostic and screening procedures, breast assessment, and breast self-examination education. The osteoporosis screening and education program provides services for women with high-risk factors for osteoporosis. Family-centered services offered by the Women's Center include parent education and a family-centered perinatal program.

Florida Hospital is a leader in parent education, offering several courses that have served as models for programs across the nation, including the Lactation Center, which has eight internationally accredited lactation consultants on staff to help breastfeeding mothers. This program supports the family-centered philosophy by offering childbirth preparation classes for the entire family, from siblings to grandparents.

REHABILITATION AND SPORTS MEDICINE

With 17 Central Florida locations, Florida Hospital Rehabilitation and Sports Medicine Centers offer the area's most comprehensive outpatient rehabilitation program. Specialty areas include stroke rehabilitation, cancer rehabilitation, spinal cord and hand injury rehabilitation, a head injury program, treatment of neurological disorders, an amputee program, an orthopedic program, and audiology services. Rehabilitation and sports medicine programs also include biofeedback services,

as well as physical, speech, and occupational therapy.

In addition, Florida Hospital is the official hospital for the NBA's Orlando Magic, as well as for the IHL's Orlando Solar Bears and the WNBA's Orlando Miracle. It also has been named the official hospital for the University of Central Florida athletic program and the official rehabilitation provider for the RDV Sportsplex. And Florida Hospital has partnered with LGE Sport Science Inc. to provide patients with the latest in high-technology medical treatment for sports-related injuries and recovery needs.

SPENCER FREEMAN

WHEN EARLY TELECOMMUNICATIONS SYSTEMS BEGAN WEAVING THEIR NOVEL WIRE WEB throughout Florida in the early 1900s, little could anyone imagine the communications impact they would have a century later. What began in 1910 with a smattering of small-business folks offering phone service for their customers in Central, South, and North Florida has evolved into Sprint—a global communications company at the forefront of integrating long-distance, local, and wireless communications services, serving as one of the largest carriers of Internet traffic. Today, Sprint has $20 billion in annual revenues and

serves more than 20 million business and residential customers.

The preeminent communications company for the 21st century, Sprint has made Greater Orlando its headquarters for the Local Telecommunications Division's Florida operations. One thousand employees work out of the company's lake-front Apopka offices. Another 2,000 Central Floridians, as well as 3,000 employees in other parts of Florida, are part of the Local Telecommunications Division. Today, Sprint supplies local service through more than 8 million customer lines in 18 states.

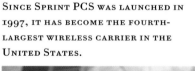

FLORIDA CONNECTION, GLOBAL REACH

Sprint's Florida presence stretches from the Panhandle to the southern edge of the state, with different divisions locating main offices in separate cities. The local telephone division in Apopka has the longest history and largest presence in the Orlando area.

The company's local telephone customers have long enjoyed exceptional customer service from a sophisticated network that offers products and services ranging from custom calling features such as Voicemail, Caller ID and Call Waiting to leading edge technologies such as high-speed Internet access. Several call centers in the Orlando area feature customer care advocates who assist customers with product and service selection, bill payment inquiries and repair questions. And, Sprint's retail centers—located throughout Orlando—offer customers one-stop shopping for local and long-distance service as well as wireless phones and service.

Sprint PCS, with its Orlando District headquartered in Maitland, is the fastest-growing digital wireless carrier in the United States and is in the enviable position of being the only carrier with 100 percent digital, 100 percent PCS nationwide services. Since Sprint PCS was launched in 1997, it has become the fourth-largest wireless carrier in the country. Its mission is simple: to create totally customized communications systems for each customer. Recently recognized by *Fortune* magazine

and *Wireless Week* for its excellence, Sprint PCS can package wireless, long-distance, and Sprint data services, simplifying service for customers and providing a competitive advantage in the wireless arena. The digital technology allows for more services including Voicemail, Call Waiting, and Caller ID. The Sprint PCS Wireless Web lets customers check e-mail, shop, and trade stock on the Internet with their wireless phone. The company's products are available at several Sprint stores in Central Florida and at partnering retailers such as Radio Shack, Dillard's, and Circuit City.

Sprint's Long Distance Division was the first nationwide, 100 percent digital, fiber-optic network in the United States and the first major long-distance player to combine voice and data services on the same network. It delivers services to 300 countries and locations, including connections to all of the world's direct-dial countries. By introducing such products as 10-cents-a-minute and Sprint Sense flat-rate calling plans, the long-distance division has always been an industry leader. For an unprecedented fifth consecutive year, Sprint received the J.D. Power and

Associates top ranking in the annual Residential Long Distance Customer Satisfaction Study.

Sprint offers customers total communications solutions, bundling varying combinations of local, long-distance, wireless, and Internet services into convenient and cost-savings packages. Voice, data, and network applications are integrated to meet individual residential customer requirements as well as specific business customer needs.

A CENTURY OF GROWTH

Sprint celebrated its 100th anniversary in 1999, tracing its roots to a clutch of small telephone companies across the state, as well as to first-time telephone operations in the Midwest. It was 1899 when the upstart Brown Telephone Company was founded by Cleyson L. Brown in Abilene, Kansas. Meanwhile, during the early 1900s, several small telephone companies were launched throughout Florida by visionaries such as grocer Carl Hill Galloway, who offered service to his Maitland and Winter Park customers.

By 1911, Brown had consolidated his company with other Kansas independents, forming the United Telephone Company. In 1967, the first Florida telephone company joined the United Telephone system family. Sixteen years later, four operating companies in Florida under the United Telephone system family joined to become United Telephone Company of Florida. In 1993, United merged with Centel and three years

later, the company officially changed its name to Sprint. With corporate headquarters in Kansas City, Missouri, Sprint now has 77,000 employees.

Today, Sprint provides a full package of products and services, including local and long-distance calling, Internet access, and wireless services to many customers throughout Florida, including much of the Orlando area.

Through its product distribution arm, Sprint North Supply, Sprint now offers more than 30,000 products from more than 1,300 manufacturers of voice, data, cable television, teleconferencing, security, and alarm systems. Sprint PCS offers a wide variety of sleek wireless phones, including one that provides voice prompts in Spanish, and

nearly all handsets allow easy access to Sprint PCS Wireless Web services.

Sprint Publishing & Advertising produces approximately 260 directories for the company's local telephone customers. Among those directories is the Central Florida edition, which is distributed throughout the Orlando area.

Sprint is a leader in providing its customers with applications such as Internet access and group video conferencing. Through its partnership with EarthLink, Sprint offers basic Internet access to rival other Internet players. The alliance creates a combined base of more than 600,000 Internet access customers.

BUSINESS CONCERN

From small businesses to Fortune 500 corporations, companies throughout Florida rely on Sprint's technical expertise and total business communications solutions. *Fortune* magazine in early 1999 named Sprint the most admired telecommunications company. The ranking was based on a survey of more than 10,000 executives, directors, and security analysts.

To help its business customers remain competitive, Sprint offers a variety of leading-edge, customized service solutions that include Internet Protocol-based technologies such as intranets, extranets, comprehensive e-commerce solutions, Web hosting, managed services, and security solutions. An e-procurement company, Go Co-Op, relies on Sprint's local division to provide

THE SPRINT PCS WIRELESS WEB[SM] LETS CUSTOMERS CHECK E-MAIL, SHOP, AND TRADE STOCK WITH THEIR WIRELESS PHONE.

THE PREEMINENT COMMUNICATIONS COMPANY FOR THE 21ST CENTURY, SPRINT HAS MADE GREATER ORLANDO ITS HEADQUARTERS FOR THE LOCAL TELECOMMUNICATIONS DIVISION'S FLORIDA OPERATIONS.

IN ADDITION TO PUBLISHING DIRECTO-
RIES FOR LOCAL TELEPHONE CUSTOMERS,
SPRINT OFFERS PRODUCTS AND SERVICES
RANGING FROM CUSTOM CALLING FEA-
TURES SUCH AS VOICEMAIL, CALLER ID
AND CALL WAITING TO LEADING EDGE
TECHNOLOGIES SUCH AS HIGH-SPEED
INTERNET ACCESS.

service and equipment that support the company's business-to-business applications. Because uptime is critical to Go Co-Op's Web-based purchasing solutions, Sprint meets the company's unique needs by placing its Internet connections on a synchronous optical network (SONET) ring to its Maitland, Florida location. SONET—a surviv-able network—ensures connectivity if a primary connection were to fail. In addition, Sprint's Advanced Network Services group monitors Go Co-Op's routers around the clock, notifying appropriate personnel and the customer in the event of a failure. This keeps Go Co-Op's business active 24 hours a day, even when an anomaly is being corrected.

INNOVATION IN EDUCATION

Several Orlando-area schools have chosen Sprint to help guide them into a new century of high-tech education. To provide more technological training to the post-secondary education market in Greater Orlando, Sprint has part-nered with Seminole Community College to install Florida's first community college asynchronous transfer mode (ATM) network. This transmission technology allows high-speed data connectivity for the institution that serves more than 30,000 students through its state-of-the-art campuses and branch locations.

And as part of a nationwide effort to recognize primary and secondary schools for their leadership in im-proving educational programs via technology, Sprint designated two

Orlando schools as "Sprint Show-case Schools." Both Southwood Elementary School and Corner Lake Middle School serve as demonstra-tion sites to show how educators can strengthen curriculum by integrat-ing technology. Playing host to other local school administrators and teachers, the schools showcase Sprint tools such as classroom tele-phone equipment and TekNetIP[SM], which uses Web-based technology to centralize and integrate all media equipment while controlling clock, public address, and electronic bulletin systems.

Sprint PCS's Education Connec-tion program donated digital wireless telephones to several Central Florida schools to help with their communi-cations needs. The phones are used to set up parent-teacher conferences, to provide quick communication in

the event of a field-trip mishap, and to aid athletic directors in reporting student injuries immediately.

COMMUNITY FIRST

Equally as important to Sprint as its technologically ad-vanced products and services is a commitment to the communities it serves. Sprint employees give back to the community in many ways. Company volunteers have helped clean up the St. John's and Wekiva Rivers and worked community events in various roles, including the col-lection of more than 1,000 pounds of food for the Let's Tackle Hunger food drive.

A long-time supporter of United Way, Sprint rallies more than 50 percent of its employees across the state to contribute more than $500,000 a year, with more than

SPRINT'S EMPLOYEES TAKE PART IN
COMMUNITY EVENTS SUCH AS THE
WEKIVA RIVER CLEAN UP.

ORLANDO

half donated to Heart of Florida United Way in the Orlando area. Sprint complemented those donations with its own $225,000 contribution to the organization.

Its Partners in Education initiative gives Sprint employees an opportunity to serve as mentors through Junior Achievement, Compact, and other programs. And Florida employees who are members of Sprint's Speakers Bureau deliver valuable consumer- and business-related information on topical subjects to community organizations. The Speakers Bureau has taught many Floridians how to avoid being victims of "cramming"—the illegal addition of products or services to a customer's account without permission—and "slamming"—the illegal practice of switching a telephone customer's long distance company without permission.

Sprint has sponsored several major activities and organizations in Orlando, including the Florida A&M University's National Alumni Association Convention, the Hispanic Business Initiative Fund, and the Red, Hot and Boom Fourth of July celebration in Altamonte Springs.

A 21ST CENTURY PERSPECTIVE

When Sprint laid its fiber-optic cable, voice traffic dominated the networks. But analysts estimate that more than 90 percent of all communications traffic soon will be data, requiring more bandwidth. Sprint is at the forefront in developing innovative solutions to today's needs.

Sprint FastConnect℠ service allows simultaneous voice and Internet services, as well as instantaneous video and audio streaming,

over one line. Just recently, Sprint introduced Sprint ION℠ (Integrated On-Demand Network) providing integrated voice, video, and data services with virtually unlimited bandwidth. No multiple phone lines or complex networks are required for this cutting-edge technology which allows customers to handle several calls, fax documents, and surf the Web simultaneously up to 100 times faster than conventional modems.

Looking toward the future, Sprint is developing effective solutions for conducting all facets of

business over the Internet. The company's e-commerce strategy is focused on residential and business customers alike. And Sprint is developing international strategies and investment opportunities in Canada, Mexico, and other areas outside the United States.

More than 100 years after its beginning in Central Florida and the Midwest, Sprint is responding to the rapidly shifting communications demands of customers and providing continually innovative technologies designed to meet those varying needs.

THROUGH EMPLOYEE VOLUNTEER PROJECTS AND FINANCIAL SUPPORT OF AGENCIES SUCH AS UNITED WAY, SPRINT GIVES BACK TO THE ORLANDO COMMUNITY.

TODAY, SPRINT PROVIDES A FULL PACKAGE OF PRODUCTS AND SERVICES, INCLUDING LOCAL AND LONG-DISTANCE CALLING, INTERNET ACCESSS AND WIRELESS SERVICES TO MANY CUSTOMERS THROUGHOUT FLORIDA, INCLUDING MUCH OF THE ORLANDO AREA.

THE ORLANDO REGIONAL CHAMBER OF COMMERCE IS FLORIDA'S LARGEST PROBUSINESS ADVOCATE, working to unite the region's business community—from sole proprietorships to Fortune 500 companies—as a world-class hub of international commerce. Drawing from the community-building philosophy of John W. Gardner, Common Cause founder and Presidential Medal of Freedom recipient, the chamber is forming alliances throughout the region to realize its goal. "We are building a better region, creating a dynamic environment for emerging businesses, and establishing a powerful forum where businesses, government, neighborhood associations,

educational institutions, and others can come together for a common good," says Jacob V. Stuart, chamber president. "A community has the power to motivate its members to exceptional performance and provide the climate in which great things happen."

PROMOTING CENTRAL FLORIDA

Since 1913, the Orlando Regional Chamber of Commerce has helped build solid business relationships throughout Central Florida. Originally known as the Orlando Board of Trade, the organization today is the largest chamber in Florida and the ninth largest in the United States. While focusing on the needs of area businesses, the chamber has contributed to Orlando's transformation from a quiet Florida cow and citrus center to an international business showcase. With some 65 employees and approximately 8,500 members, the chamber will lead businesses from Port Canaveral

to Tampa Bay into the 21st century with a steady focus on technology, workforce, and transportation—the key issues that face Orlando's ever changing community.

"Sharing thoughts and ideas will stimulate creativity and cohesiveness as we advance the theme

of working together as a region," says Ellen S. Titen, president of E.T. Consultants and 2001 chamber board chairman. "As new, innovative partnerships form, there will be significant progress toward building and sustaining economic strength."

Technology will play a critical role in strengthening the region, and that is where the Central Florida Innovation Corporation (CFIC) comes in. Established to increase the base of high-paying jobs in the area, CFIC provides outreach, consulting, and investor services to nurture growth of high-tech industries, according to Ed Timberlake, senior vice president of Bank of America and 1999 chamber board chairman.

"To us, technology is critical to the economic growth and viability of our area," says Timberlake, chairman of the not-for-profit CFIC. "The economic development of the future is the CFIC model of creating and building companies that offer high-value jobs to the area." The

CLOCKWISE FROM TOP:
TV PERSONALITY AND ANIMAL EXPERT JACK HANNAH SPEAKS AT AN ORLANDO REGIONAL CHAMBER OR COMMERCE TRUSTEE LUNCHEON.

BUSINESS COLUMNIST JOHN KOENIG ADDRESSES THE REGIONAL BOARD OF ADVISORS. EACH HALF-DAY PROGRAM ADDRESSES A KEY COMMUNITY BUILDING ISSUE.

THE CHAMBER'S BIZSHOW, THE LARGEST BUSINESS SHOW IN THE SOUTHEAST, ATTRACTS HUNDREDS OF EXHIBITORS AND THOUSANDS OF ATTENDEES.

chamber projects that by 2015 more than 2.7 million area workers—up from 1.5 million current jobholders—will be filling those positions and additional roles currently available in the Central Florida workplace.

"As Orlando grows, it becomes more and more evident that human capital is the most vital resource we need to prosper," says Jim Dunlap, who is president of Huntingdon National Bank Florida and will serve as 2002 chamber board chairman. "It is imperative that we attract the talent we need to remain competitive, and that we develop, expand, and upgrade job skills for all workers. The Orlando Regional Chamber will work closely with the education system and the private sector to develop the region's workforce."

Always Innovating

WorkForce 2020's Academies of Learning—a chamber initiative—brings local, state, and national workforce experts together to help companies be proactive in resolving the challenges of hiring, training, and retaining entry-level workers. The initiative has been so successful that it has been replicated in eight Florida cities, including Miami and Jacksonville. With a recent grant from the U.S. Chamber of Commerce, the Orlando Regional Chamber will help roll out the program in other cities across the country.

Innovation is not new to the chamber, which has worked for years to find solutions to the many business challenges facing the area. The creation of the Small Business Chamber in 1995 was designed to meet the needs of companies with fewer than 40 employees—companies that comprise 80 percent of the chamber's membership. In addition, the chamber has recently formed valuable partnerships with the African American Chamber of Commerce, the Hispanic Chamber of Commerce, and other key groups to give members and their businesses networking opportunities.

To help pave the way for precedent-setting business growth, the chamber also has developed several nationally recognized, award-winning community leadership programs: Leadership Orlando, Leadership Central Florida, and Youth Leadership. More than 2,500 of today's Central Florida business leaders are graduates of Leadership Orlando, which introduces participants to the inner workings of the Orlando area and opens doors to valuable business contacts. Leadership Central Florida, the first program of its kind in the nation, focuses on regional issues and builds partnerships to strengthen communities in nine area counties.

One of the newest chamber leadership initiatives—Senior Partners—allows workers and businesspeople age 55 and older to share their years of experience with chamber members. And *FirstMonday*, the chamber's award-winning monthly chronicle of business issues, is the first chamber publication in the country to share information on the Web as it is being delivered to members on the first Monday of each month.

As the Orlando Regional Chamber of Commerce develops its innovative programs and pioneers new initiatives, its mission remains clear: to maintain a strong foundation, build on the region's strengths, provide an innovative communications network, and create a solid community connection from which to flourish.

CLOCKWISE FROM TOP LEFT: DR. ANGELOS ANGELOU PRESENTS A FRAMEWORK FOR REGIONAL DEVELOPMENT.

300 BUSINESS AND COMMUNITY LEADERS ATTENDED THE CHAMBER'S FIRST ANNUAL REGIONAL LEADERSHIP CONFERENCE, AN EVENT FOCUSING ON THE DEVELOPMENT OF THE CHAMBER'S REGIONAL PERSPECTIVE.

THOUSANDS JOIN THE CHAMBER FOR HOBNOB, GIVING ORLANDO'S BUSINESS COMMUNITY THE OPPORTUNITY TO HAVE FUN AND RUB ELBOWS WITH ELECTED OFFICIALS AND CANDIDATES RUNNING IN FEDERAL, STATE, AND LOCAL RACES.

RLANDO UTILITIES COMMISSION (OUC—THE *Reliable* ONE) HAS BEEN A VITAL PART OF THE COMMUnity since 1923, serving the citizens of Orlando with a dependable flow of electricity and water at competitive rates. As OUC moves into the 21st century, the municipal utility continues to strengthen its commitment to forward-thinking expansion, improvement in service delivery, and heartfelt community support. OUC's heritage dates back to 1922, when the City of Orlando bought Orlando Water & Light Co., a privately held company in operation since 1901. City leaders issued $975,000 in bonds to purchase and improve the utility. In 1923, the state

BY TREATING WATER WITH OZONE, A STRONG AND SAFE DISINFECTANT, ORLANDO UTILITIES COMMISSION (OUC) REDUCES THE USE OF CHLORINE IN ITS WATER SYSTEM AND REMOVES HYDROGEN SULFIDE, A NATURALLY OCCURRING COMPOUND THAT CAN CREATE AN UNPLEASANT TASTE AND ODOR (TOP).

OUC'S SLOGAN, THE *Reliable* ONE, IS NOWHERE MORE APPARENT THAN IN THE UTILITY'S ELECTRIC DISTRIBUTION BUSINESS UNIT, WHERE WORKERS MOVE QUICKLY TO RESTORE POWER WHEN OUTAGES OCCUR (BOTTOM).

legislature granted the city a charter to establish OUC, which would operate the system. Voters soon approved an additional $575,000 in bonds to expand the utility.

Orlando's initial $1.55 million investment has grown into an electric and water utility with more than $2 billion in assets and annual operating revenues in excess of $500 million. Meanwhile, the utility's number of customer accounts has skyrocketed from 5,000 to more than 165,000.

OUC is run by its customers. The utility annually returns to its owners—the City of Orlando and its

citizens—payments making up a sizable portion of the city's general fund, which in turn helps pay for police and fire services, parks and playgrounds, traffic engineering, and other community services.

OUC's governing board, the commission, is comprised of five members, including the mayor of Orlando, who is an ex officio member. Nominees for the commission are submitted by the city's nominating board, with the commission either accepting or rejecting them. Nominees approved by the commission must then be ratified by the city council.

All commission members, with the exception of the mayor, may serve no more than two consecutive four-year terms and serve without compensation. Many industry observers believe this structure has given OUC a high degree of stability, enabling the governing board to make hard decisions based on sound business principles rather than on politics.

THE *Reliable* ONE

Adopting the slogan The *Reliable* One was a bold move, and not one taken lightly by employees of OUC. Nowhere is this more apparent than in the utility's Electric Distribution Business Unit, where workers move quickly to restore power when outages occur. The business unit also routinely replaces aging transformers, switches, and cabling across its 400-square-mile service area to avoid any unnecessary problems.

With its new commercial lighting division, OUConvenient Lighting, OUC has increased street light installation and maintenance across its service territory. The utility handles extensive street lighting contracts with large commercial accounts and

such government agencies as the Greater Orlando Aviation Authority, City of Orlando, and Orange County.

Also boasting exceptional reliability is OUC's water production and distribution business. The utility's advanced ozone water treatment process produces great-tasting tap water—proudly dubbed H_2OUC—and makes it even easier for OUC to surpass the ever demanding drinking water regulations set by federal and state authorities. By treating water with ozone, a strong and safe disinfectant, OUC reduces the use of chlorine in its water system and removes hydrogen sulfide, a naturally occurring compound that can create an unpleasant taste and odor.

PREPARING FOR DEREGULATION

With deregulation of the electric industry looming in Florida's near future, OUC is preparing for the inevitable changes. The utility's customer service arm, OUCustomer Connection, is securing long-term service agreements with local businesses as it develops innovative energy efficiency programs for both residential and commercial customers.

To help hotels, office buildings, and other large commercial

innovative, friendly, dependable service is certain to help the utility maneuver in the ebb and flow of a competitive marketplace.

SUPPORTING THE COMMUNITY

Each year, OUC lends a helping hand to charities and civic organizations across Central Florida. In its quest to make a difference in the community, OUC supports the Heart of Florida United Way, United Arts, March of Dimes, Orlando Humane Society, Orlando/ University of Central Florida (UCF) Shakespeare Festival, Salvation Army, and Second Harvest Food Bank, among many others.

A proud and energetic group, OUC employees routinely volunteer their valuable free time to participate in such fund-raisers as the Junior Achievement Bowl-a-Thon and the American Cancer Society's Relay for Life.

As OUC takes pride in its past achievements, the utility is also positioning itself for the challenges of industry deregulation. Of course, competition is nothing new to OUC; the organization has always worked hard to distinguish itself by running one of the most dependable electric and water companies in Florida. And that track record, coupled with OUC's increased focus on customer service, promises an even brighter future for The *Reliable* One.

EACH YEAR, OUC LENDS A HELPING HAND TO CHARITIES AND CIVIC ORGANIZATIONS ACROSS CENTRAL FLORIDA.

customers reduce their air-conditioning costs, OUC is circulating chilled water to these facilities. OUCooling, a partnership between OUC and Trigen-Cinergy Solutions, saves money for property owners by relieving them of the need to install their own chillers. Customers also avoid maintenance headaches and enjoy

lower energy costs—with improved reliability.

At the same time, OUC's electric service, among the most reliable in the nation, continues to attract the attention of nearby communities that are exploring ways to improve their own electric system reliability. OUC's reputation as a provider of

THE OUCOOLING PLANT IN DOWNTOWN ORLANDO CIRCULATES CHILLED WATER TO OFFICE TOWERS, HOTELS, AND OTHER COMMERCIAL BUILDINGS, REDUCING THEIR AIR-CONDITIONING COSTS.

CORRECT CRAFT, INC.

HE ALLIES WERE IN THE THROES OF WORLD WAR II AND DESPERATE TO GAIN A FOOTHOLD IN GERMAN territory when Correct Craft, Inc.® received the assignment that launched its reputation as a world-class boatbuilder. General Dwight D. Eisenhower needed a fleet of storm boats to cross Germany's Rhine River in March 1945, and the boats had to be built in fewer than three weeks. The U.S. Army Corps of Engineers asked Walter C. "W.C." Meloon, who founded Correct Craft in 1925, to produce 300 of the boats in fewer than 20 days. The company not only came through, despite the short time and against unimaginable odds, but the firm also built

an additional 100 boats when other companies failed to meet their deadlines.

QUALITY, PERFORMANCE, VALUE

oday, the name Correct Craft is synonymous with fine-quality water ski and wakeboard boats, and the Orlando company's Ski Nautique® is revered by recreational boating enthusiasts worldwide. As interest in water sports explodes, thousands of customers exploring the new frontiers of wakeboarding and ski "flying" look to Correct Craft for their boating equipment.

Correct Craft has been recognized continually for its product innovation, quality, performance, and value. In fact, all current world waterskiing slalom and jump records have been set by skiers traveling in the "no wake zone" of a Ski Nautique.

W. C. MELOON'S FIRST POWERBOAT WAS A FORD MODEL T ENGINE AND AIRCRAFT PROPELLER ON A 16-FOOT ROWBOAT, C. 1918.

THE NUMBER ONE CHOICE OF TOURNAMENT AND RECREATIONAL WAKEBOARDERS THROUGHOUT THE WORLD IS THE 2001 SUPER AIR NAUTIQUE.

Headquartered in Orlando with nearly 300 employees in its local manufacturing division, Correct Craft builds six different models each year and sells them to customers in 39 countries on six continents. In 2000, the company's sales reached 61 million, and its worldwide market share grew to about 30 percent.

Run by W.C. Meloon's grandson, Walter "Walt" N. Meloon, Correct Craft has become a world leader in water ski and wakeboard boat manufacturing, and is the oldest boatbuilder still owned and controlled by the same family. "My grandfather had a basic philosophy about work: you always did the impossible first, and when you completed that, all the rest was done," says Meloon, president and chief executive officer. "He was a man who knew no impossible task."

FROM PORTSMOUTH TO ORLANDO

eloon's great-grandfather, Walter Nathanial Meloon, was a carpenter by trade, and worked in the 19th-century Portsmouth, New Hampshire, shipyards. Meloon's grandfather,

W.C., built his first powerboat in 1918, fashioning it from a rowboat with a Ford Model T engine driving an old airplane propeller.

In 1925, W.C. Meloon moved to Florida and, when the real estate boom that drew him went bust, established the Florida Variety Boat Company in Pine Castle, just outside of Orlando. With an abundance of lakes dotting the Central Florida area, forming a boat company seemed the logical thing to do.

The company did not make much of a splash in the beginning, as times were tough and the main demand was for rowboats and outboards for fishermen. In 1930, Variety Boat became Pine Castle Boat and Construction Company and, during the Great Depression, the firm built docks and boathouses, dredged lakes and beaches, and even designed and built a system of canals. Eight years later, when W.C. Meloon heard a radio ad touting "the correct heel for your shoe," the proverbial lightbulb went off. He quickly renamed his company Correct Craft, and the firm was incorporated in 1947.

During the depression-era summers of the 1930s, W.C.'s sons,

Walter O. and Ralph Meloon, took to the road with their families on a marketing tour unlike any other. They headed to New England, traveling farmers' fence lines in their 1924 Dodge with a hand-built trailer hauling their boat. They publicized and sold boat rides for a quarter in every town with a lake, helping to keep the Meloon family afloat financially and boosting their company's profile.

By the time Correct Craft received its historic assignment from Eisenhower, the small company was producing about 48 boats a month. The job to build 300 in 20 days for U.S. troops required closing one of Orlando's main roads—Orange Avenue—so the project could spill into the street. The Meloons, devout Christians, always closed business on Sundays to rest; when government officials demanded they go to a seven-day workweek to complete the assignment, W.C. Meloon refused to comply. However, he kept his contract and produced 400 plywood assault boats on schedule.

The unwavering principles of Correct Craft's owners have been cited by many teachers of business ethics and have even been documented in *Business, Government, and Society: A Managerial Perspective*, a textbook by George and John Steiner. The book recalls an incident in 1957 when the company received a U.S. Army contract for 3,000 fiberglass boats. By this time, Walter O. and Ralph Meloon were managing daily operations, and a government inspector demanded that they set up a special account for "inspector's expenses." It was a blatant request for a bribe and, after praying for guidance, the Meloons refused to comply. As a result, inspectors rejected 640 boats based on "trivial blemishes," and Correct Craft lost $1 million on the contract. The company, owing $500,000 to 228 creditors, was forced to file for bankruptcy in 1958.

Correct Craft struggled for 25 years to repay its debts completely. Its Titusville plant, which had been building a line of motor yachts, was sold. In 1961, the tide began to turn. Correct Craft pioneered the waters of the world with its flagship Ski Nautique, and became the leader in water ski boat manufacturing.

It was a time when the world, especially Central Florida with its hundreds of area lakes, had become more and more enamored of the thrill and beauty of waterskiing. In fact, more than 20 years earlier, the Meloons had helped generate interest in the sport by supplying boats to Cypress Gardens, the very first attraction to popularize waterskiing and family recreational boating.

Before the Ski Nautique, competitive skiers had been using twin outboard ski boats that had to be refueled several times daily. To promote his new find, Walter O. Meloon

▲ JOEY MEDDOCK

contacted 15 of the world's best water-skiers, and offered them a Ski Nautique at half price if they would use the fuel-efficient boat in all their training sessions and competitions. All but one took him up on the offer, and soon the Ski Nautique came to be known as the tournament inboard ski boat.

The company continued to make headlines with several innovations: the first-ever ski boat with a center-mounted tow pylon; the first ski boat with tracking fins on the hull; the first ski boat with a safety rearview mirror; the first ski boat with cruise control; and the first totally dedicated wakeboard boat—the Pro Air Nautique®. Correct Craft won the prestigious IMTEC (International Marine Trades Exhibit & Conference) Innovation Award-Boat Category of 1998 awarded by Boating Writers International—a leading voice of the world's marine journalists—for the Pro Air Nautique Total Wake Control™ (TWC™) hull, which improves wake size and shape.

With hard times just a memory, the Meloons now celebrate their convictions and embrace their success. Today, Walter N. Meloon runs Correct Craft, with his father, Walter O. Meloon, and his uncle, Ralph Meloon, serving on the board of directors. Ralph Meloon is credited with a key role in developing competitive waterskiing tournaments internationally, and travels more than 100,000 miles a year for the company.

CLOCKWISE FROM TOP:
A WAKEBOARDER PERFORMS BEHIND THE 2001 SUPER AIR NAUTIQUE AT THE AMERICA'S CUP.

RUN BY W.C. MELOON'S GRANDSON, WALTER "WALT" N. MELOON, CORRECT CRAFT HAS BECOME A WORLD LEADER IN WATER SKI AND WAKEBOARD BOAT MANUFACTURING, AND IS THE OLDEST BOAT-BUILDER STILL OWNED AND CONTROLLED BY THE SAME FAMILY.

THE 2001 SKI NAUTIQUE IS THE HALLMARK OF THE CORRECT CRAFT'S NAUTIQUES TOWBOATS.

BOATS FOR A NEW MILLENNIUM

More than 75 years of marine innovation have brought Correct Craft to a new millennium, a time when enthusiasm for waterskiing, wakeboarding, and recreational boating is greater than ever. Ski "flying" is the newest rage, with skiers sailing through the air at distances up to a world-record-setting 299 feet off a special ramp.

Always a step ahead of the industry, Correct Craft's flagship Ski Nautique and the company's entire product line are smarter, bolder, and more exciting than ever. The Nautique Smart Pod™ 2001 has the first keyless ignition and security system, and integrates analog and digital displays in an ergonomically redesigned cockpit and helm. Other Nautique highlights include optional bench or arena-style seating in the Nautique Super Sport™ and Super Air Nautique®; a newly designed Flight Control Tower™ on the Pro Air Nautique® and Super Air Nautique; and luxurious trunk storage on the Ski Nautique.

Correct Craft, over the years, has elevated waterskiing to entirely new levels by sponsoring major tournaments, including the Masters Waterski Tournament at Callaway Gardens, arguably the most prestigious tournament in the world. The televised tournament has spanned more than four decades and attracts a television audience of millions.

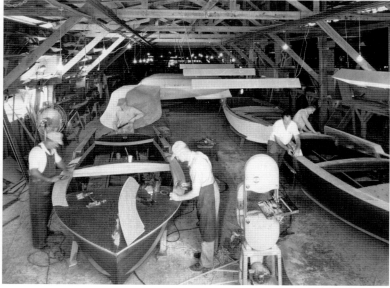

In 1977, the company formed its own sponsored water ski team, which today includes world-champion water skiers Bruce and Tom Neville and world-champion slalom skier Andy Mapple. In addition to competitions, Correct Craft Nautique water ski and wakeboard boats are used exclusively at SeaWorld® Adventure Parks across the country, thrilling ski show audiences for more than 15 years.

Under the Meloon family's leadership, the company has established a network of nearly 100 dealerships with an average customer satisfaction rate of more than 98 percent.

Never forgetting their family values, the elder Meloon brothers have created a weekend seminar, Turnaround Ministries, in which they share the lessons and skills they have acquired through years of hardship. Before audiences of Christian business owners, the seminar teaches the philosophy that "it's always too soon to quit." The Meloons preach that bankruptcy, despite its social stigma, actually can be a preparation for better things to come. And it is hard to ignore their example.

Correct Craft strongly supports the water sports industry not only with its impact on the industry overall, but with gifts as well. The company has contributed $100,000 to the American Water Ski Educational

WALTER C. MELOON'S FIRST DORY, APPROXIMATELY 14 FEET IN LENGTH, C. 1925

Foundation—the largest gift received by the group—making boats available to skiers who might otherwise not have access to them. Recently, Correct Craft founder Walter C. Meloon was honored posthumously by the Florida Department of State and the Florida League of Cities as one of the state's Great Floridians for 2000 for his significant contributions to the history and culture of the state.

The future holds great promise for Correct Craft, as more and more people plan their leisure activities around water sports and recreation. Currently operating from a 125,000-square-foot facility, Correct Craft is

preparing to double its manufacturing space and its production as well. As the company expands into a new world headquarters by 2003, boating enthusiasts everywhere can continue to expect the uncompromising quality and innovation—upheld by four generations of Meloons—that have made Correct Craft a boating leader.

Says Walt Meloon, "My grandfather made a commitment to build boats for the glory of God. To make that commitment, you must live by biblical principles and ethics, and when we build a boat, we have to remember that a job worth doing is worth doing right."

TEAM NAUTIQUE'S TONI NEVILLE RUNS THE SLALOM COURSE BEHIND THE WORLD-FAMOUS 2001 SKI NAUTIQUE.

HUGHES SUPPLY, INC.

OR SOME THREE-QUARTERS OF A CENTURY, HUGHES SUPPLY, INC. HAS HELPED ITS CUSTOMERS BUILD, repair, and replace facilities and infrastructures relied upon by millions of people. Whether the customer is a professional purchasing agent, local contractor, commercial organization, industrial concern, or government agency, leading wholesale distributor Hughes Supply has been there to provide products and support to ensure that the job is done right. The NYSE-listed company attributes its success to two basic beliefs: always put people and relationships first—whether they are customers, associates, or manufacturers—and be willing to adapt with the changing times.

PEOPLE FIRST

When electrical contractors Harry and Russell Hughes founded the company with their father, Clarence Hughes, in 1928, they knew firsthand the important role that a quality distributor plays in handling its customers' needs. Unable to find a dependable distributor for all their product and service requirements, the Hughes family decided to enter the distribution business themselves.

With a small loan and a wealth of determination, the father-and-sons team built their business on customer service and product availability. Instead of making customers come to them, the family loaded their inventory in the back of a wagon and drove to the job sites.

The service level established years ago has been the foundation of Hughes' success and continues to drive the company. "It has always been my family's belief that if you put people first—employees, customers, vendors—then success will follow," says David Hughes, chairman and CEO. "This philosophy has worked for more than 70 years, and we anticipate that it will continue to work well into the future."

Today, more than 8,500 Hughes associates, including a sales network of some 2,000 highly trained product specialists, are dedicated to building relationships. In addition, the Hughes team represents 11,000 leading manufacturing partners across the country and around the globe.

AGILITY IN CHANGING TIMES

Even a strong emphasis on business-to-business relationships is not enough, however, to protect a company from changing economic climates. In 1991, a formidable economic downturn, particularly severe in Florida, initiated the development of a new business model for Hughes: diversification. It was at this point that the management team of Hughes chose to pursue product and geographic growth through acquisition. Since that time, Hughes has grown from 50 branches scattered throughout three states to almost 500 branches across the nation and in Mexico.

"The only constant in business, as in life, is change," says Tom Morgan, president. "Hughes is willing and prepared to adapt to changing times regardless of the challenges."

As the company entered the new millennium, times changed once again. In this age of Internet economy, Hughes continues to push to the forefront, setting the industry standard. The company has made significant investments in developing its information technology systems and forming relationships with major e-business distribution partners.

Today, the company distributes more than 300,000 products throughout the world. These markets generate $200 billion annually. As a market leader, Hughes is just beginning to realize the limitless potential for growth.

"Our history in the wholesale industry, coupled with our willingness to explore new business models and opportunities—well, it's simply an unbeatable combination," says Hughes.

HUGHES SUPPLY, INC.'S HEADQUARTERS, IN ORLANDO SINCE 1928, AS IT LOOKED IN THE LATE 1950S (RIGHT).

DAVID H. HUGHES, CHAIRMAN AND CEO OF HUGHES SUPPLY, INC. (BOTTOM LEFT)

HARRY AND RUSSELL HUGHES WITH ONE OF THEIR ORIGINAL DELIVERY TRUCKS (BOTTOM RIGHT).

LOCKHEED MARTIN, THE LARGEST AEROSPACE AND DEFENSE COMPANY IN THE WORLD, TRACES ITS roots back to three daring men with a vision. In 1909, aviation pioneer Glenn L. Martin created a company around a modest airplane construction business, and then built it into a major airframe supplier to U.S. military and commercial customers. In 1961, Martin merged his company with American-Marietta Corporation, a leading supplier of building and road supplies, to become Martin-Marietta. ⚜ In 1913, around the same time as Martin's first successes in commercial aviation, Allan and Malcolm Loughhead (who later changed their name to Lockheed)

flew the first Lockheed plane over San Francisco Bay. In 1932, the modern-day Lockheed Corporation was formed after the fledgling company was reorganized.

In March 1995, the two companies that had grown up with the aviation era came together to form Lockheed Martin Corporation. In 1996, the company expanded again with the acquisition of Loral Corporation, a defense electronics and systems integration business.

In all, the new Lockheed Martin comprises all or portions of 17 heritage companies, making it one of the world's leading diversified technology companies. Employees design everything from fingerprint identification technology to sophisticated air traffic control systems.

THE FLORIDA CONNECTION

While Lockheed Martin is headquartered in Bethesda, Maryland, Florida is home to 14,500 professionals—10 percent of the firm's total workforce—representing all sectors of the company. Lockheed Martin is the largest defense contractor in the state, with 110 locations in 47 cities. Orlando is headquarters for four operations: Enterprise Information Systems, Missile and Fire Control-Orlando, Information Systems, and Integrated Business Solutions (IBS).

Enterprise Information Systems is responsible for providing technology-based information services to Lockheed Martin's various businesses. Products and services include networking communications, business process reengineering, electronic commerce, client/server applications, project management, training services, application development, Web-based technologies,

multimedia management, and data management.

Missile and Fire Control-Orlando develops, manufactures, and supports advanced combat systems, and is a world leader in electro-optics, smart munitions, and anti-armor and air defense technology. Key customers include the Department of Defense; the U.S. Army, Air Force, Navy, and Marine Corps; and international clients approved by the State Department.

Information Systems offers customers world-class information systems development, testing, and demonstration capability, including one of the largest simulation display facilities in the United States. The integrated technical demonstration suite can simultaneously link aviation, armor, and war-gaming simulations into a complete battle scenario.

IBS, part of Lockheed Martin Global Telecommunications, delivers leading-edge commercial technologies to clients such as Nike, Gateway, and General Motors. IBS provides clients with information technology design, development, integration, operations, and training.

A RESPONSIBILITY TO THE COMMUNITY

Although Lockheed Martin is a corporation with a global reach, it takes the time to give back to the communities where its employees live and work. Essential to this commitment is the principle of investing in the future through programs that reflect the company's responsibility as a good corporate citizen and neighbor.

Lockheed Martin's Philanthropic Council continually invests in the quality of life in these communities, and employees reach out in a range of worthwhile activities. Each of the four Orlando divisions has its own philanthropy budget, and the effort is pulled together to create one voice in the community. In all, Lockheed's philanthropic grants to local and state organizations amount to nearly $750,000 annually.

Through its partnerships with both communities and civic and social organizations, as well as its partnerships in business, Lockheed Martin has established itself as the premier corporation in the aerospace and defense industry.

WHEN THE MARTIN COMPANY OPENED AN OFFICE IN ORLANDO IN 1956, IT BEGAN A LONG LEGACY OF GIVING BACK TO THE CENTRAL FLORIDA COMMUNITY. TODAY, THE EMPLOYEES OF LOCKHEED MARTIN CONTINUE THAT LEGACY BY DONATING COUNTLESS HOURS AND DOLLARS IN SUPPORT OF COMMUNITY PROGRAMS AND SERVICES.

ANK MERGERS AND ACQUISITIONS MAKE HEADLINES DAILY AS THE BANKING INDUSTRY CHANGES AT AN astonishing pace. For SunTrust Banks Inc., the 1998 merger with Crestar Financial Corporation strengthened its foundation, creating the ninth-largest banking company in the United States. Today, the sizable entity offers consumer and commercial banking services to more than 3.3 million customers in Florida, Georgia, Tennessee, Alabama, Virginia, Maryland, and the District of Columbia. ▨ Though its 27 separate banks have been consolidated into a single SunTrust Bank with assets of approximately $93 billion, L. Phillip Humann,

SunTrust chairman, president and CEO, emphasizes that SunTrust continues its long-standing tradition of locally focused service. In Central Florida, SunTrust employs nearly 4,500 people at SunTrust Bank Central Florida, SunTrust BankCard, and STI Capital Management.

A STRONG FINANCIAL FOUNDATION

SunTrust Bank Central Florida is the region's largest financial institution. It has been a part of the community since 1934, when, in the midst of the Great Depression, Linton E. Allen founded SunTrust, then called First National Bank at Orlando. Allen's business philosophy was "Build your community and you build your bank."

During the 1950s and 1960s, the bank boomed with the development of several affiliate banks. In 1973, First National, its affiliates, and its holding company were renamed SunBanks of Florida, Inc. SunBanks continued to build on a foundation of strong performance and customer satisfaction. In 1985, SunBanks of Florida merged with the Trust Company of Georgia and later with Third National Bank Corporation of Tennessee, forming SunTrust Banks, Inc. But it was not until 1995 that all SunTrust subsidiaries adopted the SunTrust name, establishing a connection between local banking institutions and their umbrella organization, SunTrust.

Locally, SunTrust continues to carry the banner of "Build your community and you build your bank." "This is a people business," says Tom Yochum, SunTrust Bank Central Florida's chairman, president, and CEO. "The best way we can do our business is by having the very best qualified people who are effective at building relationships. Being professional, meeting or exceeding the customer's needs, helping them preserve and enhance their wealth–that's what banking is supposed to be. That's what we do at SunTrust."

COMMITTED TO COMMUNITY DEVELOPMENT

As SunTrust has evolved, the bank's strength has helped Orlando become a national and international destination for businesses and visitors alike. In the summer of 2000, SunTrust was the presenting sponsor of the 2000 Amateur Athletic Union (AAU) Junior Olympic Games, held at 25 venues in the five counties of Central Florida–Orange, Osceola, Seminole, Lake, and Volusia. The event's economic impact on Central Florida was estimated at more than $31 million.

Through the decades, SunTrust has helped the city earn its magical reputation by working to attract Lockheed Martin (formerly Martin Marietta Aerospace), Walt Disney World, the University of Central Florida (UCF), and the Orlando Magic to the community, as well as by playing a role in the Orlando Navy Re-Use Commission.

SunTrust's other civic endeavors include financing the expansion of the Orlando International Airport

SUNTRUST HAS BEEN A VITAL MEMBER OF THE CENTRAL FLORIDA COMMUNITY SINCE 1934.

and the Orange County Civic Center, transforming the Tangerine Bowl into the Citrus Bowl, founding the University of Central Florida, and attracting the first Minute Maid plant to Central Florida.

The bank's commitment to service extends beyond daily business calls. By concentrating efforts on four main areas—economic development, education, the arts, and health and human services—SunTrust pursues creative solutions to economic and social challenges. Philanthropy, through financial and in-kind donations, volunteering time and talent, and board involvement, is a significant part of SunTrust's past, present, and future contribution to Central Florida.

Annually, SunTrust staff members devote more than 150,000 hours to community service, building upon

the idea that if the community succeeds, SunTrust does as well. These banking professionals serve on more than 200 community boards of directors, and the company serves as a patron of the arts, giving more than $1 million to support United Arts, a funding mechanism that supports such organizations as the Bach Festival Society, Civic Theatre of Central Florida, Orlando UCF Shakespeare Festival, Orlando Museum of Art, Southern Ballet Theatre, Orlando Opera Company, Orlando Science Center, Orlando Philharmonic Orchestra, and other area arts organizations.

Additionally, SunTrust is involved in educational support—from elementary, middle, and high schools to community and four-year colleges and universities—throughout the bank's five-county

service area. SunTrust is also a big supporter of Junior Achievement and programs such as YMCA Black Achievers, which provide students with college and career planning.

In 1999, Central Florida charities received more than $1 million in SunTrust financial contributions through United Way, making SunTrust part of the Million Dollar Club. For the third consecutive year, SunTrust was the area's fourth-largest giver to United Way, and the top contributor among financial institutions. Another $1 million in SunTrust contributions benefited local charities such as March of Dimes, American Cancer Society, Orange County Historical Museum, United Cerebral Palsy, and other programs.

"As proved by the long history of SunTrust's community outreach, involvement, and support, we believe in investing where we live and work," says Yochum. "We're here for the long term. We find that our investment pays big dividends for all of our constituencies—our shareholders, customers, community, and employees—and everyone wins."

ANNUALLY, SUNTRUST STAFF MEMBERS DEVOTE MORE THAN 150,000 HOURS TO COMMUNITY SERVICE, BUILDING UPON THE IDEA THAT IF THE COMMUNITY SUCCEEDS, SUNTRUST DOES AS WELL.

PHILANTHROPY, THROUGH FINANCIAL AND IN-KIND DONATIONS, VOLUNTEERING TIME AND TALENT, AND BOARD INVOLVEMENT, IS A SIGNIFICANT PART OF SUNTRUST'S PAST, PRESENT, AND FUTURE CONTRIBUTION TO CENTRAL FLORIDA.

THE FIRST RECORD OF A YOUNG MEN'S CHRISTIAN ASSOCIATION (YMCA) IN ORANGE COUNTY DATES BACK to 1887. During the next 50 years, the YMCA faded and was resurrected two more times—in 1905 and 1925—but it was not until 1942 that Orlando established today's vibrant Central Florida YMCA. For more than half a century, the YMCA has been a force in Central Florida, improving the lives of men, women, children, families, and communities. With more than 81,000 members in a six-county service area, Central Florida YMCA has 22 family centers, including the Wewa Outdoor Center; the Refuge at Ocklawaha, a natural retreat center; and the YMCA Aquatic and Family Center.

Though YMCAs are best known for health and wellness leadership, today the Central Florida YMCA builds community by bringing people of all ages, faiths, races, and economic levels together for common causes and interests. This effort includes the hard work and dedication of more than 6,000 volunteers and nearly 200,000 program participants.

Central Florida YMCA's innovative programs represent a large portion of the organization's improvements. For instance, more than 3,000 children participate in the YMCA's after-school programs each day, with about one-third receiving assistance from the Central Florida YMCA Youth Scholarship Fund. Much of the YMCA's work is done in small groups—such as classes, clubs, committees, task groups, teams, support groups, and families—that build leadership skills, encourage the ability of family members to give and take, and support a sense of community that is central to the Central Florida YMCA.

"The Central Florida YMCA is in the business of building strong kids, strong families, and strong communities," says James W. Ferber, president and CEO. "We do this through the support and commitment of community volunteer leaders who work side by side with YMCA staff to achieve one primary goal—strengthening the Central Florida community."

CHILDREN AND FAMILIES

The Central Florida YMCA is one of the few places in the area where families can come together to participate in a wide variety of wholesome activities that help develop a stronger, closer family unit. Perhaps the biggest impact on the community is in the lives of children and families at risk.

From the YMCA's Midnight Basketball to its youth mentoring, open lines of communication are critical. A special collaboration with Orange County Public Schools allows teen mothers and dropouts to complete their high school education at the Tangelo Park and Downtown Orlando YMCA family centers.

The YMCA's Neighborhood Centers for Families Program, in collaboration with Orange County government, reaches at-risk neighborhoods, and an after-school program in 11 Orange County middle schools provides positive role models and a safe, nurturing environment to more than 2,000 students.

Among the YMCA's most innovative programs are: the Central Florida YMCA Black Achievers Program in seven communities; the Central Florida YMCA Achievers Program—Developing Hispanic Leaders—through education, mentoring, and career development; and the Back on Track suspension program, keeping suspended students off the streets. More than 100 community partners team up with

ONE OF THE CENTRAL FLORIDA YMCA'S MOST INNOVATIVE PROGRAMS IS THE BLACK ACHIEVERS PROGRAM—AVAILABLE IN SEVEN COUNTIES.

the Central Florida YMCA to meet the needs of area residents. In cooperation with Heart of Florida United Way, funds raised by community volunteers and an internal YMCA Home Mission Fund provide a variety of services to underprivileged Central Florida communities.

COMMITMENT TO CHRISTIAN VALUES

In 2000, the Central Florida YMCA Youth Scholarship Campaign raised more than $1 million to provide 25,000 children and families the opportunity to experience character-building YMCA programs that promote the organization's core values: caring, honesty, respect, responsibility, and faith.

Strong faith and deeply rooted Christian values drive the Central Florida YMCA, and Christian principles are promoted in all of the organization's programs, services, family centers, and relationships. Each year, the Central Florida YMCA's Celebration of Prayer breakfast joins thousands of people from all faiths, ages, and races together in prayer and fellowship. Most YMCA Family Centers have a chapel for members to spend quiet time.

The YMCA recognizes baby boomers and seniors as an important community segment as well. A partnership with the Winter Park Health Foundation put the Central Florida YMCA in charge of operating the foundation's two wellness centers in Winter Park and Oviedo. This partnership allows the YMCA to impact the mental and physical well-being of older adults and to incorporate the older generation into the scope of Christian influence.

A LOOK TO THE FUTURE

One of the fastest-growing YMCAs in North America, the Central Florida YMCA continues to seek innovative ways of bringing families and neighbors together, forging partnerships with community organizations and businesses. A good example is the YMCA's family center at Lake Nona, which is in partnership with the City of Orlando, Orange County Public Schools, Orlando Regional Healthcare Systems, and Lake Nona Property Holdings. This YMCA location is part of the North Lake Park Community Center, a state-of-the-art community center in the middle of a city park that is also the site of an elementary school. The unique arrangement brings children, parents, and teachers together every day, strengthening families and building healthy lifestyles.

Another pioneering expansion of family programs and services is the Refuge at Ocklawaha, a natural retreat center in nearby Ocklawaha, Florida. The Central Florida YMCA manages the bed and breakfast, located deep in the Ocala National Forest, which is the first facility of its kind in Florida, and includes canoeing, horseback riding, cultural activities, boat tours, swimming, and more.

"Innovative partnerships have helped us to inspire a revolutionary concept of community building, with strengths brought together to ensure that our goals of building strong kids, strong families, and strong communities are met successfully," says Ferber.

SINCE TUPPERWARE PRODUCTS WERE FIRST INTRODUCED IN AMERICA IN THE LATE 1940S, THE COMPANY has grown from just a handful of direct sellers in the United States to about 1 million worldwide. Headquartered in Orlando since 1954, Tupperware International sells products today in more than 100 countries, with a demonstration starting every two seconds. Eighty-five percent of the company's sales are generated outside the United States, making Tupperware a truly global brand. "A bold, new Tupperware is emerging, with yesterday's achievements and today's successful business strategies coming together to create a company for the future," says Mark

Shamley, director of community and public affairs.

Three important factors have led to the company's initial success, and they promise even greater success in the future. First, Tupperware products are well designed, with an emphasis on quality and versatility. Second, customers are educated through the world-famous Tupperware demonstration offered by enthusiastic and knowledgeable consultants who appreciate and trust the products they sell. And third, selling Tupperware offers a solid opportunity for its sales force to earn money.

To help promote future growth, the company's direct selling business has been integrated with televised sales programs, kiosks in malls, and e-commerce to help expand the earnings opportunity for the sales force. "We want customers everywhere to see Tupperware as contemporary and supportive of today's lifestyles, and we want to serve consumers when, where, and how they want to be served," says Dave Halversen, senior vice president of business development and communications.

HEADQUARTERED IN ORLANDO SINCE 1954, TUPPERWARE INTERNATIONAL SELLS PRODUCTS TODAY IN MORE THAN 100 COUNTRIES, WITH A DEMONSTRATION STARTING EVERY TWO SECONDS.

FOR THE CHANGING TIMES, TUPPERWARE PRODUCTS ARE MORE FUNCTIONAL AND BEAUTIFUL THAN EVER. IN A TRIBUTE TO BOTH THEIR FUNCTIONALITY AND THEIR DESIGN, THE PRODUCTS CONTINUE TO BE ACQUIRED BY SOME OF THE MOST PRESTIGIOUS MUSEUMS IN THE WORLD.

The company's sales consultants know and love the Tupperware line of products, taking pride in offering information that helps customers save time and money, as well as taking pleasure in sharing the tools of opportunity so others can succeed. Tupperware's compensation program, incentives, and bonuses are structured to motivate the sales force and stimulate success throughout the system, from trips and prizes to significant incomes. Since 1995, Tupperware's independent direct sellers have earned nearly $4 billion.

WORLDWIDE EXPANSION

Direct sellers give Tupperware a competitive advantage, with a worldwide market of more than $85.4 billion. Tupperware offers a broad range of high-quality, functional products in contemporary colors and styles that address food storage, preparation, and serving, along with home decoration, environmental, and children's products. These products can be launched quickly, with instant feedback from consumers. The knowledgeable sales force provides a level of product information, solutions to everyday challenges in the home, and custom-

er service almost unequaled in the retail environment.

A worldwide management team has been brought together with key leadership and talent to lay the groundwork for the company's future success. Tupperware is now adapting its method of direct selling to more than 100 markets, targeting its product lines to meet local demand and publishing catalogs in many languages.

The heart of Tupperware's direct selling system is its Orlando world headquarters, the destination for Tupperware distributors, managers, and consultants from all over the world. Each year, the company's Hall of Fame honors the achievements of the top distributor, top manager, and top consultant from each country in which Tupperware operates.

The Orlando campus is also the headquarters for Tupperware North American and Latin American division operations, and one of three design centers. Headquarters for Tupperware Europe, Africa, and Middle East division operations is in Switzerland, and the Tupperware Asia Pacific division is headquartered in Honolulu.

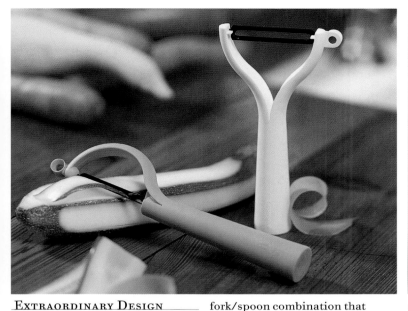

Extraordinary Design

For the changing times, Tupperware products are more functional and beautiful than ever. In a tribute to both their functionality and their design, the products continue to be acquired by some of the most prestigious museums in the world, including the Museum of Modern Art in New York and the Victoria and Albert Museum in London. Tupperware products also continue to receive prestigious design awards in the United States, Europe, and Japan. From museum shelves to kitchen shelves, Tupperware's designs provide a striking balance between form and function.

And Tupperware is in touch with unique cultural demands, creating pieces that address the specific needs of different countries. The ingenious children's lunch box for the Japanese market includes chopsticks and a fork/spoon combination that doubles as the latch. The kimchi keeper, for storing the Korean national dish of pickled cabbage, expands as gasses accumulate during fermentation.

Giving Back

Since its inception, helping others has been the hallmark of a career in Tupperware, offering opportunities to women, assisting customers with products and information to care for their families, and supporting charities with fund-raising events and direct donations. Tupperware's worldwide management team, as well, is strongly committed to giving back to its communities and helping those in need.

Around the world today, children in one out of every five families are living in conditions of war, poverty, disease, famine, homelessness, and abuse. To reflect a shared responsibility for children in distress, Tupperware established the Give a Child a Chance program to focus corporate donations and charity marketing activities. Tupperware's management and sales force have joined together on a number of projects to support Give a Child a Chance: building a residence for orphans in Germany; contributing homes for abandoned, abused, and orphaned children in Mexico and Malaysia; and supporting and educating girls in the Central African Republic. In the United States, Tupperware has adopted the Boys and Girls Clubs of America for its local charitable and cause-related marketing focus.

With a strong strategic direction, a focus on quality products, a team of enthusiastic employees, and a civic-minded orientation, Tupperware has charted its course for success in the years to come.

WHETHER IT IS A PEELER, BLENDER, CEREAL STORER, OR THE CLEVER SHAPE-O, TUPPERWARE CREATES PIECES THAT PROVIDE A STRIKING BALANCE BETWEEN FORM AND FUNCTION.

IN JULY 1954, WHEN ORLANDO'S FIRST TELEVISION NEWSCAST HIT THE AIRWAVES ON WDBO-TV, CHANNEL 6, broadcast technology was still in its infancy, and compelling local news was rare. The area's pioneering news crew did not have access to portable television cameras to help them cover the action between Orlando and the vast expanse of Florida's east coast. Instead, the WDBO crew showed Polaroid snapshots to illustrate stories like car crashes, civic club events, and big-news merchant thefts of $100. Only two 15-minute newscasts a day — at 6 p.m. and 11 p.m. — told tales of the city and beyond, with black-and-white artwork and lots of wire service stories tossed in.

CHANGING WITH THE TIMES

Channel 6 started with 25 full-time and five part-time workers who had little knowledge of this new field. Programming on WDBO-TV was limited to 56 hours a week, including shows from all three then-existing networks: CBS, ABC, and Dumont. Within two years, the station was on the air all day, broadcasting to approximately 90,000 television sets in the area.

WKMG-TV, CHANNEL 6, BEGAN AS WDBO-TV IN 1954 WITH ONLY A HANDFUL OF WORKERS AND REPORTERS.

Within 10 years, Orlando was a boomtown closing in on 500,000 residents, and the number of televisions in the market had jumped to 250,000. Most were tuned to Channel 6, which was by then broadcasting in full color.

The 1960s were considered the golden age of television, with entertaining network shows that today are considered classics: *I Love Lucy*, *The Ed Sullivan Show*, *The Twilight Zone*, and many more.

In addition, Channel 6 offered popular local programming, including *The Central Florida Showcase*

interview program, and *Hunting and Fishing* with good-old-boy commentary on these two popular outdoor pastimes. And every weekday morning, Channel 6 news reporter Nancy Stillwell became Miss Nancy of *Romper Room*.

In 1982, WDBO Radio was sold along with the original call letters. Expecting to be sold to Columbia Pictures, the television station chose the new call letters WCPX to identify it with its soon-to-be owner. In a sur-

prising turn, Channel 6 was sold instead to Rockefeller Center, Inc., which then handed it off to First Media Corp. In 1997, Post-Newsweek Stations bought Channel 6, changing the call letters a year later to WKMG in honor of Katharine M. Graham, chairman of The Washington Post Company executive committee.

A HOUSEHOLD NEWS TRADITION

Since first hitting the airwaves, the station has recorded history for all to see: Walt Disney's announcement that he would build a kingdom of theme parks in Orlando, *Apollo 11*'s moon landing, the first space shuttle launch, and the *Challenger* disaster. The station also made its own history as the first station in Central Florida to provide network news, hire a female reporter, hire the first African-American weekday news anchor in the city, send a reporter to cover state government in Tallahassee, and use helicopters and airplanes for news gathering.

Nearly 50 years after its founding, the fledgling WDBO-TV operation has evolved into WKMG-TV, a household news staple bringing cutting-edge coverage to more than 1 million Central Florida families. Live news is

FIFTY YEARS AFTER ITS FOUNDING, WKMG-TV IS AN ESSENTIAL PART OF CENTRAL FLORIDA LIFE, COVERING THE NEWS FOR MORE THAN 1 MILLION FAMILIES.

delivered each morning, afternoon, evening, and night, with special round-the-clock reports during hurricanes, tornadoes, fires, and other major news events affecting the lives of viewers. Still a CBS affiliate, WKMG-TV focuses its far-reaching lens on 10 Central Florida counties: Brevard, Flagler, Lake, Marion, Orange, Osceola, Polk, Seminole, Sumpter, and Volusia.

Today, the station's news team deploys a satellite news truck, a fleet of microwave trucks, and a Bell Jet Ranger helicopter to get the news to viewers quickly, making WKMG The One to Watch. In addition, Channel 6 is the only station in Central Florida with real-time triple Doppler radar, which gives viewers live radar coverage from three sites around the state at one time. This unique technology allows viewers and WKMG's staff of meteorologists to track critical developments in the region's fast changing, and often dangerous, weather statewide.

"We've pioneered news coverage in Central Florida," says Jeff Sales, vice president and general manager. "WKMG is growing along with Central Florida. Our mission today is to build on the station's tradition of excellence in journalism and commitment to our community by delivering the best local news and programming. We are excited about the future. High-definition television and expanded Internet services will bring incredible change, with the ultimate goal of bringing more and better services into viewers' homes."

Growing with the Community

At the dawn of a new millennium, WKMG-TV prides itself on the growth and innovation in its up-to-the-minute news coverage and quality programming. Channel 6 now employs a staff of some 200, including a team of reporters and anchors, many with long ties and keen insight into the growing Central Florida community.

The station boasts the largest full-time group of investigative and consumer reporters in Central Florida, with a special team called the WKMG Problem Solvers. The members of this team address a wide variety of issues with one key difference: they get involved with their stories, helping to seek resolution to viewer concerns, rather than just reporting on them.

In a nod to a job well done, in March 2000, WKMG's news staff earned six awards from the Associated Press for excellence in journalism.

WKMG-TV offers its audience a multitude of sports—from golf to professional football and basketball. The CBS television network and syndicated programming wrap up the station's programming package with top-quality dramas, situation comedies, prime-time specials, and other entertaining shows.

As in the past, WKMG-TV is committed to a future of keeping Central Florida well informed and entertained. The station remains dedicated to carrying on its tradition of giving back to the community by

providing clothing to needy children; organizing food drives; presenting up-to-the-minute, continuous, live coverage of emergencies; and offering WKMG News Helpline phone banks.

The FCC defines a broadcaster's mission as providing programming for the "interest, convenience and necessity" of the viewing audience. Every day and in every way, WKMG has embraced that mission. More important, WKMG-TV believes its role is to help make a difference in and for Central Florida.

FROM SPORTS, WEATHER, AND CULTURAL EVENTS, TO TRACKING ELECTION RESULTS, WKMG-TV HAS ALWAYS PIONEERED NEWS COVERAGE IN CENTRAL FLORIDA.

TODAY, THE STATION'S NEWS TEAM DEPLOYS A SATELLITE NEWS TRUCK, A FLEET OF MICROWAVE TRUCKS, AND A BELL JET RANGER HELICOPTER TO GET THE NEWS TO VIEWERS QUICKLY, MAKING WKMG THE ONE TO WATCH.

PORT CANAVERAL IS OFTEN CALLED ORLANDO'S SEAPORT, AND HOLDS THE DISTINCTION OF BEING THE world's only quadramodal transportation hub, moving passengers and freight between land, sea, air, and space transportation modes. Since the arrival of the first cargo ship in 1955, Port Canaveral has grown from a small shrimp and oil port to an international cruise and cargo port. Managed and maintained by Canaveral Port Authority, the port's first-class facilities and commitment to controlled growth have given it a reputation for excellence and innovation. ❧ Centrally located between Jacksonville and Miami on Florida's Atlantic Coast, Port Canaveral is next to Kennedy Space Center,

home of NASA's space shuttle fleet, and Cape Canaveral, where the majority of military and civilian satellites are launched. Each year, some 3.8 million passengers arrive and depart from Port Canaveral's six major cruise terminals—only a 45-minute drive east from Orlando—making a key impact on Central Florida tourism and positioning the port as a dominant force in the Florida-Caribbean cruise market.

Today, Port Canaveral is the world's busiest cruise port, accommodating the ships of Disney Cruise Line, Royal Caribbean International, Carnival Cruise Lines, Sterling Casino Lines, and SunCruz Casino. With terminal capacity to double the passengers through the port and a new, larger terminal on the drawing board, Port Canaveral is projected to continue its rapid growth. Included in this projection is a 6,200-passenger luxury ship by World City America, Inc. and Westin Hotels & Resorts.

Port Canaveral's cargo business is expanding with continued growth of its primary imports, including petroleum, lumber, cement, and

NOT JUST FOR CARGO AND CRUISE SHIPS, PORT CANAVERAL, MANAGED BY CANAVERAL PORT AUTHORITY, OFFERS VISITORS MORE RECREATIONAL FACILITIES THAN ALL OF FLORIDA'S 14 OTHER SEAPORTS COMBINED.

newsprint. The port also imports thousands of tons of rebar, wallboard, and asphalt yearly to support Central Florida's construction industry. The port is a leading exporter of scrap metal, citrus, and citrus products—from juice concentrate to fresh grapefruits. The addition of the port's new, $9 million container facility rounds out the ocean transportation needs of Central Florida; the facility lowers transportation costs by serving as a feeder to the transshipment hubs in Charleston, Savannah, Miami, and Freeport, Grand Bahamas.

Port Canaveral's Foreign Trade Zone (FTZ) 136 is the only FTZ in the nation offering space transportation. At its Kennedy Space Center and Cape Canaveral Air Station launch facilities, FTZ 136 houses two commercial payload processing operations where satellites and other payload arrive from around the world before traveling into space. FTZ 136 also plays a critical role in the recovery of the shuttle's two solid rocket boosters.

More than 35 nations trade through Port Canaveral, with 16

countries—including Russia, Norway, England, and Venezuela—engaging in both import and export activity. Port cargo has doubled in the past 20 years, with annual growth of about 5 percent.

"When Port Canaveral first opened, it was a sleeping giant, and now the giant is wide awake," says Malcolm E. McLouth, Canaveral Port Authority executive director. "The port will play an increasingly important role in tourism and the overall economic growth of Central Florida."

RESIDENTS AND TOURISTS REAP BENEFITS

Canaveral Port Authority grants long-term leases to more than 200 businesses. Seafood processors, boat manufacturers, restaurants, and other operations are located in the marine-related commercial park, and more than 20,000 residents of East Central Florida are employed in port-related business.

Keeping residents and visitors in mind, Port Canaveral has developed more recreational facilities than all

of Florida's 14 other seaports combined, with three public parks and another one in development, offering swimming, camping, fishing, and other recreational opportunities. The popular 35-acre Jetty Park includes a 4.5-acre beach along the Atlantic Ocean, with lifeguards and a lighted fishing pier that extends 1,000 feet into the Atlantic Ocean. The port provides an informative Web site at www.portcanaveral.org.

Three marinas are located within the port's harbor, with another three marinas along the barge canal, within the park's jurisdiction. Boat chartering services offer a variety of excursions as well. Several major deep-sea fishing tournaments are

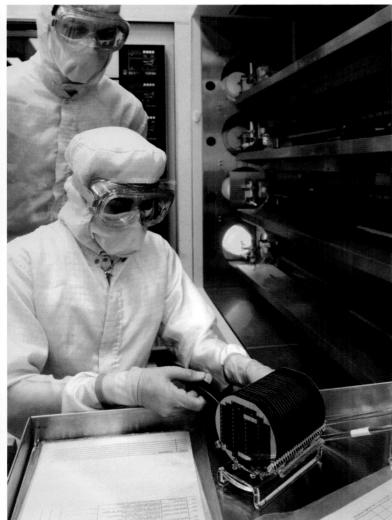

held throughout the year at Port Canaveral, including the annual Florida Sport Fishing Association's Offshore Tournament, the largest single-day fishing tournament in the world.

The U.S. Coast Guard is stationed at Port Canaveral, and the port provides logistic support to the Military Sealift Command and Naval Ordnance Test Unit. Each year, the port hosts more than 300 submarines and surface warships of the U.S. Atlantic Fleet and other navies.

In keeping with its commitment to the environment, Canaveral Port Authority implemented several measures to ensure protection of the endangered Florida manatee, which

often can be seen feeding and playing in port waters, as well as sea turtles and right whales.

A Thoughtful Past, A Vibrant Future

Although the idea of creating Port Canaveral was formulated in the late 1800s, construction on the Canaveral Port District—in north and central Brevard County—didn't begin until the 1950s. In 1953, the Florida legislature subdivided the port district into five geographical districts, each with an elected commissioner as its representative. These commissioners govern the port, and have jurisdiction over fiscal, regulatory, and operational policies.

In 1986, Canaveral Port Authority took a major step toward self-sufficiency by ceasing to levy taxes that had been collected annually from property owners in the port district. Another major milestone in the port's history came in May 1995, when Disney Cruise Line agreed to construct a $27 million terminal for its brand-new cruise business. It became the first terminal built to a cruise line's specifications for its exclusive use.

The port had 10 employees when it first opened. Today, some 150 employees keep day-to-day business in motion for the port's many operations. As Port Canaveral continues growing, it prides itself on providing major economic benefits and public recreation facilities while promoting environmental responsibility.

Canaveral Port Authority's major goal is to provide a meaningful, stable, and growing employment base for area residents. The authority expects to accomplish this goal by controlling land use within the port to maximize the economic benefit and use of natural and man-made resources, while protecting the health, safety, welfare, and environment within the port.

TODAY, PORT CANAVERAL IS THE WORLD'S BUSIEST CRUISE PORT, ACCOMMODATING THE SHIPS OF DISNEY CRUISE LINE, ROYAL CARIBBEAN INTERNATIONAL, CARNIVAL CRUISE LINES, STERLING CASINO LINES, AND SUNCRUZ CASINO.

PORT CANAVERAL'S FOREIGN TRADE ZONE (FTZ) 136 IS THE ONLY FTZ IN THE NATION OFFERING SPACE TRANSPORTATION.

Central Florida has witnessed a lot of changes in the past five decades. The area has grown from an agricultural community and retirement haven to a national center for space science and technology and the world's number one tourist destination. WESH, Florida's Channel 2, is a dynamic element of the area's phenomenal growth. ▌ Since 1956, WESH-TV has served Central Florida with outstanding programming, innovative news coverage and an ongoing commitment to excellence. At WESH, Where The News Comes First isn't just a slogan; it's a mission statement and a call to action. ▌ "At NewsChannel 2, we are dedicated to responsible news

coverage of Central Florida," says longtime news anchor Wendy Chioji. "We have more specialized reporters than any other station in the area, and they bring their depth of knowledge to the stories they cover every day."

The first area station to deliver live news coverage via helicopter and the first in the area to own and operate a live Doppler weather radar system, WESH Channel 2 is committed to presenting straightforward, live coverage of breaking news and weather. The NewsChannel 2 team of meteorologists, all certified by the American Meteorological Society, is highly regarded in the region for its accurate and dependable weather reports.

"Among our station's strengths are its vision and its commitment to staying on the cutting edge of technology," says 30-year WESH veteran Dave Marsh. "In the late 1970s, we were the first local station with weather radar. In 1996, we installed our current live Super Doppler radar—the first live Doppler in Central Florida and the most accurate system in the world. In 2000, we were first again with Predictor 2, a more accurate way

to preview tomorrow's weather. And while technology is important, our greatest advantage is our experienced team. We're all dedicated to keeping Central Florida families safe."

The station's highly specialized broadcast journalists are committed to keeping viewers informed. They work for the only station in the Central Florida market with designated reporters covering education, health, consumer issues, space, and the environment. In addition, WESH-TV staffs news bureaus throughout its nine-county

coverage area of Orange, Seminole, Osceola, Volusia, Brevard, Lake, Marion, Flagler, and Sumter counties with experienced reporters knowledgeable about the areas in which they work and live.

Through the years, WESH NewsChannel 2 has expanded its news programming to offer viewers increased options in news viewing and expanded coverage of local news. NewsChannel 2 produces news around the clock with newscasts each day, starting in the early morning, and continuing at noon, in the evenings, and late at night.

Hitting the Airwaves

A Hearst-Argyle-owned television station, WESH has a rich broadcast history. On Monday, June 11, 1956, WESH debuted with its first programming. Named after radio pioneer and founder W. Wright Esch and launched by new owner John H. Perry Jr., WESH first transmitted from its 350-foot tower at the station's Holly Hill studio with a power of 12,500 watts. Its equipment was bare bones: one black-and-white studio camera and a 16mm film projector.

CHIEF METEOROLOGIST DAVE MARSH IS JUST ONE OF THE MANY PROFESSIONALS THAT MAKE UP THE WESH NEWSCHANNEL 2 TEAM.

THE FIRST AREA STATION TO DELIVER LIVE NEWS COVERAGE VIA HELICOPTER AND THE FIRST IN THE AREA TO OWN AND OPERATE A LIVE DOPPLER WEATHER RADAR SYSTEM, WESH CHANNEL 2 IS COMMITTED TO PRESENTING STRAIGHTFORWARD, LIVE COVERAGE OF BREAKING NEWS AND WEATHER.

By November 1957, the station had become an NBC affiliate and had increased power output to 100,000 watts by utilizing a 1,000-foot tower in Orange City. The first NBC program broadcast by the station was a NCAA football game.

FCC approval in 1960 allowed the station to begin operating from its Winter Park studio and, in 1962, WESH transmitted NBC color programming for the first time. In 1966, Cowles Communications, Inc. purchased the station, and three years later all of the station's local programming made the breakthrough to color. By 1970, WESH had mounted its first weather radar unit atop its Winter Park studio tower.

Television technology rapidly improved in the 1970s and 1980s. And, in 1979, WESH became the first station in the area with aerial coverage using its SkyEye helicopters. In July 1980, the station launched transmissions from its brand-new, 1,740-foot tower in Orange City. That same year, WESH became the first station in the market to transmit live coverage of news from the Space Coast. In 1985, the station was the first in Central Florida with satellite news gathering capabilities and, in 1991, WESH moved into its current state-of-the-art facility with its landmark Doppler tower along I-4 in Winter Park.

WESH IS PIONEERING NEWS COVERAGE IN CENTRAL FLORIDA WITH A COMPREHENSIVE INTERNET PRESENCE, A MODERN STUDIO, AND OUTSTANDING ANCHORS SUCH AS WENDY CHIOJI.

REACHING FOR THE STARS

Covering America's space program has been a priority since NASA's creation in the 1950s. WESH was the first station to open a fully staffed news bureau on the Space Coast, the first to speak live with astronauts in orbit, and the only station with a reporter who covers space on a full-time basis. WESH has earned the distinction as the station of choice for complete coverage of the space program.

NewsChannel 2's dedicated news team and other station employees have contributed to Central Florida by organizing the yearly Share Your Christmas food drive since 1985, building more than 25 Habitat for Humanity homes, and establishing scholarships for students in the nine-country area the station covers. Its news anchors make appearances regularly to benefit a wide variety of causes throughout Central Florida.

As the television industry moves into the digital world, WESH is positioning itself as a leader in the industry. In February 2000, newschannel2000.com, Central Florida's leading Web site for breaking news and weather, was launched. In early 2001, WESH will complete construction on a new, 1,695-foot digital television tower in East Orange County. WESH broadcasts its digital signal on Channel 11, while continuing to broadcast its conventional analog signal on Channel 2.

WESH is leading the way in providing advertisers with unique new ways to reach customers. By using television to drive viewers to other media platforms like the Internet, WESH has created new opportunities for media convergence packages to both local and national advertisers.

It takes a station with dedication and vision to lead the way in one of the fastest-growing television markets in the country. WESH NewsChannel 2 upholds its pledge to millions of viewers to always be the station Where The News Comes First.

CENTEX ROONEY CONSTRUCTION COMPANY

THE LARGEST CONTRACTOR AND CONSTRUCTION MANAGEMENT COMPANY IN FLORIDA, CENTEX ROONEY Construction Company's projects run the gamut—from public schools and universities to Orlando International Airport facilities and Disney theme-park attractions. ❧ Acclaimed for its work for education, hospitality, criminal justice, and office and retail centers, Centex Rooney is headquartered in Fort Lauderdale, with two offices in Orlando and six other offices throughout the state. The firm is one of the oldest and largest commercial contracting companies in the southeastern United States, employing more

CENTEX ROONEY CONSTRUCTION COMPANY IS ACCLAIMED FOR ITS WORK ON EDUCATION, HOSPITALITY, CRIMINAL JUSTICE, AND OFFICE AND RETAIL CENTERS. BASS PRO SHOPS' OUTDOOR WORLD (RIGHT) IS ONE OF CENTEX ROONEY'S MORE RECENT RETAIL CENTER DEVELOPMENTS IN ORLANDO.

than 430 people, including 170 in Central and North Florida.

Founded in 1933, the Frank J. Rooney Construction Company was acquired in 1978 by Centex Corporation (NYSE: CTX), a $6 billion-per-year, Fortune 500 building organization. The company's 1999 operating revenue for Central Florida exceeded $194 million, with statewide revenues topping $600 million.

A TRADITION OF EXCELLENCE

From the time Centex Rooney laid its Central Florida foundation in 1958, the company quickly established itself as a prominent commercial builder. The firm's early projects included downtown Orlando's Florida Gas Building, the Old Pan America Building, and the State Regional Service Center.

Projects like the Titan IV Rocket Facility at the Kennedy Space Center and the Celebration Learning Center in Osceola County exemplify the can-do attitude shared by Centex Rooney's employees. Successes like the Castle of Miracles and World of Wonders at Give Kids the World Village demonstrate the company's

commitment to giving back to the Central Florida community.

Centex Rooney prides itself on its experience and ability to offer construction methods designed to satisfy a client's most demanding construction requirements. The company's services and capabilities are diverse enough to maximize project value while meeting the toughest timelines and budget constraints. To help its workforce remain at the leading edge of industry and professional standards, Centex Rooney devotes nearly 17,000 hours each year to employee training and education.

A PRESTIGIOUS PORTFOLIO

From whimsical attractions to academic institutions, Centex Rooney has completed prestigious construction projects successfully with a client-focused philosophy of quality performance and on-time delivery. The company's slogan—Begin with Centex Rooney, End with Quality—is paramount to the principals, managers, superintendents, engineers, estimators, and schedulers who make up project teams.

"We've come a long way, as now Central Florida is a major hub for our business units," says Michael Wood, executive vice president of the company's Central and North Florida division. "Centex Rooney will continue to make a strong business and civic impact in this community, and we anticipate many exciting challenges ahead."

Centex Rooney focuses on the educational institutions that are part of the company's work. The Orange County Convention Center, University of Central Florida Residence Hall and Academic Villages, Seminole Community College Oviedo Campus, and numerous projects for Orange and Osceola county public schools have all benefited from Centex Rooney's ministrations.

CENTEX ROONEY WORKED EXTENSIVELY WITH WALT DISNEY IMAGINEERING TO CONSTRUCT THE WILDERNESS LODGE RESORT AT WALT DISNEY WORLD IN ORLANDO.

The company's $66 million expansion of the state's oldest active courthouse, Osceola County Courthouse, is one of Centex Rooney's most exciting endeavors. After building a new, 255,000-square-foot courthouse and government center, the firm is completing a total, period-specific restoration of the 111-year-old original building.

Centex Rooney has constructed numerous Disney theme venues and even assisted in the creation of Cinderella's Castle in 1971. Other notable projects include Orlando International Airport terminals, Osceola and Polk county jails, and the Marriott Orlando World Center expansion.

GARNERING ACCLAIM

Centex Rooney's efforts are recognized continually throughout the industry. The company has earned the Project of the Year award and several recent Eagle Awards for Excellence in Construction from the Associated Builders and Contractors (ABC) of Central Florida. Centex Rooney also has been named Contractor of the Year worldwide by the U.S. Army Corps of Engineers, and has been ranked the number one construction firm by *Florida Trend* magazine.

Centex Rooney's holding company, Centex, was named America's Most Admired Company in the engineering and construction category by *Fortune* magazine in 1999 and 2000, and has been ranked the number one company for domestic general building contracts by *Engineering News Record*.

A CULTURE OF CITIZENSHIP

We are proud to be active participants in the civic and community programs of Central Florida," says President Al Petrangeli. "We view this involvement as a must for our company as well as for our employees."

Centex Rooney encourages civic and community participation by its employees and others through its various projects. The company has served on the executive board for the National Conference of Community & Justice; on the boards of directors for the American Cancer Society, Central Florida YMCA, Kissimmee/Osceola County Chamber of Commerce, and Seminole Community College Foundation; and on the board of trustees of Give Kids the World.

Centex Rooney is a founding participant of Orange County's A Gift for Teaching Foundation, and the company has contributed to Leadership Orlando, Osceola County Children's Home, and the advisory board of the University of Central Florida College of Engineering. "We understand the importance of having a healthy community," says Wood.

Between 1993 and 2000, Centex Rooney built the $2.5 million Castle of Miracles—an interactive play area—and the $16 million World of Wonders, a 16-acre village expansion that includes a movie theater, interactive train station, and welcome center for families with terminally ill children visiting Orlando-area attractions. The company not only managed much of the projects' development and construction, but also helped keep Give Kids the World's total costs under $7 million by soliciting donations and services in-kind.

GROWING WITH CENTRAL FLORIDA

As a general contracting firm with a breadth of experience, Centex Rooney eagerly anticipates the challenges of the next decade. With the best employees in the business, a proven partnering and total quality management program, and its client-oriented philosophy, the company is positioned to maintain its leadership in the industry.

THE GRAND FLORIDIAN BEACH RESORT HOTEL, CONSTRUCTED BY CENTEX ROONEY, IS A LUXURIOUS 903-ROOM VICTORIAN-STYLE RESORT, CONSISTING OF SIX FIVE STORY BUILDINGS OCCUPYING MORE THAN 750,000 SQUARE FEET ON A 40-ACRE PENINSULA. TO DATE, THE FIRM HAS BUILT MORE THAN 16,000 HOTEL ROOMS IN CENTRAL FLORIDA.

CENTEX ROONEY HAS ALSO WORKED WITH THE UNIVERSITY OF CENTRAL FLORIDA IN CREATING NEW RESIDENCE HALLS (LEFT) AND THE GREATER ORLANDO AVIATION AUTHORITY IN THE CONSTRUCTION OF A NUMBER OF MAJOR ADDITIONS TO ORLANDO INTERNATIONAL AIRPORT, INCLUDING THE LANDSLIDE TERMINAL (RIGHT).

1960-1979

1962	ORLANDO MAGAZINE
1962	DEMETREE BUILDERS
1963	PATTERSON/BACH COMMUNICATIONS, INC.
1963	UNIVERSITY OF CENTRAL FLORIDA
1966	TRINITY PREPARATORY SCHOOL
1970	LAKE HIGHLAND PREPARATORY SCHOOL
1971	ORLANDO SANFORD INTERNATIONAL AIRPORT
1971	WALT DISNEY WORLD RESORT
1972	CITRUS CLUB
1972	RISSMAN, WEISBERG, BARRETT, HURT, DONAHUE & McLAIN, P.A.
1974	ALBERTSON'S INC.
1974	PBS&J
1974	PROGRESSIVE COMMUNICATIONS INTERNATIONAL
1974	THOMAS W. RUFF & COMPANY
1975	ADVANTOR CORPORATION
1976	GREATER ORLANDO AVIATION AUTHORITY
1977	DATAMAX CORPORATION
1977	ZOM
1979	SAWTEK, INC.

IN 1962, ED AND ARTICE PRIZER MADE A CHANGE IN THEIR LIVES THAT ALSO CHANGED THE FACE OF ORLANDO. Ed Prizer had left a successful career with the Associated Press to purchase a small guide for visitors in Orlando. What he got was a 24-hour-a-day job in which he struggled to avoid red ink and faced competition from all sides. ❧ But what he and his wife created was *Orlando* magazine, one of the nation's first true city/regional publications, which chronicled and encouraged the rise of a sleepy southern town into a major metropolis known worldwide for its attractions, growth, and quality of life. ❧ But in the early 1960s, the big draw was warm weather. Small motels along U.S. Highway 17-92 in Winter Park and

on the South Orange Blossom Trail drew tourists who often stayed the entire winter. Ads in the magazine sold for $3.95, and content consisted of things to do in Orlando that week. The Prizers ran the business from their home.

GROWING WITH ORLANDO

By 1966, the magazine was up to 60 pages and advertising sales had doubled. But Ed Prizer had one more idea that would bolster the business and lay the groundwork for today's *Orlando* magazine. He noticed that many people staying in the small motels weren't tourists, but were people planning to relocate. Instead of simply aiming his publication at the visitor market, Prizer began running articles for both new and current residents.

Prizer's plan proved successful. In 1969, he increased the dimensions of the magazine from a small, pocket-size guide to the current standard magazine format. The first cover in this format featured an office building on Lake Eola, heralding an editorial direction that would focus the magazine's content on Central Florida's business, growth, and development.

With advertising and subscriptions booming, the Prizers were able to lease office space and hire a staff. By the 1980s, *Orlando* magazine was one of the largest city/regional publications in the nation, with issues routinely running more than 200 pages in length.

Prizer sold the business in the late 1980s, but he remains active as publisher emeritus. And, although its content now encompasses lifestyle, as well as business and development stories, the magazine's concept remains the same: to provide information for decision

making and to reflect dynamic Central Florida in all its aspects.

Orlando magazine—owned by Abarta Media, based in Miami—also publishes *WHERE Orlando*, *ABCs of Education*, *Orlando Home Design*, and a variety of other magazines. The staff includes many veterans who began their careers with Prizer, as well as talented young writers, artists, and marketing professionals who are taking the publication into the 21st century.

The future was bright when the Prizers came to Central Florida in 1962. It's even brighter today, thanks to their vision and dedication.

IN 1963, WHEN ORLANDO WAS STILL A SLEEPY CITRUS TOWN AND DEALS WERE MOST OFTEN SEALED WITH A FIRM handshake, Charles D. Patterson founded the agency now known as Patterson/Bach Communications, Inc. Patterson hired Tim Bach in 1986 as art director; Bach eventually became owner and president in 1996. Some four decades later, Patterson still serves many of his original clients. ⚐ Since its inception, Patterson/Bach's team of professionals has taken a unique approach to doing business, aiming to differentiate itself from faceless corporations full of egos and hierarchies. The company philosophy is straightforward: communicate, be on time, and care for the client. Bach, who personally meets

with each client, is quick to point out just how unique the company is. "We have no titles on our business cards because, for every project, our approach is inclusive of each team member," Bach says. As a testament to this philosophy, the epicenter of the firm's office in Winter Park is a custom-made conference and presentation center where staff members meet and creative juices flow.

CLIENTS AROUND THE GLOBE

Much of Patterson/Bach's strength comes from its diverse, worldwide client roster. "We don't focus on a particular industry," says Bach, "so when a client comes to us, we can be objective and look at the big picture." Current clients range from software companies such as Thru-Put Systems, which writes database development software for analytical labs, to a furniture manufacturer in Mexico, to a company that customizes aircraft interiors for royalty worldwide. A key Central Florida client is the Orlando-Orange County Expressway Authority.

COMMITMENT TO QUALITY

We provide the most creative concepts in the city," says Bach. "We look at a particular product or service, develop a creative concept, and then choose the most intrusive medium to communicate. You might have the best strategy, but if no one pays attention, it doesn't matter. Developing strong, creative concepts and selecting sound marketing strategies are just the first steps. We are also a service company. We strive to make every client feel as if they are our only client."

Bach also points out that the Internet has dramatically changed the agency business, as the firm was one of the first to embrace new technology. "The Web is now a key component in all of our recommended integrated marketing and communications strategies," Bach says.

COMMUNITY COMMITMENT

Bach encourages employees not only to spend quality time with family and friends, but also to volunteer in the community. Volunteerism and business blend in Patterson/Bach's commitment to RESPECT, a program that empowers teens to abstain from early sexual activity. "As an agency, we're helping young people and giving back to our community," says Bach. The firm has contracted to do public relations and advertising for this state-funded program, which aims for national prominence. The name RESPECT was created by the Patterson/Bach team in hopes that teens will "respect their bodies, their futures, and the decisions of others," Bach explains.

The agency has also donated countless hours and creative services to the Orlando Museum of Art's *A Palette for the Senses* fundraiser and to the United States Blind Golf Association. Bach serves on the governing council for the Osceola County Abstinence Only Education Partnership, which oversees the

RESPECT campaign, and on the board of directors for Central Florida's prestigious Montverde Academy, a private boarding school.

Through the years, Patterson/Bach Communications, Inc. has risen from a small, creative agency to a full-service communications powerhouse, offering integrated marketing, advertising, and public relations programs. The company has found itself ranked in the top 25 agencies in Central Florida, according to the *Orlando Business Journal*'s 2001 *Book of Lists*, and the organization enjoys steady growth. "We want to keep the pace manageable, while never sacrificing the personal touch," says Bach.

CLOCKWISE FROM TOP: PATTERSON/BACH COMMUNICATIONS, INC. IS COMMITTED TO RESPECT, A PROGRAM EMPOWERING TEENS TO ABSTAIN FROM EARLY SEXUAL ACTIVITY.

E-PASS BILLBOARD PROMOTING ELECTRONIC TOLL COLLECTION DEVICES FOR THE ORLANDO-ORANGE COUNTY EXPRESSWAY AUTHORITY

THE PATTERSON/BACH COMMUNICATIONS CONFERENCE/PRESENTATION EPICENTER IS WHERE THE CREATIVE JUICES FLOW.

TRUE PIONEERS IN CENTRAL FLORIDA REAL ESTATE DEVELOPMENT, DEMETREE BUILDERS INC. started building homes just as World War II was ending and soldiers were returning to their families. "My dad and his uncles, brothers, and cousins were building 20 houses a week in Tallahassee, St. Petersburg, Jacksonville, and Orlando," says Mary Demetree, president of Demetree Builders, one of Central Florida's most successful real estate development companies. Her father, William C. Demetree, still serves as chairman of the board. "My grandmother was an immigrant from Lebanon," says Mary Demetree. "She couldn't read or

speak English, but she loved land. With five children, she would save her pennies to make a deposit on a piece of land in Tallahassee. She formed a family trust."

William Demetree was just 26 years old when he launched his real estate business in 1948. Two years later, he founded Demetree Builders Inc., a multimillion-dollar home-building company, in Jacksonville, Florida. The company's early efforts focused on building houses for the families of men returning home from World War II.

In 1962, William Demetree moved to Orlando to direct the company's business in the rapidly expanding Central Florida real estate market. By the time Walt Disney had zeroed in on Central Florida, Demetree had already built a prosperous real estate network in central and northeastern Florida, and he and his partners sold 12,400 acres of land to Disney for Walt Disney World.

During the ensuing boom, Demetree development and construction companies completed more than 13,000 hotel rooms, dozens of mixed-used commercial

DEMETREE BUILDERS BUILDS HOMES FOR ALL INCOME LEVELS (TOP).

DEMETREE BUILDERS HELPS NEW HOMEOWNERS WITH ALL AREAS OF HOMEOWNERSHIP (BOTTOM).

projects, and thousands of multi-family and residential homes in Central Florida.

CONTINUOUS EXPANSION

More than 50 years after its founding, Demetree Builders' land-use knowledge and entrepreneurial vision have been built into numerous

skylines, office centers, suburbs, and shopping centers throughout Florida. The Demetree companies have been involved in a myriad of real estate and construction projects throughout the United States and Puerto Rico.

Mary Demetree, who started her career in 1981 as executive vice president of the family business, now heads both Demetree Builders and Demetree Real Estate Services Inc., a real estate management and development company that actively acquires properties, as well as offers brokerage and property management services. The property management division has in-depth experience with multifamily residential communities and is involved with some 2,000 apartment units, as well as with shopping centers, industrial properties, convenience stores, and miniwarehouses.

In addition to utilizing her expertise in real estate, Demetree directs the company's investments in areas that include cellular systems, hotels, restaurants, and malls.

A business partner in the popular Winter Park landmark, Park Plaza Gardens restaurant, Demetree is also a venture capital partner in WonderWorks—a themed attraction in Orlando's tourist corridor—and in e.School Systems, a nationwide satellite response system.

COMMITMENT TO
PHILANTHROPY

As trustee of the William C. Demetree Jr. Foundation, Mary Demetree oversees disbursement of grants to nonprofit organizations. Among the recipients have been the Apopka Family Learning Center, Arthritis Foundation, BETA House, Campus Crusade for Christ, Morning Star School, Southeastern Guide Dogs, and St. Jude Children's Hospital.

William Demetree serves on the Boys Town Advisory Board of Central Florida, and has also served on boards for Orlando Regional Healthcare System, the Orlando Science Center, and Catholic Social Services.

Today, a major focus for Demetree Builders is on homes for first-time buyers. "Our goal is to work with nonprofits to help place first-time buyers in their own homes," says Mary Demetree.

Demetree Builders' trademarks— attention to detail, superior service, and mutually rewarding business relationships with employees, part-

ners, and clients—will continue to keep the company on a steady, upward climb.

CLOCKWISE FROM TOP LEFT:
THE FIRST UNION BUILDING IS ONE OF MANY CENTRAL FLORIDA LANDMARKS.

WILLIAM C. DEMETREE, SR., FOUNDER, DEMETREE BUILDERS, INC.

MARY L. DEMETREE, PRESIDENT, DEMETREE BUILDERS

DEMETREE BUILDERS BUILDS HOMES FOR THE FIRST-TIME HOMEBUYER.

To hear the old-timers tell it, the first time Charles Millican—the University of Central Florida's (UCF) charter president—tried to find the site that would one day be the UCF main campus, he missed it by five miles. That was in the summer of 1965. Orange trees outnumbered Central Floridians back then. The Adamucci site—as the land had become known after New Jersey contractor Frank Adamucci sold it to the state for half price specifically for the university—comprised 1,200 remote acres practically in the middle of the wilderness. There were no signs pointing Millican the right way and few people in the area for him to ask for directions.

How Things Have Changed

Some 35 years after Millican's foiled trip, 37 years after Governor Farris Bryant signed Legislative Bill 125 to officially create the university, and 32 years after the first students began taking classes, UCF is as much a part of the Orlando and Central Florida landscape as Lake Eola and theme parks. By 2010, UCF's enrollment is projected to be 48,000 students, making it one of the largest universities in the United States.

Those future students—and the ones who have come before them—will leave an imprint on the community that no one could have imagined three decades ago. For instance, the Central Florida Blood Bank taps UCF students more than any other group, and LEAD Scholars—the university's brightest students, chosen for their interests and experience in leadership, academic excellence, and service—engage in

This high-tech classroom is just one of many innovations that adds to the University of Central Florida's (UCF) reputation as one of the most wired universities in the country (top).

UCF's signature landmark is the newly renovated fountain, which is the focal point for the 1,415-acre main campus (bottom).

one-on-one mentoring with children as part of their curriculum. Scientists at UCF are conducting research the university's founders wouldn't have dared to dream of. Today, approximately 60,000 graduates live and work in the region.

"Monday, Oct. 7. Write it down. Remember it as the day that changed Orlando and central Florida forever," said the *Orlando Sentinel* in an October 1968 editorial. "An impressive site now at its birth, Florida Technological University [as UCF was named until 1978] will within 10 short years make an impact on our area such as nothing else ever has and perhaps nothing in the future ever will rival. Even Walt Disney World. For on Monday our area took that giant step of maturity toward becoming a center for major influence on the minds of men and women. Ours has been a growing metropolitan area, and now it's a complete one."

Living Up to the Hype

At last count, students from 47 states and 112 nations were enrolled at UCF—a far cry from the home-grown charter student body of 1,948. The university has grown to 1,415 acres for its main campus—with branch campuses in Daytona Beach, Cocoa, Palm Bay, south Orlando, Clermont, and Ocala, as well as an academic center in the heart of the city of Orlando.

UCF has blossomed into six academic colleges: Engineering and Computer Science; Arts and Sciences; Education; Business Administration; Health and Public Affairs; and Honors. UCF is also the home of the internationally

respected School of Optics/Center for Research and Education in Optics and Lasers, as well as the Florida Solar Energy Center.

At the same time, UCF is earning a strong reputation for its theater, film (*The Blair Witch Project* was created by five alumni), and sports programs. In football, for instance, the Golden Knights could be close to joining a major conference. In baseball, UCF came within one game of earning a berth to the 2000 College World Series.

When John Hitt became president of the university in 1992, he brought with him a vision that would make UCF one of the nation's best schools. Among those goals is becoming America's leading partnership university. "I like the challenge of delivering a superior product with a little less than an average cost," Hitt said, shortly after arriving. "Maybe that appeals to me because I like the competitive challenge that comes with being the underdog."

UCF cannot be considered an underdog anymore. The partnerships the university has developed are changing the way higher education and industry work together. One of the most compelling examples is the Florida High Technology Corridor Initiative. The project represents a unique relationship between UCF, the University of South Florida, and companies along Interstate 4 from Tampa to Daytona. Both universities support high-tech companies through research and education, and, in return, the companies supply funding for the universities and jobs for thousands of Floridians.

UCF also participates in alliances with—among others—area hospitals for the university's physical therapy program, the space industry for engineering, Disney-MGM and Universal for film, and Darden Restaurants, AT&T, and Walt Disney World for the College of Business Administration's Business Education 2000 (BE2000).

In 1967, the year before the university opened its doors to students, Millican said: "I am strongly aware that one need only turn toward the eastern horizon, toward the thick thumb of Florida that serves as a launchpad of the missile age, to find that this place and this time in history have their own stupendous significance. But the past is nothing without its validity as a path to the future. This generation has a rendezvous with space and the stars. We must set our course and move forward. What makes a man try the impossible? It's a touch of the divine in every one of us."

The same, it seems, can be said for a university.

L ONG RECOGNIZED AS ONE OF THE TOP COLLEGE PREPARATORY SCHOOLS IN FLORIDA, TRINITY PREPARATORY School has quadrupled in size since the first classroom bell rang in 1968. Just as Orlando began a tremendous surge in population in the late 1960s, community leaders founded Trinity as an independent school for students who wanted a top-quality college preparatory education. Canon A. Rees Hay, Trinity's headmaster emeritus, was one of those early visionaries. "Canon Hay's goal was to have a school that possessed the same qualities that he found in his own northeastern prep school experience," says Trinity Headmaster Craig Maughan. Today, nearly 800 students in grades six through 12

attend classes on the 100-acre campus located east of Winter Park. Trinity is accredited by the Florida Council of Independent Schools, and is a member of the National Association of Independent Schools and the National Association of Episcopal Schools.

"Trinity Prep has grown with Orlando," says Maughan. "The master plan that we developed in 1993 has transformed the campus and enhanced the facilities for students and faculty."

CAMPUS EXPANSION

T rinity's recent expansions include the new Education Center with administrative offices, computer labs, and facilities for fine and performing arts with an 800-seat auditorium. The school also boasts a new state-of-the-art Olympic-size swimming pool for Trinity's award-winning swimmers.

The most recent addition was the Athletic Center, which opened in January 2001.

Beginning with sixth grade, students are immersed in an atmosphere of high expectations, mutual respect, and nurturing teachers. Learning is mostly hands-on, from computers to science lab. Beginning with ninth grade, students have a greater emphasis on preparing for college, with nearly two dozen advanced placement courses offering college-level work. A low student-teacher ratio throughout all seven years keeps Trinity students on track.

College counseling is an important component of the Trinity experience, and parents are encouraged to participate as students evaluate their college choices. Many of the nation's top colleges—Harvard, Brown, Dartmouth, Stanford, Vanderbilt, Duke, and Davidson—count Trinity graduates as students and alumni.

BEYOND ACADEMICS

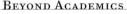

S tudents at Trinity are encouraged to balance academics with athletics and other activities. Student athletes compete in baseball, basketball, cross-country, football, golf, soccer, softball, swimming, tennis, track and field, and volleyball. Trinity traditionally has been a leader in sports, winning many conference and district titles and state championships.

The school's affiliation with the Episcopal Church provides a basis for the students' spiritual development and a commitment to ethics, responsibility, and service. Students participate in a wide variety of community service projects, including Habitat for Humanity and United Cerebral Palsy.

Exceptional academics and superior extracurricular activities are only part of the picture. "I am most proud of the faculty and students who make up the Trinity family," says Maughan. "The respect that exists at Trinity between faculty and students, coaches and athletes, and advisers and advisees is what truly makes this a special place for learning."

IN LITTLE MORE THAN 30 YEARS, TRINITY PREPARATORY SCHOOL HAS BECOME ONE OF THE TOP COLLEGE PREPARATORY SCHOOLS IN FLORIDA, PROVIDING STUDENTS WITH A COMPLETE, WELL-ROUNDED EDUCATION.

LOCATED ON BEAUTIFUL LAKE HIGHLAND IN DOWNTOWN ORLANDO, LAKE HIGHLAND PREPARATORY SCHOOL (LHPS) is situated on 22 acres at the site of the old Orlando Junior College. Founded in 1970, this nondenominational, Christian-oriented, private day school, with a student population of more than 1,750, consists of grades prekindergarten through 12. When the Board of Trustees founded LHPS, they envisioned a school based on Christian principles, democratic ideals, and a belief in the free enterprise system. With a strong, unwavering commitment to this goal, the school routinely reaffirms its mission statement, "Within an atmosphere of love, concern, and mutual respect, Lake Highland is

committed to instilling Christian values, to inspiring patriotism, and to preparing students for college and lifetime learning through academically challenging programs and affirming competitive experiences."

The LHPS campus houses nine buildings to accommodate the lower, middle, and upper schools. The newest of these buildings is the administrative, math, and science building, completed in the summer of 2000. This 55,000-square-foot facility has five math classrooms, a computer lab, two physics labs, two chemistry labs, three biology labs, a general science lab, a music room, a band room, a school store, and administrative offices.

The school's Olympic Aquatic Center was completed in 1999, containing the prefabricated pool used in the 1996 Olympic Games in Atlanta for water polo matches. New, matching panels were used when the pool was installed to extend it to its current 50-meter size. The complex was awarded a Gold Brick for excellence in architectural design by the Downtown Development Board, and is becoming known as one of the top aquatic complexes in the Southeast.

HELPING STUDENTS EXCEL

The school's faculty and staff include 248 full- and part-time employees. The faculty prepares and teaches some 150,000 hours in the classroom and some 75,000 hours outside of the classroom—as coaches and club sponsors—per year. In addition, many faculty members are presenters at national and international conferences.

Voted the Best of Orlando for private schools in 1998 and 1999 by *Orlando Magazine* readers, LHPS offers transportation, financial aid, and a Learning Differences program, available to students who qualify. LHPS is accredited by the Southern Association for Schools, National Association of Independent Schools, and Florida Council of Independent Schools.

LHPS students routinely participate in extracurricular clubs and activities, including more than 39 athletic programs, and have received state and national recognition in both academics and athletics. LHPS science students have received international recognition and, with more students selected to go to the International Science Fair than any other school in the country, LHPS ranks first in the nation in that arena. LHPS athletes, winners of the 1999

Floyd E. Lay Sunshine Cup Award, were voted number one in Division 2A for all sports.

With assistance from the school's fully operational College and Career Center, 100 percent of LHPS gradu-

THE CROSS, OVERLOOKING BEAUTIFUL LAKE HIGHLAND, IS A SYMBOL OF THE CHRISTIAN VALUES INSTILLED ON THE LAKE HIGHLAND PREPARATORY SCHOOL CAMPUS.

ates receive placement from major colleges and universities. The class of 2000 received more than $3 million in scholarship offers. "The education of the whole child—academically, spiritually, and physically—is considered the most important goal at LHPS," says Randall Rex, alumnus and vice chairman of the Board of Trustees. "We desire that our graduates are not only successful in their academic endeavors, but become successful young adults who give back to the community."

AERIAL VIEW OF LAKE HIGHLAND PREPARATORY SCHOOL IN DOWNTOWN ORLANDO (LEFT)

LOWER SCHOOL STUDENTS ENJOY THE PLAYGROUND (RIGHT).

HAVING GEARED UP IN THE EARLY 1940S AS A NAVAL AIR STATION JUST OUTSIDE SANFORD, FLORIDA—AND having taxied through decades of transition—Orlando Sanford International Airport has taken off as a primary commercial airline and general aviation airport. As a result of its heavy international air charter traffic, domestic charter service, and commercial nonstop service to several U.S. cities, Orlando Sanford International Airport now welcomes more than 1 million passengers each year. In 1999, the airport was ranked by Airport's Council International as the fourth-largest international passenger airport in the state of Florida,

and the 23rd largest in the United States. The airport just completed a major terminal expansion that allows it to handle 3 million more passengers a year. Well equipped to compete with other major air carrier airports, Orlando Sanford International Airport is actively pursuing additional airlines for its $80 million, 350,000-square-foot passenger terminal. The terminal houses five international gates and seven domestic gates, with three gates designated for joint use by either domestic or international passengers.

To keep operations running smoothly, the Sanford Airport Authority embraces its unique public-private partnership with TBI, a British-based international airport manager. While the authority operates the entire airport, TBI develops and services air carrier business, and manages the airport's two terminals.

"TBI is a business partner with tremendous worldwide clout and recognition in the airline industry," says Victor White, executive director of the Sanford Airport Authority. "Together, we've been able to accomplish great things."

IN 1999, PAN AMERICAN AIRWAYS BEGAN A NEW DOMESTIC OPERATION AT ORLANDO SANFORD INTERNATIONAL AIRPORT, WITH COMMERCIAL SERVICE TO ITS PORTSMOUTH, NEW HAMPSHIRE, HEADQUARTERS, IN ADDITION TO CHICAGO, ST. LOUIS, ALLENTOWN, AND BANGOR, WITH STILL MORE NEW DESTINATIONS ANTICIPATED.

WELL EQUIPPED TO COMPETE WITH OTHER MAJOR AIR CARRIER AIRPORTS, ORLANDO SANFORD INTERNATIONAL IS ACTIVELY PURSUING ADDITIONAL AIRLINES FOR ITS $80 MILLION, 350,000-SQUARE-FOOT PASSENGER TERMINAL.

SERVING ALL OF CENTRAL FLORIDA

Situated on more than 1,800 acres in northwestern Seminole County, Orlando Sanford International serves all of Central Florida, including Seminole, Lake, Osceola, Orange, and Volusia counties. The airport's four runways are equipped to handle the smallest private planes and the largest commercial jet aircraft; the touchdown of 370-passenger Airbus A330s is a daily occurrence at Orlando Sanford

International. The airport, just 18 miles northeast of downtown Orlando, maintains a commerce park, as well as several hundred additional acres recently made available for development.

Orlando Sanford International boasts the most general aviation operations in the FAA's seven-state southern region, and is ranked fifth in the nation. The airport's general aviation success is due primarily to a large volume of pilot training at Delta's Comair Aviation Academy—one of the largest pilot training centers in the world, located at the airport—and to the presence of several key, fixed-base operators.

"We're very excited about our future growth opportunities," says Larry Gouldthorpe, president of TBI's Sanford-based operation. "With the heavy tourism market and booming local economic development, we expect heavy demand from both leisure and business travelers."

A DISTINGUISHED HISTORY

Originally built in the 1940s as Naval Air Station (NAS) Sanford, the airport's two runways and adjacent facilities were used to train navy fighter and

ORLANDO SANFORD INTERNATIONAL'S
RAPID GROWTH HAS ALLOWED IT TO
CONTRIBUTE MORE THAN $91 MILLION
IN DIRECT ECONOMIC INVESTMENTS
PER YEAR.

dive-bomber pilots during World War II. After the war, the airport became known as the Sanford Airport.

The navy returned to the airport during the Korean War and added additional land, giving the airport more than 1,600 acres of total space. Until 1968, the NAS was used as a training base for attack and reconnaissance aircraft. At that time, the City of Sanford negotiated with the federal government to reacquire the airport, and then began the long process of rebuilding it. In 1971, the Sanford Airport Authority was established to operate the airport.

In 1990, the airport received a huge boost, when Comair Aviation Academy set up shop. By 1994, private domestic charter flights into Sanford were common. One year later, public domestic charters began traveling from Orlando to Atlantic City, Biloxi, and the Bahamas.

In 1996, international charters from the United Kingdom began pouring passengers through the airport's five new international gates. In 1999, Pan American Airways began a new domestic operation at the airport, with commercial service to its Portsmouth, New Hampshire, headquarters, in addition to Chicago, St. Louis, Allentown, and Bangor, with still more new destinations anticipated.

PROVIDING CONVENIENT AIR TRAVEL

Today, travelers choose Orlando Sanford International over other airports because of reduced fares, rapid customs processing–as many as 900 passengers per hour–and more convenient ground transportation. At Orlando Sanford International, it only takes an average of 35 minutes for international visitors to travel from aircraft to highway, beginning their vacations in a fraction of the usual processing time.

Much of Orlando Sanford International's leisure traffic is seasonal, and the airport employs nearly 2,000 people between April and October, the peak tourism months. Orlando Sanford International's rapid growth has allowed it to contribute more than $91 million in direct economic investments per year. Indirectly, more than $815 million is pumped into the economy through the airport's activity.

The perks Orlando Sanford International offers to Central Florida residents are a big draw for the airport's patrons. The GreeneWay– the beltway surrounding Central Florida–makes catching a flight a breeze. Travelers also enjoy unlimited free parking a few steps from the terminal, and baggage carts are

available at no charge. Restaurants, retail and duty-free shops, multiple game rooms, and other conveniences help provide a stress-free travel experience.

With an eye on the future, Orlando Sanford International Airport plans to add airlines, extend runways, improve infrastructure, and acquire land for additional expansions. Says White, "Our customers are foremost, and we plan to create the best of all worlds for them and provide the highest level of service delivery."

TRAVELERS CHOOSE ORLANDO SANFORD
INTERNATIONAL OVER OTHER AIRPORTS
BECAUSE OF REDUCED FARES, RAPID
CUSTOMS PROCESSING AND MORE CON-
VENIENT GROUND TRANSPORTATION.

SITUATED ON MORE THAN 1,800 ACRES
IN NORTHWESTERN SEMINOLE COUNTY,
ORLANDO SANFORD INTERNATIONAL
SERVES ALL OF CENTRAL FLORIDA, IN-
CLUDING SEMINOLE, LAKE, OSCEOLA,
ORANGE, AND VOLUSIA COUNTIES.

IN 2001, WALT DISNEY WORLD RESORT CELEBRATES THREE DECADES OF ASTONISHING GROWTH. IN THE mid-1960s, when Walt Disney quietly chose Central Florida for his company's most ambitious project, this sleepy southern outpost was forever changed. Today, Walt Disney World is the world's foremost destination resort, with more than 50,000 employees, or "cast members," and an infinite number of magical experiences awaiting its guests. ⚜ Disney was fond of telling people, "Remember, it all started with a mouse." The immense popularity of Mickey Mouse, who made his cartoon debut in 1928, launched the Walt Disney Company into worldwide prominence and resulted in the opening of

Disneyland in Anaheim in 1955, followed in 1971 by the opening of Walt Disney World Resort.

Disney was quick to point out that the Orlando area's year-round good weather and availability of land at a reasonable price—27,443 acres purchased without fanfare from 100 area property owners—were the deciding factors that brought the project to Central Florida. "There's enough land here to hold all the ideas and plans we can possibly imagine," said Disney, incorporating his dreams into the 43-square-mile master plan.

Disney did not live to see his dreams realized, dying in 1966 shortly after the ground breaking for Walt Disney World Resort. His brother, Roy, saw to it that Disney's dream became a reality, opening Magic Kingdom Park on October 1, 1971.

Since that day, the resort has added three more theme parks: EPCOT in 1982, Disney-MGM Studios in 1989, and Disney's Animal Kingdom Park in 1998. Along with the theme parks, Walt Disney

World Resort features three unique water parks, more than two dozen resort hotels, restaurants, recreation opportunities (including five golf courses), and dazzling nighttime entertainment.

But what truly makes Walt Disney World Resort special are its friendly cast members, quality service, training, and creativity. "The true source of Disney's magic is the people behind it," says Al Weiss, president of Walt Disney World Resort.

SHARING THE MAGIC WITH THE COMMUNITY

As the largest employer in Central Florida and a significant contributor to the community, Disney is committed to embracing and supporting the needs of the diverse community with efforts focused on children and families, education, and the environment.

Perhaps the most visible assistance to the community is Disney VoluntEARS, a program in which cast members volunteer their time to community service projects created to address the needs of nonprofit organizations. VoluntEARS participants contribute close to 8,000 hours each month to events all across Central Florida.

CLOCKWISE FROM TOP: WALT DISNEY WORLD RESORT'S MAGIC KINGDOM PARK HAS BEEN DELIGHTING MILLIONS SINCE OPENING IN 1971.

TODAY, WALT DISNEY WORLD IS THE WORLD'S FOREMOST DESTINATION RESORT, WITH MORE THAN 50,000 EMPLOYEES, OR "CAST MEMBERS."

WALT DISNEY HAD THE VISION, THE IMAGINATION, AND THE HELP OF A MOUSE IN CREATING WALT DISNEY WORLD.

Each year, the Walt Disney World Community Service Awards honor the efforts and contributions of many Central Florida organizations that provide meaningful aid to youth, senior citizens, families, artists, civic groups, and disadvantaged citizens. Central Florida nonprofits receive a total of $500,000 to help further their growth and to enable them to continue to make a difference in people's lives.

Other significant community assistance efforts include donating excess building material to needy organizations. The resort also provides prepared meals and unserved food from kitchens throughout Walt Disney World Resort to more than 40 nonprofit organizations through the Disney Harvest program. Disney Harvest supplies 500,000 balanced meals every year to many of Central Florida's hungry.

EDUCATION INITIATIVES

As part of Walt Disney World Resort's pledge to education, Disney's Teacherrific Awards honor outstanding local educators. To date, nearly $2 million in awards and grants have been distributed to the schools of teachers who have demonstrated innovative and effective teaching practices.

For students, Disney's Dreamers and Doers program brings recognition and inspiration to remarkable students who embody the personal characteristics that Disney himself admired: courage, confidence, curiosity, and constancy. And Disney Scholars awards more than $200,000 in scholarships each year to deserving Central Florida students.

More than 1.8 million elementary school children in Central Florida have seen *The Disney Crew*, a traveling show specially scripted to convey the dangers of alcohol and drugs. Geared to third graders, the program tackles the complex issue of substance abuse with the use of animated puppets.

KEEPING CENTRAL FLORIDA GREEN

Always working to make the world a better place to live, Disney's conservation efforts include The Disney Wilderness Preserve, a joint partnership between government, private industry, and the not-for-profit community. The preserve was implemented to protect 8,500 acres of environmentally significant land; Disney donated it to the Nature Conservancy so it can be managed and restored for future generations. The company also funds worldwide conservation projects through the Disney Wildlife Conservation Fund.

Even with all the work Walt Disney World Resort does to help its community, the company is not willing to rest on its laurels. "Our cast members feel a sense of responsibility to their community," says Weiss. "Helping to enrich Central Florida is important to us. We've accomplished a lot, but there's more to do."

CLOCKWISE FROM TOP: WALT DISNEY WORLD IS DEDICATED TO SERVING THE CENTRAL FLORIDA COMMUNITY THROUGH SUCH PROGRAMS AS DISNEY VOLUNTEARS.

The Disney Crew, A TRAVELING SHOW DEDICATED TO EDUCATING CHILDREN TO THE DANGERS OF DRUGS AND ALCOHOL, TACKLES THE COMPLEX ISSUES WITH THE USE OF ANIMATED PUPPETS.

THE DISNEY WILDERNESS PRESERVE, A JOINT PARTNERSHIP BETWEEN GOVERNMENT, PRIVATE INDUSTRY, AND THE NOT-FOR-PROFIT COMMUNITY, WAS CREATED TO PROTECT 8,500 ACRES OF ENVIRONMENTALLY SIGNIFICANT LAND.

I N 1969, LOCAL DEVELOPER FRANK HUBBARD INVITED A HANDFUL OF CLOSE FRIENDS TO A PICNIC ON THE unfinished top floor of the CNA Tower—18 stories in the air, perched on steel rafters, and overlooking downtown Orlando. Hubbard had a vision to share with them: He wanted to organize a private club to set the standard of excellence in Central Florida. The pinnacle of the newest high-rise seemed like the perfect place to pitch the idea. ⚜ Those friends were among the founding board of governors for the Citrus Club, which opened in 1972 with Hubbard as founding board chairman. The club's name was inspired by the area's bounteous crop of grapefruit and oranges, and to commemorate the

THE VISION OF FRANK HUBBARD, THE CITRUS CLUB IS ONE OF THE MOST ELEGANT PRIVATE CLUBS IN CENTRAL FLORIDA.

opening, Hubbard commissioned a unique copper sculpture that reflects Orlando's early days of citrus farming. The artwork, now aged with a valued patina, adorns a wall in the Citrus Club's foyer, symbolic of the club's rich tradition.

Today, there are nearly 2,600 Citrus Club members, many of whom are second generation. The CNA Tower now is the Republic Bank Tower/Citrus Center, with the club occupying the entire 18th floor. In 1985, the Citrus Athletic Club, a private fitness facility, opened on the building's lower level. The Citrus Club, Citrus Athletic Club, and executive offices currently occupy 26,000 square feet of the building.

AN OASIS OF CIVILITY

T he elegant club's cordial staff immediately greets members and guests for breakfast, lunch, dinner, or cocktails as they step off the elevators on the 18th floor. Black-and-white photographs of Orlando's early days line the hallway that leads to six private rooms that are available for business meetings and parties. Though men still must wear jackets for dinner, the club now houses the Citrus Grille, a casual dining room for lunch. In addition, the recently expanded cocktail lounge

gives every generation an informal place to relax, with a welcoming bar and a big-screen digital television tucked in the corner.

Still, the formal main dining room continues cherished rituals, including Friday and Saturday night dinner and dancing with live band music. At every meal, guests find attentive service and an intimate atmosphere, as well as the many delights of the executive chef's vibrant culinary creations.

A CHANGING DEMOGRAPHIC

F or nearly 30 years, the Citrus Club has grown and evolved with the city. Orlando has changed a lot since the early 1970s, when women could be members, but had to be escorted to the club. Today, the club still maintains its policy of membership by invitation, and ac-

complished women are a solid part of the club's select group of business, professional, and community leaders.

The club's social events reflect the membership's changing demographics, with a monthly newsletter that showcases dozens of opportunities, everything from holiday celebrations for the entire family to the Citrus Wine Society and business networking. The coed athletic club, with exercise rooms, fitness equipment, classes, and massages, is just as busy at lunchtime as the upstairs dining room.

And although the circle of Citrus Club friends has expanded through the decades, the founding values have not changed. Today, as in 1969, "trust, honesty, caring, respect, fairness, loyalty, and diversity of people and thought" are still the hallmarks of this Orlando landmark.

EIGHTEEN STORIES ABOVE DOWNTOWN ORLANDO, THE CLUB OFFERS DINING EXERCISE FACILITIES, LIVE MUSIC, DANCING, AND ATTENTIVE SERVICE.

FOUNDED IN MIAMI AS A FOUR-MEMBER FIRM IN 1960, PBS&J IS THE LARGEST CONSULTING ENGINEERING firm in Florida. PBS&J remains an employee-owned firm with 2,400 employees located in 60 offices across the United States and overseas. The firm is consistently ranked among the top 10 percent of design firms in the nation. ❧ PBS&J's founders were civil engineers who were passionate about their profession, and emphasized quality work, client service, and integrity. To motivate and retain key employees who would continue their legacy of values, the firm's founders began an innovative employee trust program in 1963. Today, this program continues to allow PBS&J to offer rewarding career

opportunities to new generations of employees. A Founders' Awards program and ongoing training initiatives also encourage adherence to the principles upon which the firm was based.

Recognizing the value of providing comprehensive consulting services to clients, PBS&J broadened its core services of general civil, sanitary, and transportation engineering to include surveying and other environmental disciplines, analytical testing, landscape architecture, program management, and planning. Today, the firm's scope of services also includes intelligent transportation systems, information technologies, and numerous specialty disciplines such as air quality, asset management, coastal restoration, and cultural resources management.

PARTNERS WITH CENTRAL FLORIDA

When PBS&J opened its Orlando office in 1974, it began a partnership with Central Florida that continues to impact the lives of area residents.

PBS&J has grown to become Orlando's largest engineering and planning firm, with more than 300 technical, professional, and support staff members in the community. The Orlando location has become the company's largest branch, and serves as headquarters for its national transportation, environmental, and civil engineering services. At the heart of the firm's success is a commitment to excellence and to the communities it serves.

PBS&J has been instrumental in helping to develop some exciting projects in the area, including the Orlando-Orange County Expressway system, the town of Celebration, the Orange County Convention Center expansion, Orlando's innovative wetland treatment system, and Orange County's newest water and wastewater treatment plants.

PBS&J IN THE COMMUNITY

Dedicated to strengthening the communities in which its employees live and work, the firm is an advocate of college-level engineering education, and was instrumental in helping to seed

ORLANDO'S LARGEST ENGINEERING AND PLANNING FIRM, PBS&J IS DEDICATED TO EXCELLENCE IN THE COMMUNITIES IT SERVES.

the University of Central Florida (UCF) Foundation, UCF's College of Engineering scholarship fund. UCF engineering students are also frequent recipients of PBS&J's Minority Scholarship Program awards. At the kindergarten-through-grade-12 education level, PBS&J supports myriad education-related events that have included the Super Bowlathon to benefit Junior Achievement, MathCounts, Project Create, and area science fairs.

PBS&J is a significant corporate contributor to United Way, as well as being a corporate sponsor of WMFE public television and radio. The firm holds an ongoing corporate drive for the Central Florida Blood Bank, and donated services for the expansion of the Center for Independence, Technology and Education. PBS&J provides grants to community organizations in which employees have continuing, active involvement. From corporate runs for charity to the Mayor's Neighborhood Grants Program, PBS&J contributes to a wide array of causes that work to make Central Florida a better place to live.

PBS&J'S SCOPE OF SERVICES INCLUDES ENVIRONMENTAL ENGINEERING AND SCIENCES, TRANSPORTATION PLANNING AND ENGINEERING, CIVIL ENGINEERING, CONSTRUCTION MANAGEMENT, COMMUNITY PLANNING, AND LANDSCAPE ARCHITECTURE.

SINCE 1972, RISSMAN, WEISBERG, BARRETT, HURT, DONAHUE & McLAIN, P.A. HAS BUILT A SOLID REPUTATION as a full-service trial law firm that wins in the courtroom. Rated AV by Martindale-Hubbell (the law directory's top rating), the firm—headquartered in Orlando with offices in Tampa and Vero Beach—specializes in civil litigation, workers' compensation, and commercial litigation. The firm's trial lawyers handle legal disputes ranging from small to multimillion-dollar cases. "For years, our firm has been known as a trial firm that actually takes difficult cases to trial and wins the vast majority of them," says Jennings L. Hurt III, managing partner and the firm's most experienced jury trial lawyer.

"While there are many civil litigation firms across the state, we're one of the few recognized for a level of courtroom expertise that allows us to continually deliver wins for our clients."

Many of the firm's 65 lawyers have received individual AV ratings by Martindale-Hubbell, the ultimate recognition of legal expertise. The firm's lawyers have a combined experience of more than 1,000 jury trials and thousands more nonjury trials. Its 250 employees in three offices cater to a growing clientele in a large geographical area of Florida—from Duval County south to Palm Beach County on the state's east coast, and across the I-4 corridor from Citrus County to Collier County on the west coast.

The firm's clients include Alamo, CFI, the City of Orlando, CNA, Cracker Barrel, Lynx, The Doctors Company, Exxon, FCCI Mutual, Greater Orlando Aviation Authority, Hartford, Hubbard, Lake County, Mobil Oil, Nemours Children's Clinic, Orange County, Pepsico, Pizza Hut, Publix, Ryder, St. Paul, SeaWorld of Orlando, Seminole County, State Farm, Target, Time Warner, Universal Studios Florida, UPS, Walt Disney World Dolphin Hotel, and many hospitals throughout Central Florida.

Over time, the firm has broadened its areas of expertise in order to fully serve the evolving needs of its loyal clients. Combining superior legal services with a straightforward team approach, the firm has successfully handled cases involving automobile accidents, premises liability, discrimination, medical malpractice, dental malpractice, nursing home litigation, fraud, general insurance coverage claims, wrongful death, wrongful termination, theft, product liability, and uninsured motorist coverage claims. The firm's experience also covers the Americans with Disabilities Act, libel and slander, malicious prosecution, sovereign immunity, property damage, pesticide litigation, false imprisonment and arrest, first-party insurance coverage claims, automobile claims, chemical sensitivity claims, bad faith, assault and battery, and arson.

The firm continues to resolve and try cases involving workers' compensation claims and the Special Disability Trust Fund—the legal foundation upon which today's broad base of services was built. In fact, many of the firm's lawyers are among the top echelon of workers' compensation lawyers statewide.

In addition, the firm's lawyers are experienced in administrative law, alternative dispute resolution, appellate practice, business law, commercial litigation, commercial transactions, construction law, corporate law, covenants not to compete, federal civil practice, franchise litigation, real estate development and transactions, real estate law, and securities litigation.

The firm is extensively involved in the defense of civil litigation matters in state and federal courts at both the trial and appellate levels. It represents individuals, corporations, self-insured employers, and insurance companies and their insureds in all types of cases.

"The reason we've grown so tremendously is that we give our clients an early, candid evaluation of the case so that they can make an informed decision about resolving it before significant money is spent on unnecessary discovery," Hurt says. "We stand by our pledge to be innovative, responsive, and committed to providing the finest legal services available."

ORLANDO ROOTS

Founded in 1972, the firm originally specialized solely in workers' compensation defense and grew to be regarded as the foremost defense firm in the state. One of the original founders, senior partner Steve Rissman, was a member of the Governor's Workers' Compensation Oversight Board. Rissman is the perpetual program chairman of the Workers' Compensation Educational Conference—the largest workers' compensation

STEVE RISSMAN (LEFT) AND BUCKY HURT (RIGHT) ARE THE GUIDING FORCES BEHIND RISSMAN, WEISBERG, BARRETT, HURT, DONAHUE & McLAIN, P.A.

JOANNE CAROLE PHOTOGRAPHY

THE FIRM HAS BUILT A SOLID REPUTA-
TION AS A FULL-SERVICE TRIAL LAW
FIRM THAT WINS IN THE COURTROOM.
IT IS EXTENSIVELY INVOLVED IN THE
DEFENSE OF CIVIL LITIGATION MATTERS
IN STATE AND FEDERAL COURTS AT BOTH
THE TRIAL AND APPELLATE LEVELS.

convention in the United States, involving three separate conventions and dozens of programs.

Since 1995, Rissman has been included among the elite lawyers in his field of workers' compensation in Woodward/White Inc.'s *The Best Lawyers in America.* Rissman also has been chairman of the Workers' Compensation Section of the Florida Bar.

By the late 1970s, the firm began taking on insurance defense cases. In 1987, Hurt joined the firm and quickly expanded its general liability defense business. His original team of four lawyers has since grown to more than 35.

As the firm's client base expanded, the east and west coast Florida offices were established to provide additional expertise and resources to allow the firm to serve clients in more than half of Florida's counties. Explosive growth throughout the 1990s resulted in the firm's acquiring the top three floors of the Capital Plaza Building at its Pine Street location next to Lake Eola in downtown Orlando.

ON THE LEADING LEGAL EDGE

To support its expansion and remain at the leading edge of legal technology, the firm has built an extensive, state-of-the-art computer and electronic network, which allows immediate case consultation and communication with clients via the Internet.

The firm also maintains an informative Web site at www.rissman. com. The site contains informa-

tion on the lawyers, their areas of expertise, and weekly updated summaries of appellate decisions in Florida courts.

Training and continuing education became a top priority as the firm set out to provide the highest level of legal services for its clients. Because of their extensive level of expertise, the firm's lawyers are frequent speakers at a variety of seminars, and members of the firm have served as adjunct professors at private and state universities.

To help serve the Central Florida

community, the firm matches the contributions of its 250 employees to United Way and Children's Miracle Network, which broadcasts its fundraiser yearly from the Walt Disney World Resort.

Rissman, Weisberg, Barrett, Hurt, Donahue & McLain, P.A. is poised to meet future challenges presented by its clients. Its size and diversity allow the firm to provide outstanding legal services, no matter how large or small the client and no matter how simple or complex the case.

THE FIRM IS HEADQUARTERED AT CAPI-
TAL PLAZA CENTER IN ORLANDO, WITH
OFFICES IN TAMPA AND VERO BEACH.

ALBERTSON'S INC.

 INCE 1974, ALBERTSON'S INC. HAS BEEN CENTRAL FLORIDA'S NEIGHBORHOOD GROCER OF CHOICE. Emphasizing the traditional values of personable customer service and top-quality, affordable merchandise, the company has flourished nationally with more than 2,500 shopper-friendly stores. Today, Albertson's is one of the largest retail food-and-drug chains in the United States and has 23 stores serving Central Florida shoppers. ⚜ With its Florida division office head-quartered in Maitland, Albertson's is committed to evolving with the changing needs of its customers while preserving the tradition upon which the company was built. Founder Joe

ALBERTSON'S INC. IS ONE OF THE LARGEST RETAIL FOOD-AND-DRUG CHAINS IN THE UNITED STATES AND HAS 23 STORES SERVING CENTRAL FLORIDA SHOPPERS.

ALBERTSON'S STORES INCLUDE A WIDE SELECTION OF PERISHABLE, GROCERY, PRESCRIPTION DRUG, AND GENERAL MERCHANDISE. SPECIALTY DEPART-MENTS SHOWCASE FLORAL SERVICES, VIDEO RENTALS, AND OTHER HIGH-DEMAND PRODUCTS.

Albertson's philosophy was to "give the customer the merchandise they want, at a price they can afford, in clean stores with great service from friendly personnel."

A leader in modeling its stores to the lifestyles of today's shoppers, Albertson's has been recognized year after year by *Fortune* magazine as one of America's most admired companies. And the company continues its mission: "to be the best supermarket in your neighborhood by creating value through superior service, quality products, and one-stop shopping at our combination food-drug stores."

TRADITION MEETS INNOVATION

When Albertson opened his first grocery store in 1939 in Boise, he changed the rules in the grocery business. Albertson introduced innovative services that included an in-store bakery, magazine racks, and home-made ice-cream offerings. In those early years, food stores typically were small and offered limited choices. Albertson had a vision

of a convenient market with lower prices that still could generate profits.

"Once in a while, a person comes along who has the vision to revolutionize an entire industry," says Warren E. McCain, retired CEO of Albertson's Inc. "Joe Albertson was such a man."

While embracing its founder's philosophy, the company has worked to continue meeting the diverse needs of its customers. Its spacious stores—averaging more than 51,000 square feet of space—include a wide selection of perishable, grocery,

prescription drug, and general merchandise. Specialty departments showcase floral services, video rentals, and other high-demand products.

Still based in Boise, Albertson's now employs some 235,000 people and operates more than 2,500 stores in 36 states across the country. Retail operations are supported by 19 company-owned distribution centers, including one in Plant City. The Albertson's: It's Your Store marketing campaign has helped make the company one of the country's most popular supermarket chains. Today,

Albertson's stock is traded on the New York and Pacific stock exchanges under the symbol ABS.

Convenient local access has been a key to the company's growing market share, and Albertson's is devoted to responding to a diverse marketplace. By striving to be a performance leader, the chain continues to earn customer loyalty and industry recognition.

To keep customers satisfied, Albertson's trains employees in customer-service skills. All entry-level employees must complete part of their orientation on multimedia computers to improve their thoroughness, consistency, and retention. Albertson's also works to develop its own leadership through its Career Advancement Program and by offering management training opportunities. An equal opportunity employer, the company works with schools, government agencies, and other groups to help hire and train employees with disabilities.

Much of Albertson's success lies in its commitment to staying on the technological cutting edge and providing streamlined customer service through information innovation. On the front end, its PC-based register system—including computerized intuitive keyboards for cashiers and color computer screens for customer-friendly display—is featured in all stores. A state-of-the-art pharmacy computer system provides enhanced drug interaction and allergy screening, insurance billing, patient counseling information, and drug verification.

To keep up with customers' cash needs, the chain operates more than 985 in-store banks. Additionally, Albertson's is testing Internet shopping in the Dallas/Fort Worth area and in Seattle.

While planning for the future, Albertson's hasn't forgotten the importance of preserving the environment for generations to come. Every store has an active recycling program and, in one year, recycles nearly 180,000 tons of cardboard and another 200,000 tons of solid waste.

Albertson's stores collect used plastic grocery bags, and the company's distribution centers save plastic pallet wrap for recycling into plastic lumber used to make benches for its remodeled stores.

Even meat and fish by-products have been recycled into protein for pet food, saving more than $1 million in trash-hauling costs. As a result, Albertson's has been recognized by several groups, including the Environmental Protection Agency.

COMMUNITY DRIVEN

Albertson's believes in being a good neighbor by contributing to the quality of life in the diverse communities it serves. One example is the company's merger with The American Stores Company. Both companies had rich histories of community support, yet when the merger was finalized, Albertson's immediately began to incorporate the best giving practices from all operating areas, resulting in a company that is making a tremendous positive impact on the neighborhoods in which it operates. Albertson's targets hunger relief, education and development of

youth, and health and nutrition in its charitable support.

Listening to its neighbors allows Albertson's to recognize diverse needs and act accordingly. In 1999, Albertson's donated more than $48 million in cash and in-kind donations through the Albertson's Community Partners Card. That figure does not include the donations of money, time, and talent that company associates individually chose to make to their favorite charities, nor the money raised through in-store promotions for various charitable causes.

For decades, Albertson's Inc. has provided the Orlando area with fresh foods, convenient locations, one-stop shopping, and excellent customer service, all with the charm of a neighborhood grocer. As it carries on the tradition begun more than 60 years ago, Albertson's remains committed to being the best supermarket in town.

ALBERTSON'S NOW EMPLOYS SOME 235,000 PEOPLE AND OPERATES MORE THAN 2,500 STORES IN 36 STATES ACROSS THE COUNTRY.

A LEADER IN MODELING ITS STORES TO THE LIFESTYLES OF SHOPPERS, ALBERTSON'S HAS BEEN RECOGNIZED YEAR AFTER YEAR BY *Fortune* MAGAZINE AS ONE OF AMERICA'S MOST ADMIRED COMPANIES.

IN 1974, AT ABOUT THE SAME TIME ATM MACHINES FIRST CAME INTO USE, A SMALL AD AGENCY NAMED Progressive Communications, Inc. (PCI) was born in Orlando. As a family-run business where quality always came first, PCI's mission was to put businesses directly in touch with consumers through well-targeted, customized newsletters. After several decades of growth during a worldwide communications explosion, PCI evolved into Progressive Communications International, a subsidiary of the Taylor Corporation—a Forbes Private 500 company and one of the largest printing groups in the country. ⚜ PCI is a one-stop direct marketing

source offering a variety of design, printing, and communications services for a diverse group of clients throughout Central Florida and across the United States. The company, now located in Apopka, Florida, has rocketed into the 21st century with impressive profits by living up to its slogan—Concept to Completion—and by emphasizing customer service.

"We are always willing to change along with our clients as their needs change, and we strive to exceed their expectations," says Troy Barnes, president. "We need to be on the leading edge so that we can help them drive their business and be profitable."

AN EXTENSIVE LIST OF SERVICES

PCI's clients can tap into an extensive lineup of marketing and communications services—from creative, prepress, and printing to finishing, mailing, and fulfillment—designed to help them convey their messages and reach their goals. Among PCI's offerings

are complete graphic design and editorial services, digital color scanning, high-resolution imaging and proofing, four-color process and complex combinations, high-quality binding and finishing treatments, complete database management, labeling, and packaging.

The company's full-service print shop produces custom newsletters, brochures, catalogs, directories, annual reports, and complete marketing packages—with posters, buttons, and more—for clients that include Sawtek, Inc.; United Healthcare; Intltrader.com; Aetna; the Florida Nurserymen and Growers Association; Evergreen Funds; Morrison Homes; and Watermark Communities, Inc.

PCI, home of two new five- and six-color Heidelberg presses, continually refines its state-of-the-art equipment. And to boost its already quick turnaround, PCI has built extensive upgrades into its Scitex prepress work flow. To maximize its graphic design power, the company continually updates its desktop technology.

As one of 86 Taylor Corporation-owned companies, PCI is a member of an elite business network, stretching from Europe to Mexico, that allows it to manage more cost-effective corporate buying power for its clients' diverse marketing strategies. PCI's corporate connections allow the company to be a stronger local communications force and a dynamic area employer, with a growing staff of nearly 100 working in its offices and warehouse.

As it continues to grow, PCI draws on its marketing expertise to contribute in several ways to Central Florida-area schools. The company donates paper and supplies, and helps area middle school students create their own newsletters.

Looking toward the future, Progressive Communications International is mapping out a strategy that will help position the company for continued growth. With continued focus on the company's vast experience, unflinching integrity, and devotion to its clients, PCI expects to remain a national leader in print and communications.

PROGRESSIVE COMMUNICATIONS INTERNATIONAL IS TODAY ONE OF THE PREMIER PRINTING, DESIGN, AND MARKETING COMPANIES IN FLORIDA.

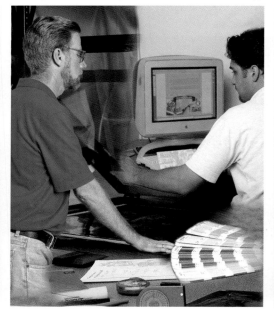

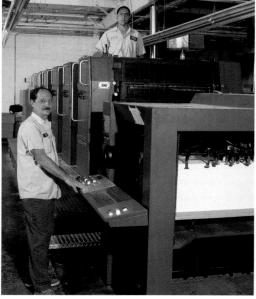

SINCE THE EARLY 1960s, ADVANTOR CORPORATION HAS BEEN AT THE FOREFRONT OF PROVIDING sophisticated security systems across the globe. The company moved its headquarters from Anderson, Indiana, to Central Florida in 1975, where 160 employees manufacture, consult, install, service, and monitor a full range of security solutions for clients ranging from Fortune 500 companies to the U.S. Air Force. Today, all of Advantor's products are developed and manufactured at its 70,000-square-foot facility in Orlando. Among industry firsts for Advantor is a revolutionary sound-activated intrusion detection system that has the highest documented

apprehension record in the security industry.

"Our vision is to make the world a safer place," says Todd Flemming, president and CEO of Advantor. "And our products range from securing nuclear power plants to helping retailers prevent loss."

CLIENTS SPAN FOUR CONTINENTS

With Advantor security systems spanning four continents, the team tracks installations worldwide. Employees travel around the world, from Fort Knox to the Russian State Depository, to assess the security needs of clients. Once Advantor professionals understand the challenges and areas of vulnerability, they design and install total security solutions. Advantor representatives are fluent in major European Community and eastern European languages. In addition, the team has successfully translated user interfaces, monitoring software, and system documentation.

"Installation of a security system, however, is just the beginning of the process," says Flemming. "Our service philosophy is that Advantor is always there." People and assets are protected around the clock, through training and through the support of Advantor's experienced technical support team, with a support center that operates 24 hours a day, 365 days a year.

COMMUNITY TIES

With employees constantly on the go, a strong sense of family prevails at the Orlando headquarters. "Most of our employees have been with us for more than 10 years," says Flemming. "At Advantor, we are innovative, enjoy having a good time, and encourage community involvement."

Advantor is a generous supporter of the United Cerebral Palsy (UCP) of Central Florida, participating in the capital campaign for the construction of a new clinic, the annual UCP gala, and the UCP-sponsored chili cook-off. In addition, employees gather every Thanksgiving to share turkey and all the trimmings with residents of a nearby nursing home. Junior Achievement is another benefactor of Advantor's support.

"Looking ahead," says Flemming, "the security industry is changing at an astonishing rate, due to technological advancements in the communications industries. There are so many new frontiers to explore and we're constantly seeking new ways to make better products for our customers."

With developments in technology come further opportunities for growth at Advantor. Dedication of employees and knowledge of the ever changing field of security systems will be the keys to this innovative company's success.

CLOCKWISE FROM TOP:
ADVANTOR CORPORATION HOSTS
RUSSIAN NUCLEAR FACILITY SITE
AND SANDIA NATIONAL LABS TO
DISCUSS SECURITY SOLUTIONS.

ON-SITE TRAINING FACILITIES ARE
USED TO EDUCATE ADVANTOR'S
CUSTOMERS.

ADVANTOR HAS CONDUCTED IN-HOUSE
MANUFACTURING SINCE 1975.

NOT SO LONG AGO, SETTING UP A BUSINESS OFFICE MEANT FINDING HARD-WALL OFFICE SPACE AND filling it with desks, credenzas, and traditional office accessories. But as businesses evolve from hierarchical setups to collaborative group environments, flexible office space with movable "smart" furniture—the hallmark of Thomas W. Ruff & Company—is setting a new standard in business environments large and small. ⚜ Thomas W. Ruff & Company, an office design leader in Orlando since 1974, deploys its team of architectural and design consultants to help businesses create office space that will support people, culture, processes,

and technology. Once the workplace design is identified, Ruff professionals recommend furniture, floor and wall coverings, and other elements that maximize space to fit a company's business needs.

"Space has to be more adaptive than in the past," says John Lukasek, vice president of sales. "Office designs are becoming more activity based and often reflect the need for think-tank types of situations. Our role is to create the ideal office environment."

The client base built by Thomas W. Ruff & Company in Florida and Ohio reflects the firm's success in providing knowledge, products, and services that fulfill its slogan, All an Office Is. Among the companies that have relied on Ruff's expertise

SINCE 1974, THOMAS W. RUFF & COMPANY HAS BEEN A LEADER IN THE OFFICE DESIGN INDUSTRY IN CENTRAL FLORIDA.

are FedEx, Harcourt Brace, Lucent Technologies, Ohio State University, Sprint, University of Central Florida, and Wendy's.

One of Ruff's largest total-service business interiors dealerships, the Orlando company offers furniture ranging from quick-ship to custom, accessories, floor and wall coverings, architectural elements for integrated interiors, and rentals. Its furnishing services include installation, project management, furniture inventory, and fabric and carpet cleaning and protection. And its management team provides clients with high-quality, cost-effective facilities while keeping furniture costs to a minimum.

As Central Florida booms with high-tech start-ups and telemarketing, reservation, and customer-support centers, Ruff is working to meet the growing demand for innovative office solutions. And as area businesses work to recruit and retain top-level employees, the company's experts can help by providing attractive, flexible work environments.

FROM OHIO TO ORLANDO

Thomas W. Ruff & Company was founded in 1936 in Columbus, Ohio, when Tom Ruff sold his first desk, ushering in a new era of workplace innovation. In the 1950s, Ruff hired Jack Gorman to work in the firm's warehouse

CHAIRMAN JACK GORMAN PURCHASED RUFF IN 1962 AND HAS SINCE RAISED THE BAR IN THE DESIGN AND CREATION OF OFFICE ENVIRONMENTS.

and taught Gorman his guiding business principle: "Service to the customer is number one."

In 1962, Gorman purchased the business and expanded its Columbus headquarters. By 1974, Gorman had extended the operation to Orlando—an area he loved because it reminded him of Columbus. Later, additional Ruff operations were established in Miami and West Palm Beach.

The company's offices and showroom in Maitland provide convenient access to downtown Orlando and the growing office communities throughout Central Florida. With more than 90,000 square feet of space, Ruff has the largest showroom facilities in the area and was ranked number one in sales of office furniture by the *Orlando Business Journal.* Ruff's experienced team can handle every aspect of a company's ongoing facility investment.

Offering the highest-quality products from Steelcase and other major vendors in the business furniture and systems market, Ruff combines unmatched expertise in design application and professional installation and services to help any business maximize its space. Small businesses and home offices find great value in Ruff's Office Furniture USA division's quick-ship program.

As part of its long-term business strategy, Ruff purchased an Office Furniture USA franchise in 1996, allowing the company to market and distribute competitively priced products to a targeted midlevel

market through a retail showroom, catalog sales, and a dedicated sales force. Recently, Ruff has partnered with Office Furniture Rental Alliance, utilizing its Central Florida distribution center, which allows the turnaround of work settings within a few days.

STRIDES TOWARD THE FUTURE

Ruff's rapid growth in Orlando recently forced the company to analyze its own Maitland building space. Staff increases had pushed office spaces onto the retail floor, and the building and furnishings needed a face-lift. As a result, the company's space was entirely renovated, and the end result provided additional showroom and office space. The renovated building features glass panels for added light, granite floors, and wood veneer walls.

"Once we moved into the new space, we could see what a huge difference it made," says Kim Ortiz, Ruff's director of design. "Our teams function better because our space reflects our business, our work style, and our image."

Many of Ruff's employees have been on board for a number of years, and the company proudly acknowledged Kathy Crynock, Gene Downing, Jim Blanton, and Brenda Blanton with 25 years in 1999. Being among the first of its kind to offer continuing education and profit sharing has been an incentive in retaining employees.

A long-standing Ruff tradition has been the company's hands-on involvement in the community.

Ruff employees donate their time and resources to local organizations such as Junior Achievement. In addition, the firm's employees contribute to United Way and other nonprofit causes like the Ronald McDonald House Easter Basket Project and Toys for Tots.

Says Mike Gorman, president, "Through personal involvement of Ruff employees, the sharing of our facilities, and direct donations, the company continues to fulfill its pledge to be a good community citizen."

GREATER ORLANDO AVIATION AUTHORITY

THE PRIMARY GATEWAY TO CENTRAL FLORIDA'S WORLD-FAMOUS ATTRACTIONS AND THRIVING COMMERCE center, Orlando International Airport is a community showcase now welcoming more than 30 million passengers a year. Today, it is the 16th-busiest airport in the United States and the 24th-busiest passenger airport in the world. Since 1976, the economic rocket booster behind Orlando International's success has been the Greater Orlando Aviation Authority (GOAA), which administers all Orlando aviation activity and has become a leader in world travel. For more than 25 years, GOAA has overseen an airport system that serves commercial,

charter, and cargo flights through Orlando International and Orlando Executive Airport. With more than 80 air carriers—including 43 commercial, 12 cargo, and 26 charter—Orlando International provides more scheduled service to domestic destinations than any other Florida airport. Its international passenger traffic has surpassed 2.5 million annually. As the aviation industry evolves with advanced air traffic technology and travel industry reform, GOAA and its full-time team of more than 600 employees prepare to meet the challenges that accompany overwhelming success.

MASTER PLANNED ON NEARLY 15,000 ACRES, ORLANDO INTERNATIONAL AIRPORT HAS ENOUGH LAND AREA TO MEET AVIATION NEEDS FOR FLORIDA AND THE SOUTHEASTERN UNITED STATES WELL INTO THE NEW CENTURY.

THE MAIN TERMINAL BUILDING IS RE-FLECTED IN ONE OF THE MANY LAKES AND WATERWAYS THAT ABOUND ON AIRPORT PROPERTY.

CATERING TO CUSTOMERS

Providing travelers with an "Orlando experience" from the moment they enter the airport is one of GOAA's primary goals. Located on some 15,000 acres eight miles southeast of downtown Orlando, the airport reflects Central Florida's character inside and out, giving passengers an immediate connection with the natural Florida environment. The modern, high-tech facilities seem to merge with the lush, tropical landscape. The terminal complex's 854-acre site is ecologically preserved and dotted with lakes and islands. In fact, among visitors' first experiences is a picturesque train ride across one of the airport's waterways to the main terminal.

The award-winning Orlando International has focused carefully on passenger convenience, minimizing walking within the main, three-story terminal and providing rapid transit to and from airside terminals. A permanent public art collection, first-rate shops and boutiques, performances by the Orlando Philharmonic Orchestra, and the facility's architectural pizzazz make the airport unique.

GOAA's initiative to integrate art into the airport's design has helped set it apart from other facilities worldwide. A recently completed fourth airside terminal in the airport's North Complex features magnificent Guy Kemper- and Kenneth vonRoenn Jr.-commissioned stained glass windows, interpreting flight from ground to air and the marriage of land and sky. Three colorful, huge floor mosaics and a wall mosaic—each comprised of more than 1 million tiles—represent an Old Florida environment, complete with fish, flowers, ferns, alligators, and frogs. The airport's original three terminals will undergo similar remodeling.

"Orlando International really is a great source of pride for the community, and there's such a sense of accomplishment surrounding it," says C.W. "Bill" Jennings, GOAA executive director. "We are known for our planning and vision, and we've created an airport on a human scale, despite the high-tech nature of travel."

GOAA also is known for its partnership with Central Florida and its diligence in managing airport land use to benefit the entire community. Orlando International plays a major role in Central Florida, creating some 54,000 direct and indirect jobs, generating $1.5 billion in wages and salaries, and providing a $14 billion economic impact on the region. The airport's current expansion programs are expected to generate more than 2,000 additional jobs.

ORLANDO

HISTORIC GROWTH

In 1981, five years after GOAA and its governing seven-member board were created, a new, $300 million terminal complex put Orlando International on the map—with 6 million passengers. Three years later, the airport's first scheduled international service to Europe by Icelandair began.

International service grew and, in 1988, a $430 million bond was issued to create an expanded terminal building, a third runway, a roadway, and tenant improvements. The following year, passenger totals climbed beyond 17 million.

In 1992, the airy, 446-room Hyatt Regency Orlando International Airport Hotel opened, and GOAA received a $39 million federal grant for future improvements. By 1994, passenger traffic had topped 22 million, and the airport received Airport Interviewing and Research, Inc.'s Airports Are for People award for outstanding customer service.

By 1996, the airport was ranked the fastest growing among the world's major airports. A $1.2 billion expansion program was approved in 1997 that included terminal, parking, and airfield improvements. The growth was necessary—passenger traffic had exceeded 27 million. *The Wall Street Journal* ranked Orlando as the fifth-largest business destination in the country.

GATEWAY FOR GLOBAL COMMERCE

Orlando International's steady growth has been instrumental in allowing Central Florida's key high-tech, film, tourism, and agribusiness industries to flourish. With its mission to advance the area as the premier gateway for global commerce, the GOAA works closely with local, state, and federal agencies, as well as its business partners, to further its success as an industry leader.

Orlando International has won praise and awards for its design and attention to customer service, convenience, and value. The facility has been ranked at the top by *Consumer Reports*, J.D. Power and Associates, and *The Wall Street Journal*. A survey by the International Air Transport Association gave Orlando International a number one ranking for airports in North America of like size and passenger volume for three years in a row during the late 1990s.

As the airport thrives and enjoys continual industry recognition, GOAA's Orlando Executive Airport is launching its own $6 million improvement project. The executive airport is an integral part of Orlando International, functioning as a reliever airport for general aviation activity.

Even as expansions at both airports continue, GOAA is gearing up for the future. Its planned Orlando International South Terminal Complex will double the size of the current facility, and will increase the overall capacity to handle 70 million passengers annually. Already, forecasters project that more than 39 million passengers will pass through Orlando International by 2006. Offering service to more than 100 cities worldwide, GOAA will continue to support Orlando as the top travel destination in the world.

THE FLOOR MOSAIC "FLORIDA VACATION" BY VICTOR BOKAS ENHANCES THE CONCOURSE CONTAINING GATES 100-109 AT ORLANDO INTERNATIONAL AIRPORT (LEFT).

THE HUB AREA OF THE FOURTH AIRSIDE BUILDING (GATES 100-129) AT ORLANDO INTERNATIONAL INCLUDES A CENTRAL AREA THAT CONNECTS TWO GATE CONCOURSES AND CONTAINS ADDITIONAL GATES, SHOPS, AND RESTAURANTS. A UNIQUE TENSION-TRUSS SUPPORTED SKYLIGHT SYSTEM BRINGS THE NATURAL SUNLIGHT INTO THE BUILDING (RIGHT).

RECOGNIZING THE IMPORTANCE OF TOUR GROUP TRANSITION, THE ORLANDO INTERNATIONAL RECENTLY EXPANDED AND ENHANCED THE FIRST LEVEL OF THE MAIN TERMINAL BUILDING.

DATAMAX CORPORATION

AT THE GROCERY STORE, MALL, LOCAL HARDWARE STORE, AND OTHER RETAIL OUTLETS, CONSUMERS HAVE COME to appreciate the conveniences that technology provides. Purchases culminate with some technological magic when the item's bar code is swiped across the machinery that reads it, and the price pops up with other key data on the register. The bar code is the Morse code of shopping, and Datamax Corporation is the Central Florida-based business force behind those encoded patterns that so efficiently and reliably interpret the final sale. ⚜ Headquartered in Orlando since 1977, Datamax designs, manufactures, and markets one of the industry's

broadest lines of products for bar code labeling, including thermal demand printers; label, ticket, and tag materials; thermal transfer ribbons; and symbology verification products. The company's products, both engineered and produced in Orlando, are sold through distributors, dealers, and original equipment manufacturers worldwide.

Ranked number one in the *Orlando Business Journal*'s listing of Central Florida's privately held manufacturing firms, Datamax serves domestic and international end users in more than 100 countries. The company's clients range in size from small manufacturing shops and single-outlet retailers to government agencies and multi-national Fortune 500 companies. Datamax's technology is used for a wide range of applications, including, but not limited to, automotive, industrial products labeling, warehousing and distribution, inventory control, enterprise resource planning (ERP), manufacturing resource planning (MRP), manufacturing,

SINCE 1977, DATAMAX CORPORATION HAS BEEN AN INDUSTRY LEADER IN THE DESIGN AND PRODUCTION OF BAR CODE AND DATA LABELING—FROM HOME OFFICE SYSTEMS TO PRODUCTS FOR FORTUNE 500 COMPANIES.

DATAMAX IS CONSISTENTLY ONE OF THE TOP PRIVATELY HELD MANUFACTURING FIRMS IN FLORIDA.

warehouse management system (WMS), medical lab labeling, pharmaceuticals, chemicals, clothing labels, theater tickets, ski-lift tickets, fishing and hunting licenses—anything that needs to be encoded with information for tracking.

Product quality, value, and service are Datamax hallmarks. The company is committed to excellence

as a world-class supplier of products and services for the automatic identification and data collection (AIDC) industry.

More than 475 employees worldwide, with some 335 in Orlando, make up the Datamax team dedicated to keeping the company on the cutting edge through innovation, vision, experience, and drive. Today, Datamax's Orlando facility also houses a sales team focused on Latin America, and a new software and connectivity lab serving as a testing ground for customer networking solutions.

MAKING ITS MARK

In 1977, Datamax opened for business in Orlando as a manufacturer of high-speed on-line transaction systems, including thermal demand printers for lotteries, gaming applications, and admissions systems. Nine years later, the company shipped its first automated ticket and boarding pass printer for the airline and travel industry, becoming one of the largest producers of the devices. In 1993, Datamax acquired the bar code

processing industries. The DMX-ST-3210™ direct thermal printer is a breakthrough product for use in the ticketing industry, and redefines on-demand printing price and performance criteria for industry-specific applications.

GROWING WITH CENTRAL FLORIDA

Datamax's success hinges on its team approach, and its employees are referred to as Team Datamax. Company benefits, in addition to 401(k) and health insurance benefits, include a variety of innovative perks such as subsidized health club memberships, company-financed golf and bowling leagues, tuition reimbursement, professional development programs, sick-child care, and a four-and-a-half-day workweek for manufacturing employees.

Company employees regularly participate in local blood drives, and Datamax has stepped up to the plate to support a number of local organizations, including New Hope's Center for Grieving Children and Children's Wish Foundation, as well as the Inner-City Games, a foundation providing enrichment opportunities for inner-city youth.

Central Florida Family magazine has consistently named Datamax one of the top 100 area companies for working families. As Datamax continues to prosper in Orlando, the company anticipates making even greater contributions to the economic growth of Central Florida.

DATAMAX TECHNOLOGY IS USED IN A CONSIDERABLE NUMBER OF APPLICATIONS, FROM INDUSTRIAL LABELING TO THEATER TICKETS.

printer products division of Fargo Electronics, forming Datamax Bar Code Products Corporation.

Business exploded in 1994 when Datamax doubled its product line with the introduction of its 32-bit thermal bar code printer, the company's first product in the high-performance market segment. That same year, Datamax marked a milestone by shipping its 100,000th thermal printer and opening its Singapore office to support the Asia-Pacific market.

In 1995, Datamax expanded its printer product offerings and introduced the first industrial thermal printer for use with environmentally friendly, liner-free labels. The company also established a sales and marketing operation in the United Kingdom to support additional international activities, and increased its global distribution network with the addition of numerous major reseller partners.

Two years later, the company received the president's E Award—the nation's highest honor for American exporting firms for competitive achievements in world markets. As the new millennium approached, Datamax created its

own industry fireworks by launching four new product lines and beginning limited manufacturing in China. The company also operates label converting facilities in the United Kingdom and in Robinson, Illinois.

Datamax focuses heavily on its new class products—the E, I, W, and S series. The company's DMX-I-4206™ is the flagship in a new class of printer products targeted at the industrial four-inch thermal printing market for applications such as ERP, MRP, WMS, distribution, and manufacturing. All of the firm's I-Class products provide greater productivity for a wide variety of applications than any other four-inch printer on the market.

The DMX-E-4203™ is a compact, four-inch printer designed for a variety of low- to medium-volume label and tag printing applications in environments such as laboratories, service shops, and shipping and mail centers. The new DMX-W-6308™, W-6208, and W-8306 printers feature tough, all-metal construction designed to withstand adverse work environments, and are ideal for heavy-duty applications in the automotive, chemical, transportation, distribution, and paper-

THREE OF THE COMPANY'S NEWEST PRODUCTS INCLUDE THE E, I, AND W CLASS LINE OF PRINTERS.

SAWTEK INC.

IT WAS THE BEGINNING OF A NEW YEAR AND THE END OF A DECADE—JANUARY 1979—WHEN FOUR YOUNG friends rented a 7,500-square-foot warehouse to launch a fledgling business. All four had started their careers at Texas Instruments and Motorola, where they had researched and designed a tiny microchip filter that would revolutionize the way the world does business: the SAW. SAW is an acronym for surface acoustic wave, and the friends' new company, Sawtek Inc., started as a supplier of both military and commercial high-performance SAW components. The same qualities that made SAW-based filters ideal for demanding military and space applications began to transform worldwide

CLOCKWISE FROM TOP LEFT: KIMON ANEMOGIANNIS BECAME CEO OF SAWTEK INC. IN 2000 AND IS DIRECTING THE COMPANY TOWARD REALIZING ITS AGGRESSIVE EXPANSION PLANS TO MEET THE GROWING WORLDWIDE DEMAND FOR WIRELESS DEVICES.

SAWTEK WAS FOUNDED IN 1979. TOTAL CLEAN ROOM, ADMINISTRATIVE, AND R&D FACILITIES IN ORLANDO OCCUPY MORE THAN 93,000 SQUARE FEET.

SAWTEK PRODUCTS ARE FOUND IN SO MANY WIRELESS PRODUCTS THAT IT TAKES A WHOLE NEIGHBORHOOD TO SHOW THEM ALL. MOBILE PHONES, BASE STATIONS, DATA TERMINALS, BROADBAND ACCESS, MILITARY AND SPACE HARDWARE, PLUS NEW PRODUCTS STILL IN DESIGN STAGES ALL BENEFIT FROM SAWTEK WIRELESS TECHNOLOGY.

telecommunications, and the explosive growth of wireless service, mainly mobile phones, sent Sawtek's business soaring.

The durability, reliability, and high sensitivity of SAW filtering reduces noise and interference for wireless systems, while making it possible for faster and more precise voice and data communication. From cellular phones to cable modem head-end systems, and from cellular base stations to wireless Internet access, the miniscule chip continues to play a vital role in the wireless revolution.

"Filtering was by no means new to radio technology when Sawtek got its start, but SAWs transformed wireless systems, and Sawtek played a big role in that," says Kimon Anemogiannis, chief executive officer. "The first commercial

cellular system began operation in the United States in 1984. No one then could forecast the explosive growth we'd see in a few short years. As phones have gotten smaller and designs more demanding, SAW became the ideal technology of choice for the major manufacturers."

A WORLD LEADER IN SAW TECHNOLOGY

By 1984, Sawtek had emerged as a major U.S. supplier of military-qualified SAW components, and by 1987, the company had entered the global commercial SAW filter market. More than 20 years since its founding, Sawtek has achieved recognition as a worldwide leader for high-performance SAW components and subsystems.

In February 1998, Sawtek further expanded with the acquisition of

Microsensor Systems Inc. in Bowling Green, Kentucky, a company that has pioneered the application of SAW devices for chemical sensing. SAW-based sensors are spawning a new generation of hand-held measurement instruments for important uses such as toxic gas detection and environmental pollution monitoring. Newer and even smaller SAW sensors designed to monitor physical parameters are also revolutionizing automotive and truck designs.

In 1999, Sawtek began a bold expansion program to serve a larger portion of the global wireless market. After establishing its reputation as a leading intermediate frequency (IF) SAW filter provider for cellular base stations and handsets, Sawtek developed highly competitive designs and greatly expanded production capacity in a new product arena: radio frequency (RF) SAW filters.

As that expansion rolled forward, two of the company's cofounders, Jay Tolar and Steve Miller, turned over operations to the next-generation management team. Anemogiannis, who leads that team, says, "All the employee-owners of Sawtek and our many other shareholders owe a debt of gratitude for the groundwork laid by our founders. Both Steve and Jay remain on our board of directors, and are part of Sawtek's guiding force."

Sawtek's world headquarters is in Central Florida, a 93,000-square-

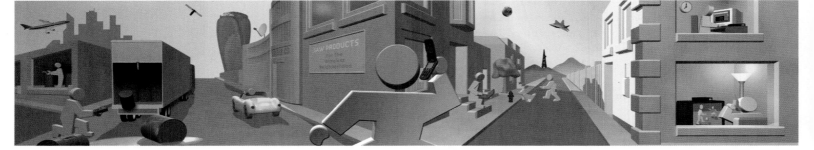

foot operation with some 500 employees. Sawtek opened an assembly plant in 1996 in San José, Costa Rica, that doubled in size in 2000 by adding newer, automated lines with enhanced, high-volume capacity. Sawtek also opened a direct sales office in Seoul to serve Korean customers, as well as other portions of the growing Asia-Pacific market region. Ongoing expansion efforts in other key international locations are also under way.

The company continues to redefine the boundaries of the global wireless neighborhood, producing thousands of different SAW devices used in everything from mobile phones and cable modems to wireless data products, broadband access infrastructure, and other applications.

FUTURE GROWTH

Central Florida benefits immensely from Sawtek's success. Many of the company's employees live in nearby Apopka, and Sawtek donates annually to the Apopka Public Schools, as well as to Valencia Community College and the University of Central Florida. Boy Scouts, United Arts, and Junior Achievement are other benefactors of Sawtek's community involvement.

The company is positioned to continue its global leadership in SAW development, offering total solutions for its customers' needs, while maintaining the same technical superiority that enabled its success as a global IF filter provider.

"The global demand for wireless products will increase substantially in the years to come," says Anemogiannis. "Mobile phones have already become the largest-selling electronic consumer item, surpassing computers and televisions." It's estimated there will be nearly 1 billion worldwide mobile phone subscribers by 2003.

Way beyond mobile phones and the wireless Internet, Sawtek is researching and developing the next generation of SAW-based components of wireless systems, called 3G, for third-generation wireless. These new products will bring wireless video, data, and voice into the daily lives of consumers and business professionals across the globe.

As the information age continues in full stride, Sawtek Inc. is well positioned to capture the tremendous opportunities it represents.

VISION, INNOVATION, AND A PASSION FOR QUALITY ARE THE HALLMARKS OF ZOM, A UNIQUE REAL ESTATE company that creates, acquires, and enhances residential and commercial properties. Since its inception as a real estate investment company in 1977, ZOM has established a reputation of stability and reliability among its capital sources and investors. In early 1990, the company made a strategic decision to expand into innovative multifamily development and property management services. ZOM's most recent premier luxury community is The Waverly on Lake Eola. The elegant, 22-story high-rise offers magnificent views of Orlando's landmark lake and urban park. Designed by world-renowned

architect Graham Gund, the high-rise is a signature address in Orlando's downtown skyline, and sets a new standard in upscale urban living.

INNOVATIVE, CREATIVE

ZOM specializes in creating unique environments where people can enjoy living, working, and playing, and we use a perceptive approach to understand a community's identity, its cultural values, its potential, and its aspirations." says Steve Patterson, president and CEO. "We strive for user-sensitive innovation and creativity, and our ambition is to create an exceptional development each time we undertake a new project."

Well-known institutions such as Lend Lease, Disney, Met Life, USF&G, and ING look to ZOM Residential Services for property management services because the company has demonstrated unparalleled service in a broad range of products and markets. Employees

are instilled with the belief that, to truly separate ZOM from the competition, they must exceed the expectations of residents and owners.

ZOM has been nationally recognized and has received multiple awards for its multifamily developments. The company has received 11 Pillars awards, including the prestigious Pillars award for Best Garden Apartment Community in 1996, 1997, and 2000. In 1999, ZOM was awarded the esteemed Pillars award for Multifamily Development Firm of the Year. ZOM has won 32 Aurora awards, including a Grand Aurora award for Best Rental Apartment Community in 2000 and a Golden Aurora for Best Development Project in 1997.

ZOM has an original approach to environmental issues as well. For the company's exemplary efforts in preserving wetlands and sustaining the quality of Florida's native environment and wildlife, ZOM was awarded the Edison Electric Institute Award, a special environmental

TAYLOR ARCHITECTURAL PHOTOGRAPHY

Pillars award, for environmental consciousness at the 2000 National Multi-Housing Conference.

In the interest of good corporate citizenship, ZOM is committed to making a difference where it builds communities. Every spring, employees celebrate Arbor Day by planting hundreds of trees at local elementary schools. "The company strives to plant more trees than it removes through its development activities, and school yards seem to be an ideal place to plant those trees and set positive civic and environmental examples," says Patterson.

ZOM continues to evolve, and separates itself from the competition with steady growth through vision in anticipating the cycles of the real estate market. The company's future investment strategies include developing urban infill residential projects, oceanfront condominiums, boutique hotels, and recreational real estate developments. "Our philosophy is to forge a trail with innovation and quality rather than follow where the path may lead," says Patterson. "ZOM develops and manages spaces in a manner that creates emotion in the hearts of those who inhabit them, and peace of mind for those who own or invest in them." It is a rare vision that sets ZOM apart.

ZOM'S BERMUDA DUNES IS LOCATED WITHIN THE PRESTIGIOUS METROWEST COMMUNITY, OVERLOOKING 2,000 FEET OF GOLF COURSE FRONTAGE.

ZOM'S MOST RECENT PREMIER LUXURY COMMUNITY IS THE WAVERLY ON LAKE EOLA. THE ELEGANT, 22-STORY HIGH-RISE OFFERS MAGNIFICENT VIEWS OF ORLANDO'S LANDMARK LAKE AND URBAN PARK. DESIGNED BY WORLD-RENOWNED ARCHITECT GRAHAM GUND, THE HIGH-RISE IS A SIGNATURE ADDRESS IN ORLANDO'S DOWNTOWN SKYLINE, AND SETS A NEW STANDARD FOR UPSCALE URBAN LIVING.

1980-1989

1980   LEISURE BAY INDUSTRIES, INC./RECREATIONAL FACTORY WAREHOUSE

1980   BARNIE'S COFFEE & TEA COMPANY

1981   KISSIMMEE-ST. CLOUD CONVENTION & VISITORS BUREAU

1981   PAYSYS INTERNATIONAL, INC.

1982   THE BRANDON COMPANY

1982   FISERV CBS WORLDWIDE

1983   ANSON-STONER, INC.

1983   CHRISTOPHER WREN CONSTRUCTION, INC.

1983   YESAWICH, PEPPERDINE & BROWN

1984   FISHER, RUSHMER, WERRENRATH, DICKSON, TALLEY & DUNLAP, P.A.

1984   ORLANDO/ORANGE COUNTY CONVENTION & VISITORS BUREAU, INC.

1985   THE PIZZUTI COMPANIES

1985   MASSEY SERVICES, INC.

1985   RADISSON PLAZA HOTEL

1987   SPACE COAST OFFICE OF TOURISM

1988   MORRIS ARCHITECTS

1989   CENTURY III

1989   FLORIDA EXTRUDERS INTERNATIONAL, INC.

ESPITE THE FACT THAT CENTRAL FLORIDIANS SPEND MANY RECREATIONAL HOURS ON LAKES, IN pools, and by area rivers, there's one more water experience few would give up: a dip in their private spa created by Leisure Bay Industries, Inc. The Orlando-based company is the largest U.S. retailer of aboveground spas and pools, as well as billiard tables, in the country, with 35 of its Recreational Factory Warehouse retail outlets located in nine states. ▼ The third-largest spa manufacturer in the country, Leisure Bay sells more than 30,000 spas and aboveground swimming pools and more than 10,000 billiard tables annually. Recreational Factory Warehouse, which has a 20,000-square-foot

Orlando showroom on East Colonial Drive, is credited with launching the spa industry in the southeastern part of the country. In addition to spas, pools, and billiard tables, the company also offers an extensive line of tanning beds, top-quality patio furniture, game tables, and accessories.

Since opening its Orlando manufacturing facility in 1986, the company has been an innovator in the design and manufacture of spas and spa cabinets. Many are designed for leisure use, but customers often use their spas for medical conditions—such as arthritis—as well.

"Our customers are discriminating, and they let us know what they like and what new features they'd prefer in their spas," says David Doebler, owner and president of Leisure Bay. Through the years, the company has developed a selection of more than 300 spas in a variety of colors, models, cabinets, and equipment packages. Leisure Bay

prides itself on its responsiveness to customer requests and needs. The spacious Recreational Factory Warehouse showrooms display a wide array of products, including 30 to 40 spas, several full-size swimming pools, and a large selection of billiard tables, at any one location.

GROWTH AND EXPANSION

Recreational Factory Warehouse was established by brothers Don and Gary Doebler in 1974 in Buffalo to sell aboveground pools. By 1979, research into customer demand pointed the pair south, and they opened their first Tampa retail outlet. The Orlando store opened one year later. By 1986, two more Florida outlets had opened, and Leisure Bay had expanded into Georgia. That same year, Leisure Bay Manufacturing was launched to build aboveground spas.

In 1995, after both Doebler brothers had retired, Don's son, David, stepped in to run the com-

pany. By 2000, Leisure Bay had established 30 additional locations. The company now employs more than 500 people, with more than 200 employees in the Orlando area.

One of Leisure Bay's top priorities is to continue providing a fun, rewarding work environment for employees in all of the company's operating divisions: manufacturing, retail, wholesale, distribution, and administration. The company is proud that, as a result of successful training, brainstorming, and leadership programs, its store managers frequently contribute ideas that lead to new product development.

MANUFACTURING INNOVATION

For many years, spa manufacturers used fiberglass behind the spa's acrylic shell to give it strength and endurance. In 1998, Leisure Bay became the first manufacturer to use an environmentally friendly, high-density substance called Black Diamond, the first

LEISURE BAY INDUSTRIES, INC./ RECREATIONAL FACTORY WAREHOUSE IS THE LARGEST U.S. RETAILER OF BOTH ABOVEGROUND SPAS AND POOLS, AND BILLIARD TABLES IN THE COUNTRY.

Many Leisure Bay employees are actively involved in the Orlando community and participate in events such as the American Diabetes Association (ADA) yearly walkathon. For three years running, Leisure Bay's employees have earned the company the ADA Golden Shoe Award for raising the most contributions, and the firm has been recognized as the largest ADA corporate contributor in Central Florida. Leisure Bay also remains active in contributing to the Children's Wish Foundation.

Because Central Florida is extremely family friendly, it's a natural location for a company that caters to providing first-rate recreational products for families, Doebler says. And as more and more people recognize the therapeutic and recreational value of spas and pools, the company is prepared to meet the growing demand. Leisure Bay Industries, Inc. plans to remain the largest retailer of aboveground spas and pools in the country by opening an additional 20 retail outlets in several markets in the coming years.

IN THE COMPANY'S 113,000-SQUARE-FOOT MANUFACTURING FACILITY ON MERCY DRIVE IN ORLANDO, LEISURE BAY PRODUCES BETWEEN 60 AND 75 NEW SPAS DAILY TO CUSTOMER SPECIFICATIONS.

alternative to fiberglass. The company's state-of-the-art, vacuum-forming system allows it to produce ergonomically correct spa shells that best match its customers' needs.

Leisure Bay designers stay on the cutting edge of spa equipment packages, adding new types of jets that rotate or pulsate with varying degrees of horsepower and fiber-optic lighting for aesthetics. Spa cabinets have also undergone a metamorphosis. Although cedar and redwood cabinets remain popular, many home owners prefer one of the latest spa innovations, the Durashell cabinet, which looks like wood but requires less maintenance.

In the company's 113,000-square-foot manufacturing facility on Mercy Drive in Orlando, Leisure Bay's research and development team designs and builds test models incorporating the latest spa innovations. And every day, the facility produces between 60 and 75 new spas to customer specifications. Other products sold at the retail outlets, such as billiard tables and tanning beds, are built to the company's specifications by carefully selected vendors.

High-quality construction of aboveground pools makes them a popular choice for many home owners. Less maintenance is required now that nearly every pool comes equipped with an automatic cleaner that, several years ago, would have

been cost prohibitive. Billiard tables continue to grow in popularity as many home owners convert dining rooms and garages into recreational areas. Leisure Bay's billiard tables all feature Italian slate with wood finish, leather pockets, and a variety of cloth colors.

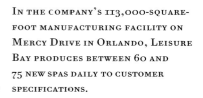

THE SPACIOUS RECREATIONAL FACTORY WAREHOUSE SHOWROOMS DISPLAY A WIDE ARRAY OF PRODUCTS, INCLUDING 30 TO 40 SPAS, SEVERAL FULL-SIZE SWIMMING POOLS, AND A LARGE SELECTION OF BILLIARD TABLES, AT ANY ONE LOCATION.

BARNIE'S COFFEE & TEA COMPANY

ANNE VALDEZ OF BARNIE'S COFFEE & TEA COMPANY SAMPLES A CUP OF COFFEE MUCH THE SAME WAY AN enologist tests a wine—inhale deeply, then slurp and spit. Cleanse the palate, and it's on to the next cup. It may not be pretty, but it exposes the full flavor of the roast to an experienced coffee planner and quality control expert like Valdez. ⚜ Long before the coffee beans themselves make it to the shelf, Valdez first must distinguish the finest beans from inferior ones. She sits at a small, round table in the Orlando-area Barnie's Coffee & Tea headquarters "cupping" coffee to determine its body, acidity, and flavor, and to guarantee that only the finest coffee beans make their way to a

Barnie's Coffee & Tea store. "Coffee from a Kenyan bean would have a winy snap to it, but with a bean from Papua, New Guinea, I would look for something a bit smoother," Valdez says. "If it's from Sumatra, it may be musty and earthy."

To stock Barnie's Coffee & Tea's shelves, Valdez relies on importers and exporters from top-growing tropical regions of Africa, South and Central America, the Caribbean, Asia, and the South Pacific. Once the beans have been selected, she determines the perfect roast level so the distinguishing varietal characteristics of each particular coffee will be the most pronounced.

ANNE VALDEZ SITS AT A SMALL, ROUND TABLE IN THE ORLANDO-AREA BARNIE'S COFFEE & TEA COMPANY'S HEADQUARTERS "CUPPING" COFFEE TO DETERMINE ITS BODY, ACIDITY, AND FLAVOR, AND TO GUARANTEE THAT ONLY THE FINEST COFFEE BEANS MAKE THEIR WAY TO A BARNIE'S COFFEE & TEA STORE.

CAREFUL CULTIVATING

Specialty coffee beans are not the easiest crop to grow, nor is the harvesting process simple. Every coffee bean is picked by hand, and one tree will yield only about one pound of coffee a year. The coffee tree begins with a seed in a nursery. The seedling is planted in just the right combination of temperature, rain, sunshine, altitude, and rich, volcanic soil.

Not until its fifth or sixth year does a tree produce a good crop of fruit—the coffee cherries. The cherries are dried and the beans extracted, then dried again.

Like grapes for fine wines, coffee beans develop their own unique qualities and are never exactly the same from year to year. The beans chosen by experts like Valdez, however, continue to earn kudos and awards from independent national coffee rating firms and media critics.

BARNIE'S COFFEE & TEA COMPANY IS DEDICATED TO KEEPING ITS TWO-DECADES-OLD PROMISE TO ITS CUSTOMERS: THE QUEST FOR A PERFECT CUP OF COFFEE ENDS WHERE THE SIGNATURE GREEN AWNING OF ORLANDO'S HOME-GROWN COFFEE COMPANY BEGINS.

Feeding the Growing Coffee Passion

The first Barnie's Coffee & Tea store opened in Winter Park during 1980 in the historic section of Park Avenue. The store offered customers a relaxing atmosphere and a chance to sample specialty coffees and teas from around the world. From that day forward, the company has prided itself on its commitment to offering the highest-quality products.

"Between 1985 and 1990, specialty coffee really took off," says Richard Ungaro, president and chief executive officer. "There's a growing niche of coffee drinkers who no longer consider coffee a commodity, but think of it as a treat. At Barnie's Coffee & Tea, a cup of coffee is a very personal thing. Some people like it with cream and sugar, some like it black. We cater to the individuality of each of our customers."

Barnie's Coffee & Tea's growing contingent of loyal customers has enabled the company to expand to more than 100 locations in 16 states with 700 full-time employees. In the metropolitan Orlando area, Barnie's Coffee & Tea stores can be found at 13 locations, including several malls.

The company has distinguished itself successfully from other coffee retailers in several ways. Primarily a mall-based retailer with heavy emphasis on hard-line products, the company offers 47 types of coffee beans and 47 types of tea imported to the stores. Coffee lovers are offered light, medium, and dark roasted coffees; decaffeinated blends; and flavored coffees, such as the top-selling Santa's White Christmas®, a combination of coconut, vanilla, caramel, and hazelnut flavors.

Barnie's Coffee & Tea goes beyond the specialty-coffee trend toward dark roasts. Ungaro points out, "Unlike other specialty coffee companies, Barnie's Coffee & Tea does not have a bias toward a dark roast, because we recognize that the difference between a light roast and a dark roast is like the difference between white and red wine. Some people like white wine, some like red wine. One is not necessarily better than the other. The same is true with dark roasted coffee and light roasted coffee."

In addition, the company's traditions include Barnie's Coffee & Tea Club, a discount program for frequent buyers, and the Coffee of the Month Club, which delivers coffee to a member's door. The company also does an impressive business in decorative gifts and accessories, such as mugs, teapots, espresso makers, coffee bean grinders, and gourmet foods.

The company's growth strategy targets coffee drinkers worldwide with plans to service business offices across the country and provide in-room coffee service to hotels and resorts, in addition to building on the successful launch of the company Web site, www.barniescoffee.com. The operating and growth strategy for Barnie's Coffee & Tea will continue to be a basic philosophy for hiring a well-trained professional staff and offering a high quality of goods in a pleasant work environment.

Contributing to the Coffee Community

Since 1980, Barnie's Coffee & Tea has supported the burgeoning population of residents who won't begin their day without a cup of top-quality coffee, or who couldn't imagine a shopping trip without a stop at one of Barnie's Coffee & Tea's many mall outlets.

But the organization contributes more than just coffee to the many communities it serves. Barnie's Coffee & Tea Company contributes donated time and money to Habitat for Humanity, finding affordable housing in local communities, as well as some coffee-growing communities throughout the world. The company also supports the United Way. Barnie's Coffee & Tea Company is dedicated to keeping its two-decades-old promise to its customers: the quest for a perfect cup of coffee ends where the signature green awning of Orlando's homegrown coffee company begins.

LEISURE AND BUSINESS TRAVELERS WHO THINK THAT THEY CAN'T HAVE IT ALL IN ONE DESTINATION need only turn to the Kissimmee-St. Cloud Convention & Visitors Bureau (CVB) for a pleasant, 21st-century surprise. Located right next door to Walt Disney World Resort, the Kissimmee-St. Cloud vacation destination offers an ideal mix of attraction thrills, family and fine dining, golf, fishing, and diverse lodging choices for business and leisure visitors eager to make their travel dreams come true. Osceola County tourism promoters continue to draw on the area's proud heritage, its vast natural resources, and its diverse offerings to promote

Kissimmee-St. Cloud to varied leisure and business travelers.

Once regarded as little more than a cow town and agricultural center, Kissimmee-St. Cloud has grown in the last two decades to become an area rich with new commercial development opportunity, much of it tied to the tourism industry. Since 1980, the area's lodging choices have more than tripled; today's travelers will discover more than 42,000 rooms, suites, villas, campgrounds, and other accommodations.

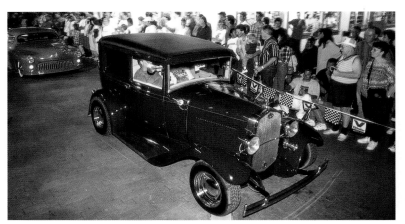

FROM CLASSIC CAR SHOWS AND MEDIEVAL DINNER THEATERS TO THEME PARKS, GOLF, FISHING, AND DIVERSE LODGING, THE KISSIMMEE-ST. CLOUD AREA HAS SOMETHING FOR EVERYONE.

RIGHT NEXT DOOR

The CVB's invitation to stay and play "right next door" to Walt Disney World Resort is attractive to millions of visitors from around the world. The location gives guests the opportunity to enjoy the world's most popular themed attractions, as well as to explore Kissimmee-area jewels such as Old Town, Boggy Creek Airboat Rides, the Arabian Nights and Medieval Times dinner theaters, the Forever Florida nature and heritage tour, and the Nature Conservancy's Disney Wilderness Preserve.

In addition to the area's diverse themed attractions, Kissimmee-St. Cloud offers a landscape ideal for

many types of outdoor activities. Sparkling lakes brim with bass for fishing enthusiasts. First-rate golf courses, horseback-riding trails, airboat tours, and guided ecological tours showcase Central Florida's beauty and amazing wildlife. The Silver Spurs Rodeo brings the area's heritage to life for thousands each year. International visitors, in particular, enjoy the charms of Osceola County and view it as a not-to-be-missed slice of Americana.

To strengthen its appeal and visitor service, the Kissimmee-St. Cloud area is undergoing a $28 million roadway face-lift dubbed the BeautiVacation Project. As a result, the west U.S. Highway 192 tourist corridor will be expanded to six lanes and 10-foot sidewalks will be added, along with safety lighting, water fountains, bus shelters, picturesque median landscaping, and benches and other street furniture.

The Kissimmee-St. Cloud Convention & Visitors Bureau, a nonmembership bureau established in 1981, is the marketing agency for Osceola County's largest and most dynamic industry—tourism. The CVB's efforts, funded entirely by Osceola County's 5 percent resort tax, support more than 600 tourism businesses, including hotels and

motels, eateries, attractions, and other hospitality service providers. More than 6 million guests stay overnight in Kissimmee-St. Cloud each year, and the revenues generated help support local parks, libraries, roads, and law enforcement.

Governed by the Osceola Board of County Commissioners, with the expert advice of the board's Tourist Development Council, the Kissimmee-St. Cloud Convention & Visitors Bureau's savvy advertising has helped spur new developments and tourism growth. Through the years, the CVB's participation in many high-profile Disney events has resulted in a close partnership with the world-renowned tourism icon.

In 1997, the CVB entered cyberspace with its www.floridakiss.com Web site. In March 2000, the bureau established a partnership with WorldRes.com to upgrade its central reservations system to include real-time, on-line Internet hotel room bookings.

"We're fortunate that millions of travelers leave here excited, satisfied, and eager to plan their next trip," says Tim Hemphill, CVB executive director. "We plan to keep giving them plenty of reasons to return and enjoy Kissimmee-St. Cloud."

IN THE EARLY 1970S, ED BRANDON AND HIS TWO SONS, JEFFREY AND STEPHEN, RELOCATED THEIR YOUNG commercial real estate company from North Carolina to Florida, eventually establishing a presence in Orlando in 1982. "We recognized opportunities for our business, and our intuitions have proved correct," says Ed Brandon. ⚜ Three decades later, the family-owned business has grown from a single operation in Miami to a network of offices in South and Central Florida, offering shopping center management, leasing, brokerage, and development services through The Brandon Company and its affiliates. Brandon Structures Inc., and Brandon Acquisitions Inc. ⚜ Though its employee base has grown, The Brandon Company's principals

still focus their attention on details at all of the firm's properties and development projects. "We are licensed general contractors, real estate brokers, and mortgage brokers, but our focus is to represent the owner's interest," says Brandon. "Our goal is to produce the highest value for the least cost."

Recognized as an industry leader nationwide, The Brandon Company's projects have ranged from rehabilitation of foreclosed properties for institutional clients to development of anchor-based shopping centers for Brandon partnerships. The company's current activities include asset management for institutional entities such as life insurance companies and pension funds, and development of neighborhood shopping centers and inner-city retail properties—many anchored by grocery stores. "Our years of experience have taught us that success is a result of being focused on a defined objective," says Brandon.

NEW OPPORTUNITIES, NEW CHALLENGES

In Florida, as in other states experiencing rapid growth, the development community often focuses its interest on expanding suburban markets. "This creates an investment opportunity, as well as a societal obligation, to refocus on the older, established neighborhoods," says Brandon. Based on its research of the needs of the inner city and established neighborhoods, The Brandon Company works with communities and municipal governments to help revitalize decaying areas, bringing retailers to markets they had not been able to penetrate. This approach holds true to the firm's commitment to provide retail goods and services where there is a need.

"Our guiding philosophy is that we should be benefiting the communities where we live and work—not building for the sake of building, but building to provide a need," says Brandon. The company was founded on Christian principles

and holds a firm belief in family and community; all of its employees are actively involved in community, church, and social activities, including support of the public school system as a Partner in Education, service on municipal boards in the areas where they work and live, and participation in the Gathering of Men, a Presbyterian organization that focuses on men's roles within the community.

"We have worked to position our companies, through long-term relationships and knowledge of our markets, to withstand the inevitable downturns in the real estate economy," says Brandon. "We welcome the opportunities ahead for the real estate development community in Florida as this new century unfolds."

THE DOWNTOWN PUBLIX IN ORLANDO IS A CLASSIC EXAMPLE OF THE KIND OF URBAN REDEVELOPMENT PROJECT THAT HAS BEEN A MAINSTAY OF THE BRANDON COMPANY'S BUSINESS (TOP).

RED BIRD SHOPPING CENTER IS NOT ONLY THE HOME TO THE BRANDON COMPANY'S MIAMI OFFICES BUT WAS ITS FIRST URBAN REDEVELOPMENT PROJECT IN THE 1980S (BOTTOM RIGHT).

THE BRANDON COMPANY'S ORLANDO OFFICE IS A REFLECTION OF ITS BELIEF IN RESTORING THE OLDER PARTS OF ITS COMMUNITIES FOR LONG-TERM USE AND BENEFIT (BOTTOM LEFT).

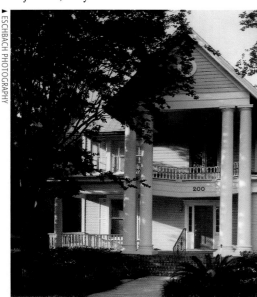

PaySys International, Inc.

SINCE 1981, CREATING AND IMPLEMENTING INNOVATIVE SOFTWARE FOR KEEPING TRACK OF MILLIONS of credit card accounts around the globe has been the focus for PaySys International, Inc., a leader in trendsetting payment processing solutions. "Today's world revolves on credit," says Chairman Stephen B. Grubb. "We provide the tools to keep it turning smoothly. We not only make the software, but also install it and maintain it. This is very specialized, mission-critical software. If our software doesn't work, the business doesn't work." With offices in Orlando; Atlanta; Melbourne, Australia; Beijing; San José, Costa Rica; Dublin, Ireland; Singapore; São Paulo; and the

United Kingdom, the company has systems installed in more than 39 countries on six continents. PaySys' list of worldwide customers includes such notables as Citibank, GE Capital Services. Neiman Marcus, Talbot's, Sears, Fiserv, MBNA Corporation, American General Financial Group, Saks Fifth Avenue, Toronto-Dominion, Transamerica, and National Australia Bank, as well as a host of others.

EXPLOSIVE GROWTH

In 1981, a young company known as Credit Card Software Inc. devised a pioneering credit card system called CardPac™, which became an instant success with financial institutions for processing private label credit cards such as MasterCard. As the company grew to become a global player, its name was changed in 1995 to PaySys International, Inc. to reflect its expanded business plans. Today, the PaySys systems are the most widely used in the world. Research and development efforts have more than quadrupled, and the company continues to create new products and processes.

"The software is very complicated and takes a long time to build," says Grubb. "And, more important, it takes a lot of expertise. That's why we've been so successful. We have terrific people capable of learning what the market requires and delivering it." Grubb notes that the company's revenues have grown more than 25 percent annually since 1995, and today employs more than 500 credit card management professionals around the globe.

A WIDE RANGE OF PRODUCTS

As the initial CardPac product became the industry standard, PaySys developed VISION21™, further revolutionizing the credit industry as it offered private label credit card processing for clients like Saks and Neiman Marcus. Those two systems were combined in VisionPLUS®, a product based at the company's Central Florida office.

The integrated VisionPLUS system is the world's dominant in-house processing system to manage retail, bankcard, and consumer loans all in one package. VisionPLUS provides speed and flexibility in all key areas of card operation, including new account processing, collections, cardholder billing, and merchant acquisition.

PaySys International, Inc. has nine locations worldwide, including the office in Maitland, Florida.

PaySys' Commercial Payment System was designed to address the growth of E-commerce, where credit and debit cards are rapidly becoming the world currency of choice. Realizing the fact that the Internet and smart cards are changing the way the world does business, the Commercial Payment System utilizes the Web in simplifying the millions of payments and data transactions that occur daily.

"With hundreds of millions of transactions a day becoming the norm, our job is not just to keep pace with our customers, but to anticipate their needs and be prepared to meet them," says Grubb.

When it comes to customer care, PaySys excels. The company provides one-on-one support on the phone, via E-mail, or at its Customer Care Web site. Because PaySys not only develops the software, but also supports it, the company's clients have access to the original developers of the software for questions and answers.

No matter where its customers are located, PaySys is committed to providing the same quality and responsive customer service that has made the company successful. PaySys has established a dedicated service team to support its growing Latin America customer base. The service team, located in Costa Rica and Orlando, puts the company in closer contact with its Latin America customers. All Latin America customer support staff are equipped with native language skills and knowledge of cultural issues.

PaySys also provides its customers with a complete line of professional services, including industry and product consulting, data and file conversions, product customization, project management, multilingual education and training, and interface development, as well as product and industry consultation.

A 15-year tradition for PaySys and its clients, Exploring Tomorrow's Revolving Credit Alternatives (EXTRA) is a global VisionPLUS user conference held in Central Florida. At EXTRA, PaySys specialists developing today's leading payment processing solutions participate in interactive sessions where new industry trends and new PaySys developments are discussed, and network with peers to build strong relationships.

EXTRA attendees explore the challenges, opportunities, and solutions facing the industry today. Respected industry speakers are also present to share their vision of future developments in the financial services industry. Everyone benefits from the broad information provided by the conference sessions.

LOOKING TO THE FUTURE

PaySys is a company looking toward the future. As a global company leading the industry, the firm understands what it takes to stay on top. Whether PaySys is organizing a user conference to share ideas with its customers or opening new offices around the world to provide its customers with quality solutions, the company is committed to being the trendsetter in payment processing solutions.

PaySys Educational Services is dedicated to providing innovative tools to aid in research and in knowledge transfer (LEFT).

Since 1981, PaySys has provided financial software solutions that are the most widely used in their category (RIGHT).

PaySys has remained the global leader in payment solutions due to the hard work, dedication, and teamwork of its employees (LEFT).

Research and development efforts have more than quadrupled, and the company continues to create new products and processes (RIGHT).

HE SOFTWARE AND SERVICES OF FISERV CBS WORLDWIDE TOUCH THE LIVES OF CONSUMERS AND businesses across a wide spectrum—from a community bank to large money center banks throughout the United States, and from the first steps into capitalism by customers in Poland, Russia, and other eastern Europe markets to the aggressive expansion of multinational customers in Latin America, Europe, and Asia. CBS Worldwide technology helps to improve the lives of more than 50 million consumers and businesses around the globe. CBS Worldwide is a growing division of Fiserv, Inc., the largest data processing provider for banks

and savings institutions in the United States. Fiserv Inc. continues to innovate—backed by revenues of more than $1.4 billion and a staff of more than 14,000 professionals. Fiserv CBS Worldwide develops, sells, and supports software for banks and other financial institutions in the United States and in more than 50 countries worldwide.

LOCAL BASE, GLOBAL PERSPECTIVE

Since its inception in 1982, Fiserv CBS Worldwide has called Orlando home. The division also has development, sales, and support offices in London, Warsaw, Singapore, Bangkok, Djakarta, Sydney, and Bogotá, and employs more than 1,000 professionals globally. The division's headquarters in Orlando is responsible for development of CBS and ICBS—complete bank automation solutions for 424 banks worldwide, whose assets range from approximately $100 million to more than $20 billion.

In addition, the company operates a large data center in Chicago, responsible for processing the ac-

counts of more than 70 banks. CBS Worldwide offers the option of managing account processing services at the Chicago data center or in the client banks' facilities.

CBS Worldwide also develops powerful and comprehensive customer relationship management and servicing software for use in multiple channels, such as bank call centers, the Internet, bank branches, and handheld devices, such as wireless phones. The Fiserv Alliant suite of products and the CBS USA Customer Servicing Desktop enable financial institutions to deliver personalized customer service for international and U.S. markets, respectively.

Fiserv Workflow helps standardize and track processes and remind representatives of important tasks, while Fiserv Computer Telephony Integration (CTI) gives agents the tools to handle client calls—along with the necessary corresponding data—quickly and efficiently.

Web-enabled products, such as Internet Banking and eCash Management, offer the retail and commercial sectors access to account information and transaction processing at

any time, from any location. CBS Worldwide also develops ATM card management and sales and teller transaction processing systems, as well as telephone banking and other electronic delivery solutions.

These integrated systems share information from a common database; communicate through a middleware layer using open, standard messaging protocol; and link every aspect of the bank's systems.

A HISTORY OF GROWTH AND PROSPERITY

CBS Worldwide has enjoyed a rich history of growth and expansion. Originally a small start-up formed in 1982, the company—then called Smith, Weiss, Delker—was dedicated to the development and support of community banking software in the United States. The firm underwent a series of expansions before being acquired by Fiserv in 1991.

With this acquisition, Fiserv obtained two powerful retail banking systems—CBS and ICBS—which added new capabilities to its financial services. Employing more than 330

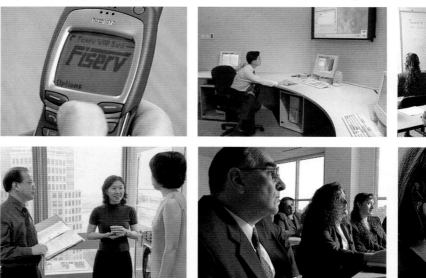

BASED IN ORLANDO SINCE ITS INCEPTION IN 1982, FISERV CBS WORLD-WIDE DEVELOPS SOFTWARE FOR MORE THAN 400 FINANCIAL INSTITUTIONS IN THE UNITED STATES AND MORE THAN 50 COUNTRIES WORLDWIDE.

Central Florida-based programmers, banking consultants, and project managers, CBS Worldwide continually takes advantage of the rich pool of Orlando-area talent.

In 1994, the British Standards Institution (BSI) granted ISO 9000 certification to CBS Worldwide, making it the first U.S.-based banking software and services provider to be recognized by the International Organization for Standardization (ISO). The globally adopted standard provides a framework to establish an effective quality system that meets industry standard quality principles.

Listening to the conversations in the halls, one gets a sense of the company's global flavor—employees from all over the world, speaking Thai, Spanish, Hindi, Polish, and many other languages.

Fiserv's reputation for rapid growth in a dynamic, global marketplace draws IT professionals from all over the world and from diverse backgrounds, including banking consulting, systems implementation, project management, and a wide range of technical areas, including Java, XML, C++, and ILE.

Fiserv leads the industry in development and implementation of team-based incentive plans and performance management programs targeted at identifying rising stars. CBS Worldwide provides a work environment that encourages growth, creativity, and satisfaction, as well as the best-trained staff in the business. The company is committed to employee development through CBS University, which offers a wide range of classes from technical skills development to interpersonal and business science skills development.

Focus on Community

CBS Worldwide is committed to building relationships in the communities where its employees live and work. The company contributes to a wide range of community and professional service programs, such as the Central Florida Blood Bank, Coalition for the Homeless, Second Harvest Food Bank, Leukemia Society, U.S. Marine Corps Toys for Tots, Toastmasters International Club, Association of Computer Professionals, and more.

With new technologies emerging every day, the financial services industry is poised for consistent breakthroughs that will transform the nature of financial transactions throughout the world. Smart cards, electronic cash, larger and more flexible payment networks, and the continual stream of more powerful computers are just a part of the technologies that will be influenced by Fiserv CBS Worldwide. The company promises a continuing reach into new markets, expanding convenience and financial control to consumers and businesses around the globe.

FISERV HOLDS ITS PARTNERS IN PROGRESS CLIENT CONFERENCE EACH YEAR, BRINGING MORE THAN 500 INDUSTRY LEADERS TO THE CENTRAL FLORIDA AREA.

CBS WORLDWIDE TECHNOLOGY HELPS TO IMPROVE THE LIVES OF MORE THAN 50 MILLION CONSUMERS AND BUSINESSES AROUND THE GLOBE.

OUNDED IN 1983 BY JOE ANSON AND MIKE STONER, ANSON-STONER INC. QUICKLY CHANGED THE advertising agency landscape in Central Florida. Over the next few years, the agency became regional in scope, adding high profile out-of-town clients like Pizza Hut, Grand Union Supermarkets, and Florida National Bank. However, in the late 1980s, after both Grand Union and Florida National Bank were sold, Anson-Stoner began shifting its focus toward the growing local market. By 1996, when Pizza Hut decided to eliminate its regional agency network altogether, the agency had added prominent locally based clients such as Universal

Studios, Recreational Factory Warehouse, and Sprint. "Our major clients used to be regional companies based outside the market," says Anson, "but the mergers, acquisitions, and corporate realignments of the late 1980s and early 1990s cost us considerable business. Fortunately, we made the transition to local headquarters operations."

Despite the fact that Orlando is not a major advertising center, Anson-Stoner's work has frequently been published alongside the best in the world. Since its inception, the agency has won literally shelves full of awards in the most highly regarded national and international creative competitions. Its body of work has also been featured in industry trade publications and the leading college textbook on advertising. Moreover, the firm has also built a solid reputation for its television and radio buying prowess—having purchased those media in markets across the country. Many clients have chosen the agency based on its experience and expertise in this area. It also is not uncommon for Anson-Stoner to

CLOCKWISE FROM TOP: ANSON-STONER INC. OFFICES ARE LOCATED ACROSS FROM ROLLINS COLLEGE IN WINTER PARK.

JOE ANSON IS PRESIDENT AND CREATIVE DIRECTOR OF ANSON-STONER.

ANSON-STONER'S MANAGEMENT TEAM (LEFT TO RIGHT) INCLUDES TERESA SCINTO, VICE PRESIDENT, FINANCE; ANDREW ANSON, VICE PRESIDENT, CLIENT SERVICES; SALLY FRITCH, VICE PRESIDENT, ACCOUNT SUPERVISOR; AND JESSICA ROBERTS, SENIOR VICE PRESIDENT, MEDIA DIRECTOR.

receive project assignments from companies that put a particular emphasis on broadcast buying efficiencies.

Through the years, the Anson-Stoner staff has also contributed its time and talents to numerous

statewide, community, and charitable organizations. Anson also serves on the Board of Directors for the Winter Park Chamber of Commerce.

MOVING AHEAD

Today, there are both similarities and change at work within the Winter Park-based agency. While Anson remains as President and Jessica Roberts, who joined the agency when it opened its doors, is still heading media—new blood is infusing the ranks, and the agency is back making regional inroads. Notable new clients include Del Monte Fresh Produce and Subway restaurants in Central Florida.

Now entering its third decade in Central Florida, Anson-Stoner looks to the future in both local and regional markets. "Times change, and we've changed," says Anson. "We used to bring in pizza for our internal brainstorming sessions. Now it's subs."

WHEN CHRISTOPHER WREN BUILDS A CLIENT'S DREAM HOME, HE WORKS TO UNDERSTAND EVERY facet of the dream. He learns about his client's lifestyle. He researches the client's likes and dislikes. In the end, he creates a monument to his client's taste, a custom home that is suited perfectly to the customer's way of life. "I pay great attention to the large design concept while honing in on the smallest details, and I build homes for my clients in the same manner I would build for myself," says Wren, the fifth-generation Central Floridian who is president and builder of Christopher Wren Construction, Inc. Wren shares his name

with the great 17th-century British architect Sir Christopher Wren, whose Latin epitaph sums up Wren's devotion to superior design and fine craftsmanship: "*Si monumentum requiris circumspice*" (if you seek his monument, look about you).

MAKING A DIFFERENCE

A consistent award winner, the Christopher Wren Construction team has built several first-place custom homes for the Home Builder's Association of Mid-Florida Parade of Homes, and has participated in several Street of Dreams national showcases. The company also has been named by *The Orlando Business Journal* as one of the top custom home builders in the Central Florida area, with homes ranging from $300,000 to $1 million plus.

The highly competitive Orlando marketplace is an exciting challenge to Wren and his team, renowned for their innovations in design, construction, and marketing. Wren's background in every area of building—from carpenter to commercial contractor and custom home builder—has been instrumental to

the company's success. "If you want to lead an orchestra, you need to play every instrument in the band," says Wren, who believes his hands-on involvement in each custom home sets him apart from other builders.

BUILDING A FOUNDATION

Wren first dabbled in custom homes in 1976 when he joined a Palm Beach County building firm. He later supervised commercial Florida projects that included the United Kingdom and Canada pavilions at Epcot in Walt Disney World Resort, as well as the University of Central Florida Library. As a general contractor, Wren worked on the Hyatt Grand Cypress Resort and other high-profile Central Florida projects.

By 1985, Orlando had emerged as a major relocation center for executive-level employees. So Wren shifted his focus to custom home building and mounted a team of the best home and interior designers, suppliers, and subcontractors in the area. His keen eye for architectural design and fine craftsmanship earned his firm many loyal customers—

including celebrities, sports heroes, and prominent CEOs—who repeatedly refer business.

PREPARING FOR THE FUTURE

In 1991, Wren's sister, Kimberly, joined the firm as a sales consultant, and soon was overseeing the company's marketing program, working closely with clients and serving as liaison to the real estate community.

As Christopher Wren Construction has grown, the company is once again accepting select commercial ventures. The company will continue to take risks such as the building of its 1999 neoclassical spec home—a $1.4 million, Chatham Manor home in Windemere that drew rave reviews, sold quickly, and earned the company new business.

Most important, Christopher Wren Construction will cater to each individual client. "Our focus will always be on the customer's vision," says Christopher Wren. "Throughout construction, our homes are executed with first-class materials in the most professional manner. Quality is guaranteed and the vision is realized."

ONE OF THE TOP CUSTOM HOME BUILDERS IN CENTRAL FLORIDA, CHRISTOPHER WREN CONSTRUCTION, INC. DOESN'T JUST BUILD HOUSES, IT FULFILLS DREAMS.

MARKET-SAVVY BUSINESSES RELY ON THE INSIGHT AND EXPERTISE OF ORLANDO-BASED Yesawich, Pepperdine & Brown (YP&B), an international marketing, advertising, and public relations firm that specializes in serving clients in the travel and leisure industries. ❦ One of the most successful and influential agencies of its kind in the country, YP&B is part of epb.communications, one of the country's largest privately held communications companies, with capitalized billings of more than $1.4 billion annually and approximately 900 employees in 12 offices across the United States and Europe. YP&B office locations include

Beverly Hills, Boca Raton, Honolulu, London, New York, Orlando, and St. Petersburg, Florida.

GROWTH THROUGH EXCELLENCE

YP&B was founded on a tradition of excellence that began in 1983, when Robinson, Yesawich & Pepperdine was established. At its inception, the company had only 35 employees. By the late 1980s, the Orlando office more than tripled in size, employing 100 full-time marketing professionals. In addition, the firm expanded its presence in New York and accelerated its national reputation as a leader in hospitality, travel, and leisure industry marketing.

By the mid-1990s, the company represented dozens of hotels, resorts, airlines, transportation companies, and tourism promotion boards. Merging with the Florida office of Washington, D.C.-based

EPB in January 1996, the agency added even more new clients to its expanding portfolio. Current assignments include hotels and resorts, destination promotion boards, attractions, transportation companies, vacation ownership/time-sharing companies, and leisure-service providers.

International clients include Marriott International, Interval International, ResortQuest International, Hong Kong Tourism Association, and the Mexico Tourism Board. Among the firm's local clients are Universal Orlando, Opryland Hospitality Group, and Grand Cypress Resort.

INDUSTRY LEADERSHIP

YP&B also coauthors the widely acclaimed *National Travel Monitor*—a nationally representative survey of the travel habits, preferences, and intentions of Americans—with Yankelovich

Partners, one of America's leading market research and consulting firms. Results of the survey are frequently reported in national news media, including *The New York Times*, *The Wall Street Journal*, and *USA Today*, as well as on *The Today Show*, Bloomberg's business reports, CNN, CNBC, and other leading news organizations.

Principals in the firm include Peter Yesawich, Ph.D., president and CEO; Jim Pepperdine, executive vice president; Jeremy "Jeb" Brown, chief executive officer of epb.communications; and Gary Sain, executive vice president. The individual successes of each of the firm's leaders contribute to the firm's position of prominence in the industry. With the promise of exponential growth in both leisure and business travel, world-class Yesawich, Pepperdine & Brown is poised to grow for years to come.

ONE OF THE MOST INFLUENTIAL AND SUCCESSFUL AGENCIES OF ITS KIND IN THE COUNTRY, YESAWICH, PEPPERDINE & BROWN IS AN INTERNATIONAL MARKETING, ADVERTISING, AND PUBLIC RELATIONS FIRM THAT SPECIALIZES IN SERVING CLIENTS IN THE TRAVEL AND LEISURE INDUSTRIES.

ORLANDO/ORANGE COUNTY CONVENTION & VISITORS BUREAU, INC.

VISITORS FROM AROUND THE GLOBE NEVER OUTGROW THE LURE OF AN ORLANDO VACATION. WITH MORE than 42 million people visiting the area each year, Orlando is home to the world's most famous theme parks, a world-class airport and convention center, and a variety of cultural venues. The Orlando/ Orange County Convention & Visitors Bureau, Inc. (Orlando/Orange County CVB), a nonprofit economic development agency, was established in 1984 with only two employees and 94 charter members. The organization has grown to a member base of 1,500 and a full range of departments—from marketing to convention sales and services—to support the agency's needs. To ensure that Central Florida remains

one of the most popular destinations in the world, the Orlando/Orange County CVB markets the area globally to increase international and domestic leisure travel, as well as convention and meeting business, for the continuous economic benefit of the community.

PROMOTING CENTRAL FLORIDA

The Orlando/Orange County CVB promotes the area in a variety of ways—from creative, integrated marketing campaigns and self-supporting publications to the organization's extensive sales efforts, trade show participation, media and travel agent tours, a comprehensive Web site, and its own Official Visitors Center. In addition, the Orlando/ Orange County CVB's offices in the United Kingdom, Latin America, Belgium, Germany, and Japan work with the Orlando headquarters to keep visitors and the travel trade up to date on the destination's offerings.

Leisure travelers aren't the only constituency the Orlando/Orange County CVB's marketing efforts reach; meeting planners are a target group as well. The convention sales staff generates more than $2 billion a year in meeting and convention bookings. As a result of the organization's efforts, the Orlando/ Orange County CVB is an eight-time winner of *Successful Meetings* magazine's Pinnacle award.

All of this hard work pays off for the local community. Visitors inject more than $19 billion into Central Florida's economy each year, and tourism generates 22 percent of the area's total employment. These jobs run the gamut from professional careers in sales, marketing, hotel management, engineering, human resources, and

many others to part-time positions for students working their way through college and seniors who want to stay actively employed. The strong tourism base has also laid the foundation for diversification of the metro Orlando economy.

"All of this tremendous growth and success would not be possible without the commitment, support, and forethought of the political leadership, business community, and local residents," says William C. Peeper, president of the Orlando/ Orange County CVB.

The Orlando/Orange County CVB's commitment to the community extends beyond its mission to strengthen tourism. It partners with several local organizations, including the Orlando Regional Chamber of Commerce, University of Central Florida, and United Arts of Central Florida, on various programs. The Orlando/Orange County CVB is a cofounder of the Central Florida Hospitality Industry Charity Organization (CFHICO), which coordinates the resources of the hospitality industry for the benefit of area charitable organizations. The agency also works closely with the Orange County Sheriff's Office and the

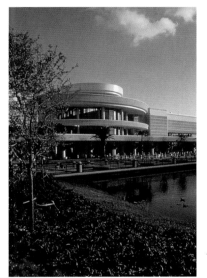

Orlando Police Department on initiatives to ensure visitor safety.

Innovation, strategic thinking, and community support are key to the continuing success of the Orlando/Orange County CVB. "We expect to develop greater demand than ever before," Peeper says. "We will stay ahead of the curve with a strong regional message that we can sustain globally, and strategic partnerships that extend our message and maximize our marketing efforts for the continued economic benefit of our community."

CLOCKWISE FROM TOP: THE ORLANDO/ORANGE COUNTY & VISITORS BUREAU, INC. (ORLANDO/ ORANGE COUNTY CVB) BOOKS MORE THAN $2.3 BILLION A YEAR IN FUTURE MEETINGS AND CONVENTIONS, INCLUDING MAJOR TRADE SHOWS AT THE ORANGE COUNTY CONVENTION CENTER.

THE ORLANDO/ORANGE COUNTY CVB MARKETS THE AREA GLOBALLY AS A PREMIER LEISURE, CONVENTION, AND BUSINESS DESTINATION.

VISITORS INJECT MORE THAN $19 BILLION INTO CENTRAL FLORIDA'S ECONOMY EACH YEAR, AND TOURISM GENERATES 22 PERCENT OF THE AREA'S TOTAL EMPLOYMENT.

ONE OF THE MOST SUCCESSFUL INDEPENDENT FILMS IN HISTORY, *The Blair Witch Project* MIGHT never have made it to the big screen without the legal expertise of the downtown Orlando law firm Fisher, Rushmer, Werrenrath, Dickson, Talley & Dunlap, P.A. In January 1999, the film's then-unknown producers and directors were celebrating their movie's Sundance Film Festival acclaim when they were blindsided with a legal dilemma. The cash-poor filmmakers sought the firm's help with a lawsuit filed by a former business associate who was seeking a movie credit and a percentage of the *Blair Witch*'s profits, as well as an injunction to prevent the film's sale and

its release in theaters nationwide. Fisher, Rushmer, Werrenrath, Dickson, Talley & Dunlap battled the injunction attempts, the movie was released, and the rest is movie history: *The Blair Witch Project* became a box office blockbuster, and the film's creators became Central Florida heroes.

PASSIONATE ABOUT THE LAW

Located in the heart of downtown Orlando at Orange Avenue and Central Boulevard, Fisher, Rushmer, Werrenrath, Dickson, Talley & Dunlap started in 1984 with only 11 attorneys, and has since tripled in growth. The firm's diverse client base includes Fortune 500 companies, local and regional organizations, and professionals subject to malpractice and other lawsuits.

The firm is AV rated, the highest rating possible from Martindale-Hubbell, the country's preeminent legal rating service. All of the firm's senior attorneys are also individually AV rated, and many are board certified in civil trial law. Many of the firm's lawyers hold positions of leadership on the Florida Bar Board of Governors, as well as on committees and boards of both the Florida Bar and Orange County Bar associations.

Fisher, Rushmer, Werrenrath, Dickson, Talley & Dunlap has always been committed to delivering first-rate legal services. Well-known for

its civil trial expertise, the firm also has gained a reputation for its appellate practice. More important, its lawyers are passionate about the law: "We have a reputation for going the extra mile—for being prepared and accepting any challenge," says Partner John Fisher.

A VARIETY OF SPECIALTIES

In the beginning, the firm's lawyers practiced primarily insurance defense litigation. Since then, Fisher, Rushmer, Werrenrath, Dickson, Talley & Dunlap has significantly expanded its areas of expertise to include a wide variety of practice areas from either the plaintiff or the defense perspective. Its attorneys are well suited to face the full gamut of legal challenges, from personal injury and wrongful death cases to complex commercial litigation, and from real estate transactions to other transactional matters.

Extensive litigation experience has made the firm a logical choice for corporate clients looking for top-notch litigation attorneys to represent their interests. With its corporate and commercial background, the firm represents

FISHER, RUSHMER, WERRENRATH, DICKSON, TALLEY & DUNLAP, P.A. PARTNERS FRANK RAPPRICH AND JIM TALLEY VISIT A SITE OF CONSTRUCTION CLIENT KVAERNER CONSTRUCTION INC.

JON ODEN PROVIDED LEGAL EXPERTISE TO HELP INSURE THE RELEASE OF *The Blair Witch Project*.

organizations in general contract matters, shareholder-partner disputes, stock and investment fraud cases, and unfair competition and trade practice cases.

Firm specialties also include real property, mediation, all areas of employment and discrimination law, professional liability suits, and insurance and bad faith cases. Fisher, Rushmer, Werrenrath, Dickson, Talley & Dunlap is also highly practiced in construction law, with clients ranging from multinational construction firms to small, family-run businesses and individual builders.

In addition, the firm's health law expertise has attracted clients to include physicians, large physician groups, and other health care entities. Attorneys at the firm have extensive experience in a wide range of medical cases, including

cancer, obstetrical, orthopedic, surgical, and cardiac claims. A team of in-house consultants provides technical assistance with medical malpractice issues.

The firm takes particular pride in its appellate practice, which has

handled some of the nation's major tort and negligence decisions. Attorneys from the firm have been entrusted with significant tort and negligence issues on behalf of the Florida Defense Lawyers Association.

THE FIRM'S SHAREHOLDERS ARE COMMITTED TO PROVIDING QUALITY LEGAL SERVICES. STANDING (FROM LEFT) JOE AMOS, CHIP COWARD, PHIL KING, GARY RUSHMER, RICK DICKSON, DAVID CORSO, JON HOLLINGSHEAD. SEATED (FROM LEFT) FRANK RAPPRICH, JIM TALLEY, JOHN FISHER, KAREL AVERILL, CHRIS BALLENTINE. (NOT PICTURED) REN WERRENRATH, LORA DUNLAP.

PASSIONATE ABOUT THE COMMUNITY

The firm's attorneys also make it a priority to give back to the community by contributing time and effort to several local charitable organizations, including Meals on Wheels and House of Hope. Many of the firm's lawyers also hold leadership positions or serve on boards of organizations such as the Central Florida Chapter of the American Red Cross.

Through the legal aid program of the Orange County Bar, Fisher, Rushmer, Werrenrath, Dickson, Talley & Dunlap and its lawyers have received awards of excellence for representing abused and neglected children and indigent clients. In 1998, the firm received the Legal Aid Society Award of Excellence. In 1999, it earned the Florida Defense Lawyers Association Community Service Award.

Every member of Fisher, Rushmer, Werrenrath, Dickson, Talley & Dunlap has committed to deliver the effective, efficient, quality legal services that have built the firm's stellar reputation. "They all bring exceptional attributes to the mix, and most of all, they have the confidence to go along with the capacity to excel—they all understand the meaning of teamwork," Fisher says. "I'm proud of what we've accomplished since 1984, and I'm thrilled about what the future holds for us."

JAMIE MOSES AND JEFF KIRSHEMAN DISCUSS A HEARING AT THE ORANGE COUNTY COURTHOUSE.

THE PIZZUTI DIFFERENCE IS MORE THAN A CATCHY AD PHRASE. THE PIZZUTI COMPANIES differentiates itself through the development of heralded downtown mixed-use projects; nationally recognized, master-planned office and industrial parks; Class A-quality buildings; and a dedication to making its communities better places to work and live. Listening, taking action, and building partnerships that spell tenant success are the watchwords upon which the company has operated since 1976. ▼ The Pizzuti Companies' recent alliance with Nationwide Realty Investors, Ltd. adds financial power to the company's solid foundation

in the development of high-quality, aesthetically pleasing workplaces. The strength of this partnership enhances Pizzuti's ability to react quickly to market demands and presents new opportunities for growth—nationally and within Central Florida.

Established in Orlando in 1985, The Pizzuti Companies, which specializes in real estate development, build-to-suit services, and property and portfolio management, partners with the best-known names in business: Veritas, Convergys, First USA, HTE, Marriott, Fiserv, Regus Business Centres, IBM, Whirlpool, HomePlace, PetsMart, and Rodenstock.

The company's core portfolio includes development of more than 18 million square feet of single-and multitenant Class A office space and institutional-grade industrial buildings, as well as more than 4,000 acres of master-planned business parks. Headquartered in Columbus, Ohio, the Pizzuti Companies has offices in Orlando, Chicago, and Indianapolis.

The company's Orlando Region develops throughout Florida and the southeastern United States under the direction of Senior Vice President Ken Simback and a team of local professionals with unparalleled qualifications.

Orlando City Center

Pizzuti's Orlando City Center will dramatically alter the city's skyline through its world-class architecture and planned amenities. Two office towers, an upscale hotel, restaurants, shops, and an inviting pedestrian plaza will grace this 5.6-acre, mixed-use development in the heart of Orlando's central business district.

Designed by internationally acclaimed Arquitectonica, Orlando City Center will set a new, higher standard for corporate and professional office space in Orlando. Construction of the first phase is planned to parallel the downtown office space needs of significant tenants.

Heathrow International Business Center

Nationally acclaimed Heathrow International Business Center (HIBC) in Lake Mary, Florida, is a 370-acre, master-planned office park

ESTABLISHED IN ORLANDO IN 1985, THE PIZZUTI COMPANIES, WHICH SPECIALIZES IN REAL ESTATE DEVELOPMENT, BUILD-TO-SUIT SERVICES, AND PROPERTY AND PORTFOLIO MANAGEMENT, PARTNERS WITH THE BEST-KNOWN NAMES IN BUSINESS, INCLUDING SUCH COMPANIES AS VERITAS AT HEATHROW INTERNATIONAL BUSINESS CENTER.

DESIGNED BY ARQUITECTONICA, PIZZUTI'S 27-STORY ORLANDO CITY CENTER WILL BE A BOLD ADDITION TO THE DOWNTOWN SKYLINE.

owned, developed, and managed by the Pizzuti Companies since 1995. Developed to its prime use, HIBC is representative of the Pizzuti Companies' commitment to good planning, urban design, and astute asset management.

To date, more than 1.7 million square feet of Class A office space has been developed within HIBC, with another 1 million square feet scheduled. A health club, a day care center, a full-service hotel, restaurants, and specialty shops complete the HIBC development program. Construction is under way on HIBC's largest office building to date. The 192,159-square-foot, five-story building is scheduled for occupancy in mid-2001.

True to its commitment to community, the Pizzuti Companies has constructed a nine-acre park within HIBC. Oval Park, with wide pedestrian walkways and lush landscaping, is available to tenants and residents, and is home to one of the region's largest annual art festivals. Pizzuti will also construct more than two miles of the Seminole-Wekiva Trailway through HIBC. The trailway is part of a system of bicycle and walking paths that will connect all of Seminole County's neighbor-

hoods with parkland and nature preserves.

HIBC's latest addition is Park Place at Heathrow, a 304-room Marriott Hotel and a 90,000-square-foot retail and entertainment venue. "We remain dedicated to developing each of HIBC's project components to the highest standard in the industry," says Simback. This unique, three-party transaction incorporated HIBC's planned hotel and retail sites into one destination venue for park tenants and local residents to enjoy.

The Marriott brings the first full-service hotel to the north Orlando area. The hotel's 11,000 square feet of meeting space is the largest in Seminole County with seating capacity for 900. A restaurant and lounge component, as well as a gift shop, health club, and business center, will contribute to the hotel's appeal.

Some things remain the same, such as good design and partnerships forged through trust and mutual success, as well as a sense of communal well-being. The Pizzuti Companies continues to define its differences by remaining steadfast in its commitment to these founding qualities.

From the day he bought the Walker Chemical and Exterminating Company in February 1985, Harvey Massey had only one goal in mind—building the finest service organization in the country, one that was not the biggest, just the best. ⚜ The Walker family originally founded the company in 1930, eventually building a business that was generating $3.9 million in annual revenues from service centers in Orlando, Cocoa, Daytona, and Fort Pierce. Since Massey's purchase, growth has been phenomenal. Massey Services provides residential and commercial pest prevention, termite protection, and lawn, tree, and shrub care to

more than 100,000 customers throughout Florida and Georgia. Today, the company has 36 service centers, more than 550 employees, and more than 450 vehicles on the road on a given day, and generates more than $35 million in annual revenues. Ironically, Massey Services is today not only one of the finest service organizations in the country, it is now one of the largest.

THE MASSEY SERVICES CORPORATE STAFF (FROM LEFT) TONY MASSEY, BUD BREWER, BARBARA CORINO, DAVID MOUGEOT, RICK BEARD, ED DOUGHERTY, DARLENE WILLIAMS, ADAM JONES, FRANK CAMBARERI, DON CLINE, JEAN NOWRY, BILL MANG, CAROL MASSEY, AND HARVEY L. MASSEY

DYNAMIC TEAM, STRONG BRANDS

Two keys to the company's success are extraordinary people—whose key contributions are reflected in a great image, a quality attitude, and uncompromising integrity—and a business model based on brand segmentation. The Massey Services brand provides residential pest prevention and termite protection, as well as residential and commercial termite protection pretreatment. GreenUP

MASSEY PERSONS BRINATI COMMUNICATIONS EXECUTIVE STAFF (FROM LEFT) HARVEY L. MASSEY, CHAIRMAN; CAROL BRINATI, PRESIDENT/CEO; AND TODD PERSONS, VICE CHAIRMAN

Lawn, Tree & Shrub Care is a freestanding brand providing residential and commercial landscape nutrition, along with weed, insect, and disease control and prevention services. PrevenTech, The Leader in Prevention Technology, provides commercial pest prevention services to hotels, restaurants, themed attractions, health care facilities, and many types of nonresidential real estate.

Another important element in the company's growth and success has been an emphasis on training and development. A professional staff of entomologists, biologists, and other scientists interacts with regulatory agencies, product manufacturers, and industry peer groups to help develop new approaches to age-old pest problems. Massey's GreenUP features agronomist-designed, customized programs that meet the needs of different turf grasses, ornamental horticulture, and soil compositions.

Massey Services has played a leadership role in redirecting the entire industry away from traditional pest control, which historically has relied on the indiscriminate application of pesticides in or around

a structure to control or eliminate pests. In June 1990, Massey Services developed a service protocol and coined the term Pest PREVENTION, an environmental service model that eliminates the conditions, avenues, and sources of pest infestation in or around a structure. The goal of pest control was always to kill pests with chemicals. The goal of Pest PREVENTION is to use no-impact or low-impact solutions and methods to keep pests from gaining access to a structure. This is now the acknowledged standard toward which the entire pest management industry is moving.

NEW DIRECTIONS

In 1997, Massey Services branched out with the purchase of Persons & Brinati Communications, an Orlando-based public relations company with a local, regional, and national client base. The firm, now called Massey Persons Brinati Communications, is operated by Todd Persons, vice chairman, and Carol Brinati, president and CEO, and is a leading provider of strategic communication and reputation management services to clients in Central Florida and around the nation.

In addition to building his own organization, Massey supports and works for a strengthened pest management industry. He and Massey Services play an important role in helping to raise the image of the industry and, in so doing, broaden the base of customers around the nation who use professionally delivered services.

The Professional Pest Management Alliance, founded in 1997 and until the end of 2000 chaired by Massey, exists to raise industry standards and awareness of the beneficial aspects of the services provided by professional pest management operators. Massey, along with many Massey Services senior executives, is a sought-after speaker at industry meetings and shows. Many Massey Services executives author articles and papers for industry trade and technical journals. And during the 1990s, Massey was named Pest Control Industry Professional of the Year and received the Industry Leadership Award.

COMMUNITY SERVICE

Massey Services also provides generous support to the communities where it does business. Massey serves on boards of directors and trustees for Stetson University, Roy E. Crummer Graduate School Advisory Council at Rollins College, Dr. Phillips Foundation, United Arts of Central Florida, National Conference for Community and Justice (NCCJ), and others.

Many other Massey Services staff members do volunteer work for a number of community-based organizations in Florida and Georgia. In addition, the company sponsors scholarships at Stetson University, University of Florida, and Valencia Community College. Massey Services also donates significant volunteer time, provides pro bono services, and makes cash contributions to non-profit organizations involved in education, children's issues, health and human services, and the arts.

As Massey Services continues to grow, founder Harvey Massey continues to place emphasis on core values that differentiate the company from others in the industry. These include the image and attitude of its people, the lengths to which the company will go to wow each and every one of its customers, and a commitment to ongoing training for all of its employees.

In addition, the company strives for performance that measures beyond excellent, and exhibits care and concern for all employees and the communities where the firm does business. These are hallmarks of the Massey culture. Massey Services is a company proud of where it came from, enthused by where it is, and excited by prospects of a future bright with promise and potential.

RADISSON PLAZA HOTEL

IN JUNE 1985, THE 15-STORY RADISSON PLAZA HOTEL FIRST OPENED ITS DOORS AND WELCOMED ITS GUESTS TO downtown Orlando with the trademark hospitality and can-do spirit that its parent company had already established. Today, loyal visitors are returning to a newly refurbished Radisson Plaza Hotel, replete with every convenience and the same warm hospitality that first won their business. Located in the heart of downtown, the Radisson Plaza Hotel offers picturesque views of Lake Ivanhoe and the Orlando skyline from its 337 newly renovated guest rooms and 27 suites. One of the area's most popular hotels for meetings, the Radisson Plaza Hotel offers 20,000 square feet of versatile function space.

The hotel features up to 18 meeting and breakout rooms, including the 5,450-square-foot Ivanhoe Ballroom. For events ranging from small conferences to large receptions, all of the hotel's meeting facilities provide flexibility, accessibility, and style. Meeting rooms are equipped with high-speed wireless Internet access and video teleconferencing equipment. A full-service business center and on-site audiovisual services make it easy to plan meetings.

Two top-level concierge floors provide guests with upgraded rooms and suites, as well as private Plaza Club lounge benefits. The hotel's premier restaurant, 'Lando Sam's Bar & Grill, features sumptuous breakfast and lunch buffets and fine dinner fare. A fully equipped health club, outdoor pool and Jacuzzi, and tennis courts round out the amenities.

As the Orlando area thrives, the Radisson Plaza Hotel is making plans for its own development. On adjoining property, the hotel expects to add 100 suites, an additional 25,000 square feet of meeting space, and a tower featuring 200 condominium accommodations overlooking the lake.

TRANSFORMED

The Radisson Corporation brand has been evolving since the roaring twenties, when its Flaming R logo helped launch the hotel company. For the new millennium, the Radisson has created a contemporary logo to express the hotel's casual, but sophisticated, style.

"We, as a company, insisted that our new logo design convey the uniqueness of our hotels and our genuine style of hospitality," says Wilson Perry, general manager. "It's an appealing image that signals that a major transformation has occurred at the Radisson." As part of that transformation, the company has launched a redesigned Web site at www.radissonorlando.com with more guest information. The company also offers an enhanced

Radisson Gold Rewards loyalty program with the opportunity to earn and redeem Gold Points from a group of businesses.

What has not changed is the Radisson Plaza Hotel's compelling customer service philosophy: genuine hospitality celebrating the "Yes, I can!" spirit of Radisson employees. The hotel backs its commitment to customers with its global guest satisfaction guarantee program.

Recently, the Radisson Corporation has enjoyed record-breaking growth, including the addition of 56 new hotels in major worldwide destinations. The company operates one of the most extensive global hotel systems with Radissons in 53 countries on five continents.

The Radisson Plaza Hotel's commitment to Orlando is strong, as well. Each year, the hotel cosponsors the annual Fine Wines and Great Food event to raise funds for Healing the Children-Florida Inc. Owner George Zaczac and his wife, Lourdes, sponsor a number of other events for the same good cause.

As the Radisson Plaza Hotel in downtown Orlando celebrates its own growth, the hotel continues to play a major role in contributing to the well-being of the Central Florida community.

THE REFURBISHED RADISSON PLAZA HOTEL OFFERS GUESTS NOT JUST WARM HOSPITALITY AND CASUAL ELEGANCE, BUT 337 GUEST ROOMS, 27 SUITES, AND 20,000 SQUARE FEET OF VERSATILE FUNCTION SPACE.

W

ATCHING SPACE SHUTTLES RISE MAJESTICALLY INTO THE BLUE IS JUST ONE OF THE MANY attractions of Florida's Space Coast. Nature is another, with 72 miles of beach housing wildlife from manatees to songbirds, and sheltered backwaters that abound with shrimp, crab, and the well-known freshwater bass. And all of this is just an hour's drive from Orlando, one of the world's top vacation destinations. ❦ "For years, the Space Coast was a well-kept secret," says Rob Varley, director of the Space Coast Office of Tourism. That changed in 1987, when Brevard County established its own tourism office to capture the multitudes of visitors

coming to Florida, and specifically to the Orlando area. The organization's $4.8 million operating budget is generated through a 4 percent resort tax on the Space Coast's 11,000 hotel and motel rooms, condos, and campgrounds.

The Space Coast Office of Tourism employs nine people, and contracts with seven outside agencies to accomplish its goals. With support from the local tourism industry, as well as from the Brevard County Commission, the organization's strategies aim at creating visibility and demand. With a combination of advertising, public relations, direct response, Internet marketing, and seasonal visitor promotions, the Space Coast aggressively pursues consumers, travel agents, tour operators, meeting planners, the sports and entertainment market, cruise enthusiasts, and nature lovers.

SYNERGISTIC MARKETING TO REACH VISITORS

Competing destinations, both domestic and international, are promoting themselves as never before. Vacationers are becoming more sophisticated, more value oriented, and more focused on special-interest activities. This presents the Space Coast with both a challenge and an opportunity. According to Varley, the Space Coast's strength is in the partnerships that have been formed with the local tourism base. "Cooperative efforts with the Kennedy Space Center Visitor Complex, the Canaveral Port Authority, and the Melbourne International Airport help us identify and target niche markets—plus, their partnerships help to stretch our advertising dollars," says Varley.

This partnership also includes sales missions and manning trade show booths under the banner of

Florida's Space Coast. The efforts are global, including hiring a British firm, Representation Plus, to promote the Space Coast to the European market. "You only have to listen to the multiple languages being spoken in local businesses to realize how much the international market has grown in importance to our overall marketing strategy," Varley explains. In addition, the Space Coast has banded together with Orlando in a seven-county partnership that promotes the Central Florida area to the global marketplace.

Thrusting the Space Coast further into the spotlight are the variety of cruise ships that sail out of Port

Canaveral—the second-busiest cruise port in the world—and the beautiful 72 miles of Space Coast beach. Three of Florida's top 10 beaches are on the Space Coast. "A significant portion of tourism funds are set aside for the renourishment and cleaning of the beach," says Varley. "It is our number one asset, and its true natural beauty is not taken for granted."

The spectacular achievements of the space program—together with approximately 3,700 miles of inland waterways, endless fishing and water sports, more than 1,400 restaurants, some 8,600 hotel rooms, and some 2,500 campsites and RV parks— all make the Space Coast one of Florida's most popular destinations.

FROM WATCHING SPACE SHUTTLE LAUNCHES TO VISITING THE KENNEDY SPACE CENTER OR JUST LOUNGING ON A PRISTINE BEACH, VISITORS WILL FIND ONE OF THE WORLD'S TOP VACATION DESTINATIONS IN FLORIDA'S SPACE COAST.

ORRIS ARCHITECTS, THE AWARD-WINNING ARCHITECTURAL DESIGN FIRM THAT ESTABLISHED a presence in Orlando in 1988, has quietly reshaped the skyline of Central Florida and lent its creative influence to dozens of area projects—from theme attractions and resorts to office buildings and retail centers. ❧ The firm chose Orlando as the ideal location to serve the burgeoning entertainment, hospitality, and commercial markets. As Orlando's boom resounds and demand increases for quality domestic and international design work, Morris Architects has been able to effectively

CLOCKWISE FROM TOP:
THE MEN WHO GUIDE MORRIS ARCHI-TECTS INCLUDE (FROM LEFT) HOSPI-TALITY STUDIO DIRECTOR GERALD KOI, DIRECTOR OF DESIGN WALT GEIGER, AND ENTERTAINMENT STUDIO DIRECTOR JAMES POPE.

THE FIRM SERVED AS INTERIOR ARCHI-TECT OF THE ACCLAIMED EMERIL'S® RESTAURANT ORLANDO AT UNIVERSAL'S CITY WALK®, WHERE THE CRISP, CON-TEMPORARY INTERIORS PORTRAY CHEF EMERIL LAGASSE'S ENERGETIC PERSONA.

THE ROMANTIC HARBORAGE OF AN ITALIAN SEASIDE VILLAGE IS RE-CREATED AT THE THE PORTOFINO BAY HOTEL AT UNIVERSAL ORLANDO, A LOEWS HOTEL.

A VIRTUAL-ADVENTURE EXPERIENCE IN A 60,000-SQUARE-FOOT, 3-D, THREE-SCREEN THEATER MEGA-ATTRACTION AT UNIVERSAL ORLANDO, TERMINA-TOR 2: 3D BATTLE ACROSS TIME™ WAS THE FIRST-EVER COMBINATION OF THREE-DIMENSIONAL CINEMATOGRAPHY, DIGITAL COMPOSITE COMPUTER GRAPH-ICS, AND LIVE ACTION.

and creatively combine art and business with technology and a passion for detail to create world-class projects.

Morris Architects' first Central Florida project—the Bank of America Building, known initially as the duPont Centre—quickly led to a succession of high-profile projects. The firm's Central Florida experi-ence includes Emeril's® Restaurant Orlando at Universal Orlando℠; Daytona USA World Center of Rac-ing; the Disney Feature Animation Building at Disney-MGM Studios; the Portofino Bay Hotel at Univer-sal Orlando, a Loews Hotel; thrill attractions such as Terminator 2: 3D Battle Across Time™ and MEN IN BLACK™ Alien Attack at Uni-versal Orlando; enhancements to the Disney Village Marketplace at Lake Buena Vista, and additions to the Orlando Museum of Art.

The firm provides comprehen-sive design services for architecture, urban planning, landscape architec-ture, interiors, signage and graphics, visualization and imaging for all phases of the design, and construc-tion process including predesign strategic planning and program-ming. Since 1995, the company has completed more than $4 billion in projects around the globe.

Established Excellence

orris Architects was founded in Houston in 1938 as Wilson and Morris Architects, and became Morris Archi-tects in 1986. The firm has estab-lished itself as one of the largest national full-service architectural practices, with offices in Orlando, Houston, Los Angeles, and Mexico City. These offices are organized into studios specializing in the de-sign of entertainment, hospitality, corporate, civic, education, health care, and public assembly architec-ture. Today, Morris Architects has completed or is designing projects both domestically and worldwide on four continents.

Hospitality Studio Director Gerald Koi established the Orlando office in 1988, overseeing the duPont Centre, a $400 million, mixed-use development. Since that time, Koi—with the help of Entertainment Studio Director James Pope and Director of Design Walt Geiger has overseen steady growth of the Or-lando office, and currently employs a staff of more than 50 professional, technical, and administrative per-sonnel who specialize in hospitality, entertainment, retail, planning, and commercial design. Morris Archi-tects' fresh approach and its staff's enthusiasm for each project truly set the firm apart in the industry.

"We have a true passion for all aspects of our work, from concept design of architecture as art to detailed technical design, documen-tation, and management of complex projects," Koi says. "We have a clear, strategic business plan based on a vision and firm values to support and promote the vision."

Other notable projects by Morris Architects located in Central Florida include Twister...Ride It Out® and Woody Woodpecker's KidZone℠ at Universal Orlando®; the Disney Institute and Amphitheater at Lake Buena Vista; Fairfield Cypress Palms Resort in Kissimmee; Hard

Rock Café and Hard Rock Live at CityWalk® Universal Orlando; the dynamic Apollo/Saturn V Visitors Center at Kennedy Space Center; the Daytona Hospitality Village at Daytona International Speedway; Leu Gardens Multi-Purpose Center in Orlando, and W. T. Bland Library in Mt. Dora.

In addition to entertainment, hospitality, and retail projects throughout Central Florida, Morris Architects has left its mark on office buildings, banking centers, libraries, and mixed-use developments.

IMAGE AND SENSE OF PLACE

Careful development of appropriate aesthetics for all projects is Morris Architects' hallmark. Each project design is personally tailored to its specific site context, with skillful integration of regional influence and contemporary needs of the client and its facility.

"Projects inserted into the community consistently respond to their neighborhoods. Entertainment projects within the regional theme parks respond to the film industry-based 'themes' developed from film directors' story lines. The influence of contemporary design on themed environments and the influence of themed environments on contemporary design in urban settings has resulted in a mutually beneficial, enriched, and informed architecture which has created memorable places," says Geiger.

A COMMUNITY-DRIVEN COMPANY

Morris Architects has funneled its talents into several community projects. The firm volunteered its architectural services to the Lake Eola

Charter School, Orlando's first such private undertaking in Central Florida; the Universal Studios® Theater at the Boggy Creek Gang Camp in Cassia, Florida; and the new Beta Center, Inc. in Orlando, an educational haven for pregnant and parenting girls in their early and midteens. The firm's staff has also raised funds for United Way since the office's inauguration in 1988, and holds an annual golf tournament with proceeds going to local charities.

An exciting lineup of Morris Architects projects stretches across Central Florida from the state's east coast to its west: Ocean Walk Resort and Ocean Walk Beach Shoppes on Daytona Beach; Daytona USA World Center of Racing: Simulator Wing at the Daytona International Speedway; Pinnacle Observation Tower in Tampa; and Thornton Park Central in the heart of downtown Orlando, where the firm has designed and will establish offices in a new mid-rise, mixed-use development that brings a lively mix of retail, entertainment, residential, office, and parking elements together as a cohesive, dynamic urban village.

The firm's innovative approach to architectural design, technical expertise, and exemplary service have earned worldwide recognition.

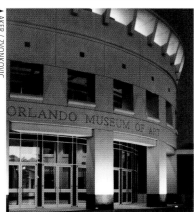

World Architecture magazine named Morris Architects as one of the top five leisure and top seven hospitality architectural practices in the world. *Engineering News-Record* ranked it among the top 10 entertainment architectural firms. Other plaudits include a ranking as one of the top 10 designers and architects by *Hotel Business* magazine, and as one of the top 150 Interior Design Firm Giants by *Interior Design* magazine.

An established reputation for excellence in architecture, continuing acclaim from members of its own industry, and a résumé of notable clients are proof that Morris Architects will continue to be an architectural leader in Central Florida as well as internationally in the decades to come.

CLOCKWISE FROM TOP LEFT: THE 100,000-SQUARE-FOOT APOLLO/SATURN V VISITORS CENTER IS A WORLD-CLASS FACILITY THAT TELLS THE STORY OF THE APOLLO SPACE PROGRAM AND THE MOON LANDINGS.

DAYTONA USA IS A 60,000-SQUARE-FOOT MOTOR SPORTS ENTERTAINMENT AND INTERACTIVE EDUCATIONAL FACILITY, WITH SPECTACULAR CINEMATIC AND VIDEO PRESENTATIONS.

THORNTON PARK CENTRAL IS A 275,000-SQUARE-FOOT PROJECT LOCATED IN THE THORNTON PARK NEIGHBORHOOD NEAR LAKE EOLA, JUST OUTSIDE OF DOWNTOWN ORLANDO.

THE RENOVATION AND EXPANSION OF THE ORLANDO MUSEUM OF ART WAS DESIGNED FOR CONTINUED GROWTH AND EXPANSION AND IT NEARLY DOUBLED THE SIZE OF THE GALLERY SPACES AND RENOVATED THE EDUCATION WING AND COLLECTION MANAGEMENT.

THE FIRST PHASE OF OCEAN WALK RESORT IS A 19-STORY TOWER, COMPLETE WITH 300 UNITS AND AN EIGHT-LEVEL PARKING GARAGE.

Florida Extruders International, Inc.

SINCE JOEL G. LEHMAN PURCHASED AN AGING ALUMINUM PLANT ON THE OUTSKIRTS OF ORLANDO IN MID-1989, Florida Extruders International, Inc. (FEI) has exploded into a rising star. After refurbishing the building, upgrading the equipment, and buying painted patio shapes from other aluminum extruders for a year and a half, Lehman began manufacturing extrusions and screen doors for patio, pool, and glass enclosure applications in 1991. Four years later, Lehman led the company into manufacturing windows and sliding glass doors. FEI has since become the largest independent aluminum extruder and one of the largest window manufacturers in Florida. The firm has been recognized in the

Orlando Business Journal's Golden 100 and Silver 50 lists of top privately held companies in the area, and as one of the largest employers among manufacturing companies. A further tribute to corporate founder Lehman and his dedicated employees has been his multiple nominations as Florida's Entrepreneur of the Year in the manufacturing category.

The company's rise from virtual obscurity can be directly attributed to Lehman's innovative approach to business. For example, patio extrusions were historically warehoused by stocking distributors and sold to specialty contractors. Since Lehman knew how to cost-effectively manufacture these products, he recognized a void in the marketplace. Lehman chose to bypass the distributor and sell directly to the contractor, therefore becoming a mill-direct distributor.

FEI penetrated the market by passing the savings on to the end users and providing them with the highest-quality products in the industry. Today, the company is a dominant supplier of these products in Florida and beyond. In

JOEL LEHMAN AND STAFF IN FRONT OF NEW MANUFACTURING AND DISTRIBUTION FACILITY. PICTURED LEFT TO RIGHT ARE: EARL MOORE, DANA LEHMAN, NINA LEHMAN-WILSON, JOEL LEHMAN, KIM LEHMAN-BARLOW, TERRY BROWNLEE, AND BARRY DOMBCHIK.

HOT TOP ALUMINUM BILLET CASTING SYSTEM

addition to large contractors, FEI's customers include many of the firm's competitors in building-products distribution, who also recognize the value of buying direct from FEI.

MANUFACTURING INTEGRATION

"**Q**uality, quality, quality," says Lehman, describing FEI's philosophy. "It all goes back to being vertically integrated and having total control over products and service. We entered an established market, yet we carved out our niche. We supply the best products, offer the widest variety of stocked lengths, and maintain reliable inventory levels, all of which enables us to provide the best service the industry has ever experienced."

The company's integration, which includes making its own raw materials in a state-of-the-art aluminum billet casting facility, results in the ability to control quality from raw material to the finished product, offer competitive pricing, and provide the most dependable service. Like quality, the words "low-cost leader" are emblazoned in the

mission statement of FEI. "Our operating philosophy includes being recognized as the best in the business, and it is shared with employees and customers alike as a reflection of the company's commitment to being the low-cost producer, and being flexible to satisfy the needs of our customers," says Human Resource Manager Kim Lehman-Barlow.

Powder coating has played a major role in the company's success. "The finish that we put on our products is at least two times greater than the coating thickness specified for most aluminum extrusions, windows, and doors," says Operations Manager Dana Lehman. This results in durable, scratch-resistant products that have provided FEI with a competitive edge from the start.

PRODUCT DIVERSIFICATION

"**F**lorida Extruders prides itself on being applications oriented, versus commodity driven," says Marketing Manager Barry Dombchik. "This philosophy ensures that both sales and manufacturing personnel understand where our products are used, and

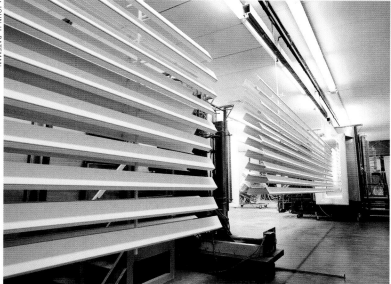

enables us to do the best job of both providing the highest-quality products and meeting our customers' requirements."

The company manufactures 40 million pounds of aluminum shapes on three extrusion presses, ranging in size from 1,250 to 2,500 tons. A fourth press is planned to be operational by 2002. Although FEI has specialized in extruding shapes for patio and pool enclosure, railing, shutter, screen door, window, and sliding glass door applications, the company has expanded its business by producing and warehousing a variety of standard industrial shapes and custom extrusions.

In 1995, FEI introduced Milestone® quality windows and sliding glass doors, and in 2000, it acquired a manufacturer of architecturally shaped windows, such as arches,

circles, and ovals, to enhance the capabilities of its rapidly expanding business. Also, Milestone products have received wide acclaim for their innovative design, stylish appearance, operating performance, and structural integrity to meet stringent Florida building codes. "As the name implies, Milestone products do set the standard," says Window Division Operations Manager Earl Moore. FEI is one of the leading manufacturers of replacement and new construction windows and patio doors in Florida.

Growing to the Top

With its unparalleled quality, service, technology, and growth, FEI's workforce has increased from 18 to more than 500 employees. Sales grew from $5 million in 1991 to $55 million in

2000. The company has increased its original 140,000-square-foot facility to 450,000 square feet of total manufacturing and warehouse space.

And FEI has an aggressive sales plan to further increase its market. "We will continue to grow our business based on our performance record, the proven ability to create new products in a saturated market, and our manufacturing formula for success," says Extruded Products Sales Manager Terry Brownlee.

Still, with future growth, some things will never change. Production Control Manager Nina Lehman-Wilson notes, "Florida Extruders will maintain its commitment to be the low-cost producer, as well as the most dependable, quality-conscious, customer-oriented aluminum extruder and metalworking company in the industry."

ELECTROSTATICALLY APPLIED (ESP) POWDER COATING PROCESS (LEFT)

2,300-TON ALUMINUM EXTRUSION LINE (RIGHT)

MILESTONE® WINDOW AND SLIDING GLASS DOOR MANUFACTURING (LEFT)

1,800-FOOT, HIGH-SPEED POWDER COATING LINE (RIGHT)

CENTURY III IS ONE OF THE MOST COMPLETE TELEPRODUCTION FACILITIES IN THE SOUTHEASTERN United States and the largest postproduction studio in the state of Florida. Century III offers film and tape production and postproduction, animation, graphics, design, visual effects, high definition television (HDTV), image motion control, digital versatile disc (DVD), satellite and fiberoptic feeds, interactive services, and Web site design, as well as various other teleproduction services. ❧ Since the company's arriving in Orlando in 1989, Ross M. Cibella has boldly taken Century III where few companies have gone before. Century III has had an explosion of

high-profile projects that keep it bustling in the highly competitive Orlando film and television industry.

Cibella has always had a vision of success. His idea to create a teleproduction studio came to life on July 4, 1976, when Century III— named in celebration of the United States' third century of independence— was born. Now, as president of Century III at Universal Studios Florida, Cibella is watching his vision become more clearly defined.

Century III is dedicated to the highest standards of excellence in entertainment, commercial and corporate production, and postproduction. In January 1989, Century III was chosen as Universal Studios Florida's exclusive supplier for postproduction and related services in a brand-new production/postproduction complex.

AWARD-WINNING CREATIONS

Century III rang in the millennium with *IllumiNations 2000: Reflections of Earth* for Epcot at Walt Disney World Resort. The company created images for the 28-foot-high video system wrapped around a globe. The exhibit is expected to have a total in-park audience of more than 70 million by 2010. However, the jewel in Century III's crown is the national Addy award— presented by the American Advertising Federation—that Century III earned for the *IllumiNations* project. This was one of the first national Addy awards to be given to a Central Florida company.

Century III has been responsible for numerous television projects with national and international appeal. Some of the company's past successes include such television series as *Super Boy*, *Super Force*, *Fortune Hunter*, and *Swamp Thing*. The company also created a 360-degree, domed theater presentation for the new Madame Tussaud's in Manhattan's Times Square.

Century III is always working on innovative projects, including two world-tour concert videos for the

Orlando-based band 'N Sync. Century III also works with a number of major television shows, concert tours, and movies, keeping company with celebrities including Rosie O'Donnell, Britney Spears, the Reverend Jesse Jackson, Sherman Hemsley, and former President George Bush.

"Century III shows no signs of slowing down," says Cibella. "Every day, we're moving closer to being the most complete teleproduction facility in the southeastern United States. Our future looks very bright."

FROM WIREFRAME TO FINAL IMAGE, CENTURY III'S PHOTOREALISTIC RENDERING OF YANKEE STADIUM IN 1928

CLOCKWISE FROM RIGHT: MARILYN MONROE IN THE *Seven Year Itch*, ONE OF 1000 MOTION CONTROL SHOTS USED IN THE TUSSAUD'S PROJECT

YANKEE STADIUM IN 1928—A LARGE FORMAT IMAGE REPRESENTING A DOME THEATER COMPOSITE WITH LIVE ACTION AND COMPUTER GENERATED ELEMENTS

A COMPUTER GENERATED MODEL OF THE EMPIRE STATE BUILDING

1990-2001

Midland Information Systems, Inc.

In 1990, when Midland Information Systems, Inc. first set up shop in Orlando, just five employees scrambled to sell refurbished IBM AS/400 commercial computers to area clients. After a decade of growth and global expansion, the high-tech and electronic component provider has nearly quintupled its staff, increased and diversified its product offering and built an impressive client base of Fortune 500 companies. ¶ Today, Midland is a key provider of quality new and refurbished IBM computers, hardware upgrades, Avaya/Lucent telephone and communication products, and electronic components such as circuits, capacitors, and memory chips. Located in a brand-new office and

warehouse in Apopka, Florida, Midland prides itself on the technological expertise of its professionals, comprehensive product inventory, and ability to be a one-stop solution provider. At a moment's notice, the company can ship computers and other products either across the interstate to Winter Park or across the ocean to Frankfurt.

"We like to say we have innovative solutions for your technology evolution," says Midland President Mike Illies. "We can find a way to get our clients what they want right away, we can save them money, and we can back the product with first-rate service."

Growing with the Technology Revolution

Midland was established in 1981 by C. Terry Swenson in Minneapolis. In 1990, the company opened its Florida location on the outskirts of Orlando.

By January 1998, Illies and his partner, Henry Rodriguez, had purchased the company and moved its headquarters to Orlando. Two months later, they added Avaya Communications/Lucent Technologies products to their inventory, stocking a wide variety of new and refurbished Avaya Communications/Lucent Technologies systems, including audio- and videoconference units, paging systems, and other equipment. By September 1998, the company had expanded to include its electronic components division. In January 2000, Midland became an IBM Business Partner with the right to sell new IBM AS/400s, RS/6000s, and Netfinity servers.

Midland recently moved to its new, 14,700-square-foot Apopka headquarters, complete with an 8,200-square-foot warehouse. There, the company's team of in-house service specialists, technical engineers, and sales staff helps clients stay ahead

of technological change by providing cost-competitive equipment solutions. Staff members test and retest products for service reliability for customers ranging from new small businesses to internationally known companies.

Since starting operations, Midland has provided more than 10,000 businesses with high-quality computers and other equipment. The company trains its dynamic sales team to know and understand its products inside out, and to guide a client to an equipment solution that may not have been an obvious one. Midland's experience with IBM AS/400 equipment ranges from sales of whole machines to processors, memory, and other items. The company also strives to be a nationwide leader as a remarketer of Avaya Communications/Lucent Technologies equipment, from sound station conference units to port carriers and data modules.

LOCATED IN A BRAND-NEW OFFICE AND WAREHOUSE IN APOPKA, FLORIDA, MIDLAND INFORMATION SYSTEMS, INC. PRIDES ITSELF ON THE TECHNOLOGICAL EXPERTISE OF ITS PROFESSIONALS, COMPREHENSIVE PRODUCT INVENTORY, AND ABILITY TO BE A ONE-STOP SOLUTION PROVIDER.

With the demands of today's competitive and rapidly changing technologies, Midland's status as a one-stop source for the latest in new and used computer hardware, communications systems, and electronic components for short- and long-term business needs gives the company a definite edge.

"Orlando is a great location for us because it's a thriving city, and it's not a saturated market for us," says Rodriguez. "It really is coming into its own technologically. Whether it's a new small business ready to equip for a launch, a growing business in need of upgrades, or a global enterprise that needs quality products and services quickly, Midland can respond to their needs."

Staying on the Cutting Edge

Midland plans continued growth from its new headquarters. In addition to the expansion of its existing divisions, the company anticipates delving into E-commerce for clients who want to buy and sell on the Internet. Most important, Midland will continue to build on its already solid reputation of expert service, quality products, extensive inventory, rapid delivery, and unbeatable value.

Midland is a member of three major computer associations that work toward ensuring that strict guidelines are followed in order to keep the industry top notch. "We have so many customers who keep coming back to us time and time again," Illies says. "We've earned their trust and their loyalty because they know we are committed to serving them."

Midland's commitment to the Central Florida community has grown as well. A member of the Better Business Bureau of Central Florida, the company and its 20-plus employees enjoy increasing involvement in local fund-raising efforts, including March of Dimes, Muscular Dystrophy Association, and Florida Hospital/American Heart Association events. "We're excited to be here," Illies says. "Not only is it a great place to live, work, and play, but it's the perfect place for us to grow right along with our Central Florida clients."

THE VACATION DESTINATION OF THE FUTURE IS HERE TODAY—UNIVERSAL ORLANDO® RESORT. Comprised of two great theme parks, a dynamic entertainment complex, and world-class on-site hotels, this new vacation resort delivers unforgettable experiences for every member of the family. ▮ It began in 1990 with the opening of Universal Studios, the world's number one movie studio and theme park and the largest working motion picture studio outside of Hollywood. Universal Studios allows guests the opportunity to go behind the scenes to "ride" the movies. Its larger-than-life approach to theme park entertainment has led to wide praise from guests

and travel organizations. Travelers rate Universal Studios tops among theme park experiences, and Rick Namey, author of Fodor's *Orlando Like a Pro* travel guide, calls it "the best theme park in the world."

The reasons are simple. From the start, the goal has been to make Universal Orlando a world-class destination offering world-class experiences. The result has been a huge success.

"We use state-of-the-art technology and tremendous creativity to bring guests the theme park experience of a lifetime," says Felix Mussenden, chief operating officer for Universal Orlando. "Our rides continue to get superb reviews, and our events—such as Halloween Horror Nights and Mardi Gras—have become a major part of what makes our park popular. Universal Studios has become a must-see in Orlando."

STATE-OF-THE-ART ATTRACTIONS

Universal Studios features dozens of rides, shows, and attractions along with street entertainment, celebrity look-alikes, and dining and shop-ping experiences. Its streets look like they're straight out of favorite films and, on any day, guests have the chance to watch movies and television shows being filmed in one of Universal's soundstages or along one of its streets.

Cutting-edge entertainment is a large part of what makes Universal Studios so successful. It made entertainment history when it opened MEN IN BLACK™ Alien Attack™ in 2000, which features Will Smith and Rip Torn from the film, along with more than 120 extraterrestrial creatures. The life-size, ride-through interactive video game is the first-ever attraction where guests' individual and collective abilities determine each ride's outcome. Players of the game—part heart-stopping thrill ride, part cosmic turkey shoot—actually step into the movie and directly affect the environment around them by firing their laser-sighted "alien zappers" at targets and scoring points. And the aliens respond,

CLOCKWISE FROM TOP:
VISITORS TO UNIVERSAL ORLANDO® RESORT CAN SAVE THE EARTH ON THE ALL-NEW MEN IN BLACK™ ALIEN ATTACK™ RIDE AT UNIVERSAL STUDIOS®.

RIDERS' SCORES DETERMINE THE ENDING AS THEY ZAP ALIENS IN MEN IN BLACK ALIEN ATTACK.

HOP IN A LOG AND HANG ON AT DUDLEY DO-RIGHT'S RIPSAW FALLS®.

Caro-Seuss-el, Green Eggs and Ham Cafe, If I Ran The Zoo, One Fish Two Fish Red Fish Blue Fish, and The Cat In The Hat.

Myths and legends come to life in The Lost Continent, a mysterious, fog-shrouded land, featuring Poseidon's Fury: Escape From the Lost City, The Eighth Voyage of Sindbad, The Flying Unicorn, and the Dueling Dragons double coaster, the world's first inverted near-miss dueling roller coasters. The Dueling Dragons are constructed with perilously intertwining paths of metal and dragon-shaped racing cars that furiously barrel towards and around each other at speeds close to 60 miles per hour, escaping collision by mere inches. The Flying Unicorn is a child-sized coaster for a gentle and fanciful aerial ride through a mystical forest, as if park visitors were flying on the back of the mystical unicorn.

Jurassic Park is a full-fledged incarnation of the novel and motion picture, a hauntingly fascinating island inhabited by the most advanced animatronic creatures ever designed—dinosaurs that respond to the humans around them. The Jurassic Park River Adventure, featuring the longest and steepest water drop ever built—plus Camp Jurassic, an interactive play area with a multitude of adventures including lava pits, amber caves, tropical rain forests, and the new Pteranodon Flyers—brings Jurassic Park roaring to life.

Toon Lagoon is a delightful land where everyone's favorite cartoon characters live when they're not in the Sunday funnies. Visitors delight in Popeye & Bluto's Bilge-Rat Barges and Dudley Do-Right's

causing chaos as the MEN IN BLACK (MIB) trainee transports spin out of control with each ricochet or direct hit.

But cutting-edge entertainment doesn't end with MEN IN BLACK Alien Attack. At Universal Studios, guests know what it's like to take a virtual adventure in TERMINATOR 2: 3-D, an attraction that earns cheers every day. The $60 million attraction *USA Today* calls "a 3-D extravaganza" is the most elaborate and technologically advanced experience ever created for the Orlando theme park.

Also at Universal Studios, guests can experience the fury of an actual tornado in Twister, be chased by a giant shark in JAWS, or take a spectacular journey into the future on Back To The Future The Ride. And only Universal Studios is home to Woody Woodpecker's KidZone, where kids of all ages find Woody Woodpecker's Nuthouse Coaster and Curious George Goes to Town alongside the Animal Actors Stage and A Day in the Park with Barney,

as well as Fievel's Playland, and E.T. Adventure.

Major Expansion, More Adventures

In 1999, Universal Orlando opened its second theme park, Islands of Adventure, the most technologically advanced theme park ever built. Adjacent to Universal Studios, Islands of Adventure brings together the most unforgettable encounters of all time and challenges guests to live the adventure. This is where the worlds of legendary myths, epic adventures, cartoon characters, and comic book superheroes come to life right before visitors' eyes. Islands of Adventure features five exciting islands: Seuss Landing, The Lost Continent, Jurassic Park, Toon Lagoon, and Marvel Super Hero Island.

A cacophony of colors, music, and mood, Seuss Landing is where the whimsical characters of Theodor "Dr. Seuss" Geisel's famous books spring to life. Attractions include

CHILDREN NEVER KNOW WHO THEY WILL RUN INTO ON THE STREETS OF UNIVERSAL STUDIOS®.

BLAST OFF FROM ZERO TO 40 M.P.H. IN TWO SECONDS FLAT ON THE INCREDIBLE HULK COASTER® (LEFT).

IT'S SMILES ALL AROUND ON THE CARO-SEUSS-EL™ AT SEUSS LANDING™ (RIGHT).

Ripsaw Falls, the first water flume ride ever to send its riders plummeting 75 feet, then down beneath the water's surface.

On Marvel Super Hero Island, guests encounter heroic battles between renowned superheroes and villains with such exciting rides as Storm Force Accelatron, Doctor Doom's Fearfall, The Amazing Adventures of Spider-Man, and The Incredible Hulk Coaster.

The Amazing Adventures of Spider-Man is the first ride in history to assimilate 3-D film, live action, and a revolutionary "roving motion base simulator" to engage guests in the famed comic book character's epic battle against the forces of evil, including a stunning, 400-foot freefall "sensory descent." Creators of The Amazing Adventures of Spider-Man refer to it as the "next threshold attraction," which combines the best of Universal Studios' famed Back To The Future and TERMINATOR 2: 3-D attractions, which are widely considered to be landmark achievements.

Using a powerfully designed special booster thrust system, The Incredible Hulk Coaster hurls riders upward with g-force power before sending them careening in wild zigzags 10 stories above the ground in a flying maze of intricate tracks, byzantine paths, and a complete weightless inversion 110 feet from the ground, before plunging under a bridge and into two deep, underground trenches. Such weightless inversion has never been attempted.

Storm Force Accelatron provides a whirling experience for anyone not tall enough for, or not wishing to face, the g-force of The Incredible Hulk Coaster. This indoor

spinning ride enlists guests to help superhero Storm harness the power of weather to battle her archenemy Magneto. Special effects create a thunderstorm of swirling sound and light, while guests spin beneath Storm Force's circular dome.

Academy Award-winning producer/director Steven Spielberg serves as creative director for Islands of Adventure and Universal Studios—two great theme parks that make one great vacation.

CITYWALK ADDS ANOTHER DIMENSION

A visit to Universal Orlando isn't complete without a trip to the resort destination's dynamic new entertainment complex, CityWalk. This two-tiered promenade of individually themed entertainment adventures captures everything from the birthplace of the Motown sound to the world of NASCAR auto racing to the world's largest Hard Rock Cafe. Set amid authentic streetscapes and native landscaping, the architectural pan-

orama wraps around a four-acre harbor fed by the resort's interconnecting waterways.

Included in CityWalk are culinary attractions such as Hard Rock Cafe, Jimmy Buffett's Margaritaville, Emeril's Restaurant Orlando, MOTOWN Café, NASCAR Café, NBA City, Latin Quarter, and Pastamoré. Additional entertainment options can be found at Hard Rock Live Orlando, Pat O'Brien's, Bob Marley—A Tribute To Freedom, CityJazz, Universal Cineplex, the Grove, and various specialty shops.

ELEGANT HOTEL CENTERPIECE

In September 1999, Universal Orlando's first on-site hotel opened, the Portofino Bay Hotel, a Loews Hotel. Featuring 750 elegantly appointed rooms, the Portofino Bay is imbued with the ambience and romantic harbor setting of the Italian seaside village of Portofino.

At their rooms, Portofino Bay guests find state-of-the-art safety,

security, and convenience, beginning with the guest room key, which also serves as guest identification and provides charging privileges throughout Universal Orlando. The Smart Room adjusts the room temperature to the most comfortable setting and automatically reports any malfunctions as they occur. This innovative feature also monitors whether a minibar needs replenishing and alerts housekeeping when the room is vacant, eliminating service-related disturbances to guests.

For those staying in one of the Portofino's Butler Villas, elegant service is the order of the day. Guests are greeted by their butler, and served fresh-squeezed orange juice or champagne, while their suitcases are unpacked for them. The butler makes all the arrangements for theme park tickets, dinner, spa appointments, pressing, and laundry service, among others.

Other amenities include eight restaurants and lounges, a 10,600-square-foot health spa, three swimming pools, two boccie ball courts, and a full-service business center. Convention facilities include 42,000 square feet of meeting and banquet space, including a 15,000-square-foot Grand Ballroom and a 7,500-square-foot Junior Ballroom.

ROCK-AND-ROLL MEMORABILIA IN NEWEST HOTEL

In January 2001, Universal Orlando opened the Hard Rock Hotel, showcasing the unique California mission architectural style, with public areas decorated with pieces from the Hard Rock's extensive collection of rock-and-roll memorabilia.

The world-famous Hard Rock Café's themes of Love All Serve All, All Is One, and Save the Planet are echoed throughout the Hard Rock Hotel. Universal Orlando's Hard Rock Hotel features 650 guest rooms and suites, a lobby lounge, an indoor bar, a pool bar, a pool snack bar, two restaurants, a fitness center, and a business center, all on a 14-acre site,

providing guests with an understated, comfortable, and casually elegant atmosphere.

In addition to enjoying luxurious accommodations, on-site hotel guests receive numerous other benefits, including special conveniences, privileges, and discounts at both Universal Orlando theme parks and select on-site restaurants.

When Universal Orlando is complete, a total of five hotels will be part of the resort complex. The three managed by Loews include the Portofino Bay Hotel, the Hard Rock Hotel, and the Royal Pacific Resort, which is scheduled to open in 2002. The hotels are connected to each other, the theme parks, and the CityWalk entertainment complex by a chain of scenic waterways. Guests may take traditional transportation or opt for convenient water taxis to and from their hotel.

Combining the creativity of Hollywood, the greatest stories of all time, soul-stirring entertainment, and unparalleled lodging accommodations, Universal Orlando creates the vacation destination for the 21st century.

CLOCKWISE FROM TOP: KIDS WILL HAVE GALLONS OF FUN IN THE CURIOUS GEORGE GOES TO TOWN INTERACTIVE PLAY AREA.

VISITORS CAN TRY TO ESCAPE THE JAWS OF A HUNGRY T-REX ON THE JURASSIC PARK RIVER ADVENTURE AT ISLANDS OF ADVENTURE.

EVERY SPRING, UNIVERSAL STUDIOS CELEBRATES MARDI GRAS WITH THE BIGGEST BASH THIS SIDE OF NEW ORLEANS.

BILL AND VONETTE BRIGHT FOUNDED CAMPUS CRUSADE FOR CHRIST—ONE OF THE WORLD'S LARGEST Christian missionary organizations—in 1951 as a ministry to college students at the University of California at Los Angeles. Since then, the movement has expanded to more than 1,000 U.S. campuses and more than 1,200 campuses around the world. However, Campus Crusade reaches beyond college students. More than 60 ministries worldwide, which include Family Life, Athletes in Action, and The *JESUS* Film Project®, fall under the umbrella of Campus Crusade for Christ. Campus Crusade's world headquarters relocated from San Bernardino to Orlando in 1991.

HEADQUARTERS IN THE CITY BEAUTIFUL

After researching 38 cities in the United States based on 56 criteria, the organization's leadership came to the consensus that God was leading them to Orlando. The leaders had all but moved to another state when they realized that God was telling them to move to Central Florida. The international airport, climate, and generosity of Central Florida's government and civil leaders helped draw the organization to the city. "Having Campus Crusade in Orlando helps establish our reputation as a caring community," says Glenda E. Hood, mayor of Orlando. "The Lake Hart facility is a beautiful testimony to Campus Crusade's fine work."

In an architectural tip of the hat to the movement's early beginnings, the headquarters resembles a college campus, tied together by a four-acre quadrangle of grass and flowers. The three buildings cover some 250,000 square feet of space. "The size of the buildings captures people's attention," says Jay Berlinsky, executive director of headquarters development. "It lets them know we are serious about reaching the world for Christ."

Accented with 25-foot pillars and two central rotundas, these classical, Roman-style buildings rise out of open meadows at the end of a winding road. Nearby, forested marshlands serve as home to otters, deer, and egrets. "The world headquarters is truly a gift from God," says Bill

Bright. "We are greatly blessed to be in beautiful Orlando, yet we must always remember this marvelous facility belongs to America and the world."

VISITORS WELCOME FOR TOURS

Visitors can take a guided tour of the VisionWalks, which includes interactive, multimedia presentations. Also, guides give guests a tour of The *JESUS* Film Project. Since the full-length feature film debuted in 1979, Campus Crusade staff members have traveled all over the world, translating *JESUS* into more than 640 languages. Today, it stands alone as one of the most widely viewed movies in the world, seen

IN 1991, AFTER AN EXHAUSTIVE, NATIONWIDE SEARCH, THE LEADERS OF CAMPUS CRUSADE FOR CHRIST CHOSE ORLANDO AS THE NEW HOME FOR ITS WORLD HEADQUARTERS.

▼ JOEL DASALLA

VISITORS CAN TAKE A GUIDED TOUR OF THE VISIONWALKS, WHICH INCLUDES INTERACTIVE, MULTIMEDIA PRESENTATIONS. ALSO, GUIDES GIVE GUESTS A TOUR OF THE JESUS FILM PROJECT.

by more people than *Titanic, Gone With the Wind, The Lion King,* or any other film. Campus Crusade strives to give every person in the world a chance to see The *JESUS* film at least once in his or her native language. The tour shows the process Campus Crusade staff members go through to make the film, as well as how they distribute it.

Tours through Lake Hart's VisionWalks and The *JESUS* Film Master Studio are offered multiple times daily, beginning in the facility's East Building. Special group tours can be arranged.

THE HUB OF THE ORGANIZATION

The Lake Hart facility serves as the hub of the Campus Crusade organization, with frequent visits from international staff members. From the organiza-

tion's Florida headquarters, more than 800 Campus Crusade staff members serve and lead more than 22,000 staff members and 489,000 trained volunteers who live all over the United States and in 186 other countries.

"Campus Crusade has made an impact in our community that is beyond calculation," says Mel Martinez, Orange County chairman. "Its executives and staff contribute countless hours as volunteers to non-profit organizations, and their beautiful campus is a welcome addition to Orange County's landscape. We are very fortunate to have Campus Crusade in our region."

The organization's new buildings in Orlando were designed to show what God is doing around the world and to challenge people to join with Campus Crusade for Christ in telling the 6 billion people on Earth about

the love of Jesus Christ. "The Lake Hart complex is a testimony to the power of faith and faithful giving," says Tom Hunt, regional director of Bell South. "It's a home base for heroes, the thousands of Campus Crusade missionaries who are taking God's word to the four corners of the earth. We in Orlando are blessed to have this wonderful center."

FROM ITS FLORIDA HEADQUARTERS, MORE THAN 800 CAMPUS CRUSADE STAFF MEMBERS SERVE AND LEAD MORE THAN 22,000 STAFF MEMBERS AND 489,000 TRAINED VOLUNTEERS WHO LIVE ALL OVER THE UNITED STATES AND IN 186 OTHER COUNTRIES.

FIRST UNION CORPORATION FOUNDER H.M. VICTOR WOULD HAVE A DIFFICULT TIME RECOGNIZING the bank he began in 1908 in Charlotte. After raising funds to start Union National by selling 1,000 shares of stock at $100 each, he set up his office at a rolltop desk in the main lobby of a Charlotte hotel. As Union National grew, it maintained a reputation for high credit quality, strong financial performance, and excellent customer service. It was this viability that kept the bank open during the 1930s when the depression caused many others to close. ⚜ Union National was the first bank in Charlotte

to open a branch office in 1947, and the bank continued to flourish until its first merger with another North Carolina bank in 1959 to become First Union National Bank. In the mid-1980s, the bank began expanding outside of North Carolina, and First Union stock began trading on the New York Stock Exchange in 1988. Successful mergers continued—with more than 70 banks and other

companies—and today Victor's Union National Bank has grown into First Union Corporation, the nation's sixth-largest bank holding company, based on assets of $247 billion as of September 30, 2000. The bank has been serving Central Florida customers and communities since 1985, when it merged with Atlantic Bancorporation. First Union later strengthened its presence in

the Orlando area when it merged with American Pioneer, FSB of Orlando in 1991.

PHENOMENAL GROWTH NATIONWIDE

Today, First Union has full-service banking offices in 11 states and Washington, D.C.; some 70,000 employees; and more than 15 million customers.

FROM HUMBLE BEGINNINGS EARLY IN THE 20TH CENTURY, FIRST UNION CORPORATION HAS GROWN TO BECOME THE NATION'S SIXTH-LARGEST HOLDING COMPANY.

IN CENTRAL FLORIDA, FIRST UNION
HAS ESTABLISHED READING PARTNER-
SHIPS WITH ELEMENTARY SCHOOLS.
EMPLOYEES VISIT SCHOOLS FOR 30
WEEKS IN A ROW, READING NEW BOOKS
TO CHILDREN AT EACH SESSION.

The bank offers a full range of financial services to corporate and consumer customers, from deposit accounts to mutual funds, and from Wall Street-type corporate financing to cash management services for businesses. The company also offers brokerage services, mortgage banking, home equity lending, and insurance to customers nationwide through its some 2,200 full-service banking financial centers, some 340 retail brokerage offices, and more than 3,800 ATMs. In Central Florida alone, there are some 100 First Union financial centers and some 165 ATMs.

First Union also offers customers convenience through 24-hour banking by phone and through on-line banking at www.firstunion.com. Due to its Internet banking options, First Union has been recognized by *ComputerWorld* magazine as one of five banks among the magazine's Premier 100 list of companies making innovative use of the Web.

HELPING THE COMMUNITY

One of First Union's core values is stellar service, and the company believes that service should extend beyond customers, clients, and colleagues to First Union's communities. "First Union has grown through mergers, but many of the staff members have remained," says

Marshall Vermillion, Central Florida president. "We have maintained the individual histories of the institutions. Our history in Central Florida may have just begun in the 1980s, but it's really much richer through the traditions of the employees."

In Central Florida, First Union has established reading partnerships with elementary schools. Employees visit schools for 30 weeks in a row, reading new books to children at each session. The books, donated to the schools, have helped Central Florida's schools receive more than 4,000 children's books as part of First Union's Reading First program. In 2000, First Union received the President's Service Award, the nation's highest honor for volunteer service, for the company's Education First volunteer program.

Another way First Union encourages employees to volunteer in schools is by providing paid time off. Every employee has four hours a month of paid time away from work to volunteer in local schools or other education programs. First Union also serves the community through investments in local community development organizations, such as the Orlando-based Florida Community Loan Fund, which supports neighborhood revitalization and affordable housing initiatives throughout the state.

OUTSTANDING WORK ENVIRONMENT

First Union's innovative benefits for employees earned the bank a top ranking among financial services companies in the 2000 *Money* magazine poll of benefits plans at Fortune 100 companies. Also in 2000, *Working Mother* magazine named First Union among its 100 Best Companies for Working Women for the fourth time because of its family-friendly programs for employees.

First Union is also committed to a diverse workplace that reflects the communities where it operates. The bank's diversity efforts are not going unnoticed; First Union received the Corporate Award in 1996 for the Advancement of Women, which was awarded by the National Council of Women. In addition, *Hispanic* magazine recognized the company as one of the top 100 companies in the nation for providing the most opportunity for Hispanics.

"First Union will continue growing in Central Florida because this is such a vibrant part of the state and our nation," says Vermillion. "We plan to open new branches and improve our coverage in the marketplace, while serving our communities through education and community development initiatives."

MASSEY CADILLAC IS PART OF THE NATION'S LARGEST AND MOST SUCCESSFUL CADILLAC dealership group. Massey Cadillac is owned by Don Massey, known both as a leader in the automotive industry with four decades of automotive expertise and as the first inductee into the Cadillac Master Dealer Hall of Fame. ⚜ Massey began a summer job at an automobile dealership when he was just 14 years old. He started selling cars in 1955, and within three years, was general manager. That experience enabled him to open his own used car lot, and he soon bought his first

Cadillac dealership, Don Massey Cadillac in Plymouth, Michigan, on the outskirts of Detroit.

Today, this megadealer is the highest-rated Cadillac dealer in the nation, with 28 branches across the country. "Massey chose Orlando in 1991 for his first Florida dealership because he considered it a major growth market," says Mark Naszradi, general manager of Massey Cadillac in Orlando.

"Our customers look forward to buying a new car and having a place to come in for service if they need it," says Naszradi. "We make it a positive experience with our top-grade, quality service, and our business keeps growing by leaps and bounds."

Naszradi was handpicked to open the new Orlando dealership. Since that opening, two more Central Florida locations have been added: Massey Cadillac Oldsmobile of Sanford and Massey Cadillac South on the Orange Blossom Trail. The original store recently expanded with a Saab franchise. Today, Massey Cadillac of Orlando is the largest Cadillac dealership in Florida and among the top five Cadillac dealerships in the country.

MASSEY CADILLAC IS OWNED BY DON MASSEY, KNOWN BOTH AS A LEADER IN THE AUTOMOTIVE INDUSTRY WITH FOUR DECADES OF AUTOMOTIVE EXPERTISE AND AS THE FIRST INDUCTEE INTO THE CADILLAC MASTER DEALER HALL OF FAME.

MASSEY CADILLAC OF ORLANDO IS THE LARGEST CADILLAC DEALERSHIP IN FLORIDA AND AMONG THE TOP FIVE CADILLAC DEALERSHIPS IN THE COUNTRY.

▶ JENNIFER FOLEY

REPUTATION FOR QUALITY

Massey Cadillac's philosophy is simple: the company's goal is to be "a caring, servicing, selling dealer." Massey's own advice to employees is to "talk to as many customers as you can, listen to as many customers as you can, and service as many vehicles as you can." The Orlando dealership consistently wins the annual Cadillac Master Dealer award for superior service and record sales.

"Massey's reputation for outstanding customer service and professionalism stems directly from the people who work in the dealerships," says Naszradi. "It's always been the people who are the key to the success of the Massey group." The Orlando dealerships employ more than 200 people and have a reputation for quality service with longtime customers.

Naszradi considers community involvement to be part of Massey Cadillac's customer appreciation program. Though the biggest benefactor of the dealership's generosity is the Arnold Palmer Hospital for Women and Children, Naszradi has been known to charitably support dozens of smaller community events at the request of customers. "We consider giving back to the community a gift to our loyal customers," Naszradi says. "We want to keep growing with Orlando and Central Florida."

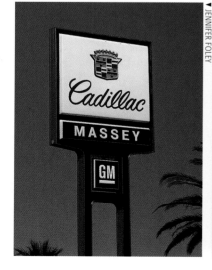

◀ JENNIFER FOLEY

◀ JENNIFER FOLEY

NE OF THE FASTEST-GROWING HISPANIC BUSINESSES IN THE UNITED STATES, AMERICAN PAVING Contractors, Inc. is a Central Florida entrepreneurial success story. In less than a decade of providing top-quality paving and concrete work throughout the Orlando area, the company has grown from five employees, including founders Pete and Raiza Tamayo, to a staff of about 30 people. The company has increased revenue from less than $500,000 to more than $3.5 million, and it has built a client base that includes Walt Disney World, Universal Studios, Florida Hospital, Florida Power and Light, and Eckerd Drugs. ✴ "Our motto is Live to Excel, and we guarantee the finest

service, quality of work, and level of professionalism in the area," says Raiza Tamayo, chief financial officer. "From the time we meet with our clients through final project completion, we give them our personal attention."

American Paving is a versatile company that provides a wide range of construction and maintenance services—from small repairs to complete design and construction. The company custom tailors sites as well, including earthwork and storm water drainage system installation, as well as concrete and asphalt paving. The firm's asphalt maintenance division provides patching, resurfacing, and paving of roads and parking lots of all sizes. In addition, the company designs and installs new concrete parking lots, driveways, and cart paths, and repairs and installs concrete curbing and car stops. It also offers seal coating, striping, and signage services.

Since 1997, American Paving has been recognized by *Hispanic Magazine* as one of the top 100 fastest-growing Hispanic businesses in the country.

Basic Beginnings

Pete Tamayo, president of American Paving, was born in Cienfuegos, Cuba, and arrived in the United States as a child in 1963. He met his wife, Raiza, at Coral Park High School in Miami, and they married in 1977. Less than 10 years later, they moved their family to Orlando and, on January 2, 1992, opened the paving business from their garage.

"The potential for growth in the Orlando area was evident," Pete Tamayo says. "It's a prime spot in the country for construction, and it's a great city for families."

In its brief history, American Paving has grown its services and rapidly expanded its client base between Central Florida's east and west coasts. The Tamayos have become a force in the Hispanic business community as well.

Pete Tamayo is on the board of the Small Business Chamber of the Orlando Regional Chamber of Commerce, has helped create the area's first Hispanic Contractor's Council, and has been named Hispanic Businessman of the Year for the Southeast region by the U.S. Hispanic Chamber of Commerce. One of his proudest accomplishments has been creating a class, in conjunction with the state's Hispanic Business Initiative Fund, to educate non-English-speaking workers who might some day become subcontractors.

Raiza Tamayo has worked closely with Junior Achievement, has been chosen chairman of the Hispanic Chamber of Commerce of Central Florida, and represented the southeastern U.S. and Puerto Rico on the U.S. Hispanic Chamber of Commerce from 1998 to 1999.

"We have grown and matured as a company to the point where we are viewed as leaders in our industry and

in our community, and that's something we're very proud of," says Raiza Tamayo. "Our goal is to increase profits, keep clients happy, and help our employees thrive."

SINCE 1992, AMERICAN PAVING CONTRACTORS, INC. HAS GROWN FROM A GARAGE-BASED COMPANY WITH FIVE EMPLOYEES TO A FIRM WITH ANNUAL REVENUES OF MORE THAN $3.5 MILLION AND A STAFF OF AROUND 30.

LOOKING AT PHOENIX INTERNATIONAL TODAY, ONE WOULD SCARCELY BELIEVE THAT LESS THAN A DECADE ago the origins of this leading global banking software company, based in Heathrow, Florida, could be traced to a single, 16-page white paper. ⚜ The document's author, Bahram Yusefzadeh, is now chairman and CEO of Phoenix International. After graduating from a small liberal arts college in the Midwest, he developed a strong interest in computer technology and began creating application software programs for community banks in the nation's heartland. Thirty years later, Yusefzadeh's knowledge of the banking industry, combined with his hands-on technology

expertise, would culminate into a concept for a new generation of banking software.

Yusefzadeh believed banks could more effectively manage their organizations and serve their customers with software that uses client/server-based technology, harnessing the power of PCs, networks, and even the Internet. When Phoenix International was founded in 1993, this was considered a bold vision; finding progressive, innovative bankers that shared this belief would prove to be a challenge. Yusefzadeh forged ahead and, with help from a core group of bankers, created what is known today as the Phoenix System.

Today, Phoenix International has grown to more than 300 employees, and is among the world's leading banking software providers with more than 150 clients in 26 different

countries. These clients include small, start-up banks; midsize to larger U.S. community banks; credit unions; and other multibillion-dollar international financial organizations. Phoenix also has offices and development centers in the United Kingdom, Singapore, New Zealand, and Australia, and operates Application Service Centers—including one in Orlando—through which the Phoenix System is offered on an outsourced basis.

BANKING ON PHOENIX

The Phoenix System was never meant to be just another banking software system. Using a totally customer-centric design and the newer client/server-based computing architecture, the Phoenix System helps bankers overcome the many problems inherent

in legacy, mainframe-based systems. In an age when consumers look for convenience and better service from their financial institution, the Phoenix System enables bankers to respond by allowing quicker and easier access to customer information using Windows-based point-and-click technology.

This accessibility to information, along with powerful reporting and decision support tools, has made the Phoenix System a strong ally for banks seeking a competitive edge through technology. Phoenix International has further advanced its product and service offerings by using Internet-based technology to offer Web site development and hosting services, its own Internet Banking product, custom-designed intranets, and an extranet that provides e-commerce services, such as

FOUNDER, CHAIRMAN, AND CEO BAHRAM YUSEFZADEH (LEFT), AND PRESIDENT AND COO RAJU SHIVDASANI GUIDE PHOENIX INTERNATIONAL.

on-line brokerage to banks and their customers.

These technology advantages have clearly been successful with bankers both in the United States and abroad. Expanding its customer base to more than 150 clients worldwide in less than five years, Phoenix has shown impressive growth and bankers are excited about the technology the company has put at their fingertips.

"The Phoenix System is easy to use, even for a computer novice," says William C. Beiler, president and CEO of Orlando-based CNL Bank. "It's an excellent Windows-based system that enables me to access management reports on a daily basis. I can look at customer activity and accounts from my desk, without bothering any of my staff."

Perhaps even more impressive is the fact that the customer-centric design that served as the Phoenix System's foundation has more than delivered on its promise of providing better access to customer information, which has, in turn, helped clients improve customer service.

"Our goal is to achieve what we refer to as 'once and done' service,"

says Bill Filer, chief financial officer of Evergreen Bank, located in Seattle. "The idea is to satisfy a customer's needs in one call or visit, without having to transfer the call, ask the customer to wait, or otherwise inconvenience them. Phoenix enables us to fulfill this service model."

COMMUNITY INVOLVEMENT

Phoenix takes pride in being a responsible corporate citizen; community involvement ranks high on the company's agenda. As a leading technology firm—with its worldwide headquarters based in Seminole County's high-growth, high-tech, Lake Mary/Heathrow business corridor—Phoenix is focused on supporting educational efforts to ensure that Central Florida continues to attract quality personnel. To this end, the company funded an Endowed Teaching Chair at Seminole Community College and recently donated a number of PCs to a local elementary school.

In addition, Phoenix employees are encouraged to participate in organizations and events that contribute to the quality of community life, including the annual United

Way Campaign, the Make-A-Wish Foundation, and quarterly blood drives at the company's headquarters. Phoenix has also supported America's Promise, a program founded by General Colin L. Powell, retired, and the living presidents, which is dedicated to building and strengthening the character and competence of America's youth with the help of commitment makers.

From Yusefzadeh's groundbreaking white paper through the company's status today, Phoenix International has committed itself to providing the global financial services industry with innovative products and services by keeping itself on the forefront of technology's ever changing landscape. The company continues to evaluate new technologies, working hand in hand with strategic technology partners such as Microsoft, IBM, Hewlett-Packard, and Unisys to ensure that the company stays ahead of the curve. Phoenix International's goal is to grow and compete in today's dynamic financial services marketplace by meeting the needs of financial institutions around the world.

THE PHOENIX SYSTEM ENABLES BANKERS TO RESPOND BY ALLOWING QUICKER AND EASIER ACCESS TO CUSTOMER INFORMATION USING WINDOWS-BASED POINT-AND-CLICK TECHNOLOGY.

TODAY, PHOENIX INTERNATIONAL HAS GROWN TO MORE THAN 300 EMPLOYEES, AND IS AMONG THE WORLD'S LEADING BANKING SOFTWARE PROVIDERS WITH MORE THAN 150 CLIENTS IN 26 DIFFERENT COUNTRIES.

To say that Knight Images (KI) got off to a modest start in 1994 would be an understatement. Like many new companies, capital was limited. Twenty-four-year-old Michael Hinn and Jim Hobart, then 28, had just enough money in start-up loans for 13 weeks of operation for their design and marketing company. And they had one major client, the University of Central Florida (UCF) Alumni Association. ▌ From that meager start, KI has developed into a full-fledged interactive communications firm, employing more than 25 talented and energetic individuals, and maintaining an average annual increase in billings of 150 percent—it has been listed three

consecutive years on the *Wall Street Journal*'s 100 Fastest Growing Companies in Florida list. The company now occupies two floors of the historic Kress Building in the heart of downtown Orlando, with the Interactive division on the second floor, and Creative and Publishing on the mezzanine. Both floors are decorated in KI's trademark primary color scheme of blue, red, and yellow.

▼ SHERI O'NEAL

WELL-ORGANIZED CREATIVITY UN-LEASHED. THAT MIGHT BE THE BEST WAY TO DESCRIBE WHAT THE MEN AND WOMEN OF KNIGHT IMAGES BRING TO THE TABLE, BESIDES THEIR TOYS.

KEEPING AHEAD OF THE CURVE

Breaking out the Web applications development is a logical progression for the company," says Hinn, president and CEO. "The rapidly changing interactive industry requires that we anticipate and react quickly to new technologies. The smaller Interactive team is able to respond to client requests in a timely and innovative fashion." KI specializes in electronic and print publishing, Web development and applications, creative services, and consulting. Hobart, CIO, says, "By separating the business units, we are able to stay fast and agile—a requirement to stay ahead of the curve."

EMPLOYEES LIVE, WORK AND PLAY DOWNTOWN, AND SOMETIMES TAKE GIANT SHAPES WITH THEM, TOO.

A PHILOSOPHY OF FUN

KI's business savvy is balanced with a casual work environment. The words "fun," "balance," "play," and "relationships" are rarely included in corporate mission statements—singly or otherwise. KI's mission statement contains all four.

"What we do every day—innovative problem solving and creative solutions to everyday communications challenges—is serious business, but, as much time as we spend at work, we feel it is important to enjoy what we do," says Hinn. "But work, even enjoyable work, isn't life. That's where balance comes in."

To support a creative environment, play is exactly what the KI team does. Each quarter, the entire company closes for an afternoon and participates in Attitude Adjustment Day, which can be anything from a visit to a local theme park to a trip to a video arcade. The group has also spent the afternoon golfing, bowling, or even go-karting. "The creative process is not a nine-to-five process," says Hobart. "And creativity does not occur in a sterile environment. Atti-

◀ SHERI O'NEAL

tude Adjustment Day helps keep our brains from getting into a routine."

CREATIVE PROBLEM-SOLVING

The company's clients ultimately reap the benefits of KI's "work hard, play hard" philosophy. Hughes Supply, for example, is a national wholesale distributor of construction materials. When Hughes approached KI to create an advertising campaign to reach a target audience in a variety of geographic areas and industry segments, the company expected a traditional ad strategy—and a big media budget. In the end, they received more than they bargained for, for less than expected.

Instead of presenting Hughes with a conventional strategy, KI created *The Source*, an 80-page, informative, timely, and useful trade publication with a quarterly circulation of 55,000. KI also built a complete on-line community, TheSourceMag.com, making Hughes' knowledge base accessible to everyone, all the time. And that big media budget was not needed. Through advertising sales, the

pany take advantage of its access to given communities—replicating them on-line and promoting TWC as a good neighbor, literally bringing neighbors together.

In 1997, the Orlando Regional Chamber of Commerce was looking for a solution to reduce the costs of promotion materials for 360 events a year and to stop inundating its audience with direct mail. KI developed a four-color business news publication to be distributed to 10,000 member businesses and chamber alliances. *FirstMonday* is by, for, and about chamber members, and consolidates all the chamber news into one place—blending the chamber's unique insight into the local business community. The best part, of course, is that *FirstMonday* supports itself through advertising and partnerships.

Examples like these are numerous, and are reflected in KI's client retention and in its more than 75 awards from professional and business organizations. "The greatest achievement of this company is that we spend every day with people we like, we do the work we enjoy, and we still make the time to spend with our families, friends, and personal dreams," says Hinn. "Like any good marriage, there is give and take. When there's a big deadline, we're all here pitching in to help get it done. At the end of the day, the people who work together here have a bond that goes beyond mere coworkers—we're all friends too."

publication raises more than $600,000 each year to design, print, and maintain itself.

Examples of this type of original thinking abound in KI's portfolio. The company's first big client, UCF Alumni Association, began as a brainstorm over coffee. KI proposed a full-color, glossy, advertising-driven magazine for all the alumni, and *Pegasus* magazine was born in July 1994. Since then, UCF has become a major client, and KI has worked on the overall branding campaign, conducting research and producing an image campaign that includes print, television, radio, outdoor, Web, and direct mail.

Rather than just redesigning a Web site for Time Warner Communications (TWC) of Central Florida, the KI staff suggested that the company

▲ SHERI O'NEAL

WHEN DARDEN RESTAURANTS' FOUNDER BILL DARDEN OPENED THE FIRST RED LOBSTER more than 30 years ago in Lakeland, no one could have dreamed the moderately priced, full-service seafood restaurant was the harbinger of a restaurant revolution. At the time, there weren't many options for diners who wanted something between fine dining and quick-service meals. Darden and his team—which included Wally Buckley, Charlie Woodsby, Al Woods, Joe Lee, Darden's brother Denham, and, later, Gus Gornto—changed that, and the hundreds of customers who lined up in front of

the restaurant every day made it clear they were on to something.

When Bill Darden was ready to try to repeat his success nationally, he took his team to Orlando, an area poised to become an economic powerhouse. Orlando was also where Darden had been a part of another seafood restaurant, the enormously popular Gary's Duck Inn.

A FLORIDA SUCCESS STORY

Red Lobster's immediate success caught the attention of Minneapolis food giant General Mills, which was eager to expand into the growing casual dining industry. The company bought the three-restaurant chain and based its restaurant division, General Mills Restaurants, in Orlando. With Bill Darden at the helm, they started a rapid national expansion,

CONCEIVED AND STARTED BY DARDEN RESTAURANTS IN CENTRAL FLORIDA, RED LOBSTER IS THE LARGEST AND MOST SUCCESSFUL CASUAL DINING SEAFOOD RESTAURANT COMPANY IN THE WORLD, AND ONE OF THE MOST RECOGNIZED AND RESPECTED BRANDS ANYWHERE.

and by 1974 there were 100 Red Lobsters nationwide. Fueled by an internally developed international seafood purchasing network that's still the envy of the restaurant industry, Red Lobster literally brought

seafood to the nation, giving millions of people their first taste of lobster and crab.

Building off that tremendous success, in 1981 the company decided to capture market share in a

OLIVE GARDEN, ANOTHER DARDEN RESTAURANTS CONCEPT THAT GOT ITS START IN ORLANDO, DOMINATES THE HIGHLY COMPETITIVE ITALIAN SEGMENT OF THE CASUAL DINING INDUSTRY.

different segment of casual dining—Italian food. General Mills Restaurants saw an opportunity to create another winning concept based on the same things that made Red Lobster so popular: quality, value, and service.

The company opened its first Olive Garden in 1982 on International Drive in Orlando, recognizing Central Florida's unique demographic mix made it an ideal place to test new restaurants. Within a few years, Olive Garden became the most successful Italian restaurant in the country.

In 1995, General Mills Restaurants separated from General Mills. The venture was named Darden Restaurants, in homage to the company's pioneering founder, who died in 1994.

Today, Darden Restaurants is the largest casual dining restaurant company in the world, with more than 1,140 restaurants across the United States and in Canada, more than 119,000 employees, and annual sales of $3.7 billion. In addition to Red Lobster and Olive Garden, Darden also has developed two more restaurant concepts: the highly successful, Caribbean-themed Bahama Breeze, and its newest sensation, Smokey Bones BBQ & Sports Bar. Like their well-established predecessors, both restaurants were created internally by the company and originated in Orlando.

DARDEN RESTAURANTS' LATEST INNO-VATION, SMOKEY BONES BBQ & SPORTS BAR, SERVES GREAT TRADITIONAL BARBECUE FAVORITES IN A RUSTIC MOUNTAIN-CABIN SETTING WITH A FUN, HIGH-ENERGY SPORTS BAR ATMOSPHERE.

RED LOBSTER INVITES GUESTS TO "GO OVERBOARD" AND ENJOY A FRESH APPROACH TO GREAT SEAFOOD, GOOD TIMES AND HOSPITALITY.

Darden is renowned for its ability to respond to the rapidly evolving preferences of today's casual dining consumers. "Our company is customer driven," says Darden Chairman and CEO Joe Lee. "We constantly listen to our guests, and work very hard not only to provide the kind of dining experience that today's consumers want, but also to anticipate how those tastes are changing to continue to meet and exceed their expectations."

Lee says the company also owes its phenomenal growth to one of the most talented and experienced leadership teams in the business—starting with Lee himself, who was on Darden's team at the first Red Lobster in Lakeland.

FINDING STRENGTH IN DIVERSITY

Bill Darden once said, "The greatest competitive edge our company has is the quality of our employees, as evidenced by the excellent job they do every day." That quote hangs on plaques across Darden's corporate campus in Orlando Central Park, and the words are still taken very seriously. The company believes its strength lies in the commitment and diversity of its employees.

"We strongly believe in embracing, fostering, and celebrating diversity, both inside and outside our company—not only because it's the right thing to do, but because it's essential for any progressive, growing business," says Lee.

Fortune magazine took notice of that commitment, ranking Darden one of the nation's top 10 companies for minorities to work for on its annual Diversity Elite list.

A SENSE OF CIVIC RESPONSIBILITY

A commitment to the communities where it operates is also at the heart of Darden Restaurants' corporate culture. Lee calls it part of the company's "civic rent." Through the Darden Restaurants Foundation and the Darden Environmental Trust, the company has poured millions of dollars into communities and environmental causes. In Central Florida alone, Darden has funded hundreds of local programs, and Darden employees volunteer hundreds of thousands of hours a year for charitable events and fundraisers all over the country.

In addition, Olive Garden's Pasta for Pennies program raises millions of dollars for the Leukemia Society of America and Red Lobster's Cops and Lobsters does the same for Special Olympics. Bahama Breeze raises funds and awareness for the Big Brothers and Big Sisters program in every city where it opens a new restaurant, and through its Drive Against Hunger program, Olive Garden donates refrigerated trucks, meals, and hundreds of thousands of pounds of food for food banks.

Industry analysts expect the casual dining industry to grow significantly during the next several years, as baby boomers reach the age of peak casual dining usage, and Darden intends to take full advantage of that trend.

"We will continue to develop more restaurant concepts and look for potential acquisitions to meet our long-term growth objectives," Lee says. "Our strategy is to continue providing the highest standards of hospitality and culinary excellence

in the industry. We are uniquely prepared for the millennium, and I am confident the 119,000 dedicated employees of Darden restaurants are prepared to fulfill our vision— to make us the best casual dining restaurant company now and for generations to come."

ACCORDING TO BILL DARDEN, "THE GREATEST COMPETITIVE EDGE OUR COMPANY HAS IS THE QUALITY OF OUR EMPLOYEES, AS EVIDENCED BY THE EXCELLENT JOB THEY DO EVERY DAY."

AT BAHAMA BREEZE, GUESTS CAN ENJOY DRINKS, APPETIZERS, AND DANCING TO LIVE MUSIC ON THE ALL-WEATHER OUTDOOR DECK.

OLIVE GARDEN IS A FAMILY OF LOCAL RESTAURANTS FOCUSED ON DELIGHTING EVERY GUEST WITH A GENUINE ITALIAN DINING EXPERIENCE, AND NO GENUINE ITALIAN MEAL WOULD BE COMPLETE WITHOUT WINE. THAT'S WHY OLIVE GARDEN HAS ONE OF THE MOST EXTENSIVE AND SOPHISTICATED WINE LISTS OF ANY CASUAL DINING RESTAURANT.

BEERS CONSTRUCTION COMPANY

HEADQUARTERED IN ATLANTA, BEERS CONSTRUCTION COMPANY AND ITS AFFILIATES CURRENTLY have 12 full-service offices in the United States, and have worked in a total of 25 states nationwide, along with Puerto Rico. Originally established in 1907 as Southern Ferro Concrete, Beers has had a strong presence for nearly a century in the state of Florida, opening its Orlando office in 1996. Providing general construction and construction management services, the company played a significant role in the building of the state as it completed many projects from 1935 to 1965, including several with Florida State University,

as well as adding the first wings on the state capitol and renovating the federal courthouse.

Beers has worked continuously in Florida since its early years, and in the early 1990s—with the success of its Healthcare Facilities Construction Group—the company reentered the Florida market with a more substantial commitment. Soon afterwards, the company opened its first full-service Florida office in Tampa. The solid foundation for unprecedented growth had been established as Beers entered its first market outside of Georgia.

As Beers began substantial projects in Central Florida with Walt Disney World's Celebration office buildings, Disney's Animal Kingdom Theme Park, and Teague Middle School, the company was faced with the need to further extend its focus in the Florida market with the opening of a second, full-service Florida office. In September 1996, Beers opened its Orlando office. Now located in the heart of downtown in the historic Fidelity Building, the company's 140-plus-employee

Orlando office recorded construction volume in 1999 of more than $100 million and exceeded $140 million in 2000.

BUILDING FOR LIFE

In its 90-plus-year history, Beers has served a variety of markets, including education, hospitality, tourism, sports, corporate/commercial, high-tech, residential, health care, and government. After only a short period in the area, the com-

pany boasts a diverse group of projects that have become a visible part of the Central Florida community. Some of the outstanding projects that Beers has constructed in specific markets include Hard Rock Café/Hard Rock Live (tourism), Nemours Children's Clinic (health care), Walt Disney World's Celebration office buildings (corporate/commercial), Universal Studios Islands of Adventure's Super Hero Island (tourism), and the Echelon at Cheney Place (residential).

Beers is continuing its strong focus on kindergarten-through-grade-12 and higher education projects, as the company has completed 37 educational projects in Orange, Seminole, and Osceola counties. The company has also entered the information age with a strong involvement in the high-tech market sector. The University of Central Florida's high-tech classrooms and the expansion and build-out of Lucent Technologies' Advanced Development and Research Facility are two of Beers' notable projects. With these high-quality projects and a host of others, Beers Construction Company is making a lasting impression on the

BEERS CONSTRUCTION COMPANY SENIOR VICE-PRESIDENT BOB McCLELLAND (SECOND FROM RIGHT), BOYS & GIRLS CLUB YOUTH OF THE YEAR LA'QUANDA TAYLOR (SECOND FROM LEFT), AND OTHER COMMUNITY LEADERS BREAK GROUND ON THE BOYS & GIRLS CLUBS OF CENTRAL FLORIDA'S DR. PHILLIPS TEEN SUPREME CENTER.

WALT DISNEY WORLD'S CELEBRATION OFFICE BUILDINGS WAS ONE OF THE CENTRAL FLORIDA PROJECTS THAT LED TO THE OPENING OF BEERS' ORLANDO OFFICE IN 1996.

J J WILLIAMS ARCHITECTURAL PHOTOGRAPHY

Central Florida community and its residents.

Fully 75 percent of Beers' projects are performed for repeat clients. This large repeat client base is due in part to Beers' constant implementation of its mission: Make Our Clients More Successful. As a result of this strong mission, the City of Orlando awarded Beers one of the first Construction Manager at Risk contracts to build an expansion to the Dover Shores Recreation Center. "This project delivery method proved to be highly cost effective, while producing tremendous results for the City of Orlando," says Jose Baerga, project manager.

COMMUNITY FOCUS

Beers' Orlando office has impressive representation within diverse community and civic organizations. In addition to memberships with all of the major professional trade associations and the tri-county chambers of commerce, the company's employees are leaders in a number of community organizations. In capacities from president to board of directors member, Beers' Orlando office has been involved with the Foundation for Orange County Public Schools, Downtown Orlando Partnership, Heart of Florida United Way, Walt Disney Memorial Cancer Institute, Jeppesen Foundation, and Economic Development Commission. A number of the company's employees have graduated from the Greater Orlando Chamber of Commerce's Leadership Orlando program.

Beers' project teams make it a point to give back to the communities in which they work. Communities will find that Beers is serious about its civic responsibility as it has built playgrounds, tutored students, contributed to the arts, helped to keep cities beautiful, and participated in pro bono construction projects. United Way is a charitable fund in which Beers employees annually lend their efforts through events such as interoffice competitions, job site meetings, bake sales, silent auctions, and kickoff events. In 1999, the company raised more than $400,000 through employee donations for United Way campaigns throughout the Southeast. The Orlando office has also been involved with such groups as Special Olympics, Toys for Tots, Ronald McDonald House, Habitat for Humanity, Boys and Girls Clubs, Restore Orlando, and Boggy Creek Gang Camp.

Beers continues to sustain its growth in Florida. The company was selected as a construction manager of the new, $80 million U.S. Courthouse in Jacksonville, and as a result, Beers recently opened its third full-service office in Jacksonville. "We are proud of what we have established in the state of Florida," says John H. Pinholster III, president. "Further, we are looking forward to what the future holds for our Orlando office. We feel confident that our goals are directly in line with making our community and state a better place to live and work."

THE UNIVERSITY OF CENTRAL FLORIDA'S $10 MILLION CLASSROOM BUILDING I, AN 88,000-SQUARE-FOOT PROJECT, IS EQUIPPED WITH STATE-OF-THE-ART INSTRUCTIONAL TECHNOLOGY AND PROJECTION SYSTEMS, AND INTERCONNECTED WITH DATA, VIDEO, AND AUDIO RESOURCES AND NETWORKS (LEFT).

IN 1999, BEERS CONSTRUCTION COMPANY WAS AWARDED AN AGC BUILD FLORIDA AWARD AND AN ABC EXCELLENCE IN CONSTRUCTION MERIT AWARD FOR ITS CONSTRUCTION AND COMPLETION OF UNIVERSAL STUDIOS' ISLANDS OF ADVENTURE MARVEL SUPER HERO ISLAND (RIGHT).

THE WORLD'S LARGEST HARD ROCK CAFÉ AND THE FIRST AND ONLY HARD ROCK LIVE WERE AWARDED A BUILD FLORIDA AWARD IN 1999. ASSOCIATED GENERAL CONTRACTORS, INC. AWARDED THE BEERS CONSTRUCTION TEAM WITH THIS HONOR FOR PRODUCING A TRULY UNIQUE DINING AND ENTERTAINMENT FACILITY, LOCATED AT UNIVERSAL'S CITYWALK IN ORLANDO.

INCE 1996, COLONIAL BANK HAS BEEN THE SUPER COMMUNITY BANK, DELIVERING HOMETOWN service to Central Florida with the resources of a larger bank. Combining an unwavering personal focus rarely found in the 21st century with the strength and technological influence of a leading regional financial institution, Colonial Bank is known for its convenient banking services managed by a responsive, personable team. With about $1.3 billion in total assets and 43 offices in eight Central Florida counties, Colonial Bank is committed to developing and providing financial products and services of the highest quality. ⚜ The region's corporate

COLONIAL BANK HAS BEEN DELIVERING CONVENIENT, PERSONAL, ATTENTIVE SERVICE TO ITS CUSTOMERS IN CENTRAL FLORIDA SINCE 1996.

headquarters, overlooking Lake Eola from East Pine Street in downtown Orlando, is the heart of the regional operation. Offices can be found in Brevard, Lake, Orange, Osceola, Polk, Seminole, Volusia, and St. John's counties. Colonial Bank, member FDIC and Equal Housing lender, provides customers with an array of services including checking and savings accounts, CDs and IRAs, retail and commercial loans, cash management, other real estate loans, investments, trust, asset management, and Internet banking.

"We can assist everyone from the individual consumer to the real estate developer, and we do it with the type of hometown friendliness you'd expect from a smaller institution, combined with the products and services you can get in a larger one," says Michael L. Sleaford, president and CEO of Colonial Bank's Central Florida region.

Colonial Bank has a long-standing philosophy of establishing local boards of directors and management who stay in touch

with the needs of the communities and customers they serve. Colonial Bank's can-do attitude, embraced by its some 325 regional employees, defines its role as a leader throughout the Southeast, where the bank has established a stronghold in the last decade.

Colonial Bank's parent company, The Colonial BancGroup Inc., headquartered in Montgomery, Alabama, is a multi-state bank holding company with more than $11 billion in assets. Colonial BancGroup has more

WITH 43 OFFICES IN EIGHT CENTRAL FLORIDA COUNTIES, COLONIAL BANK CONSISTENTLY PROVIDES SUPERIOR FINANCIAL PRODUCTS AND SERVICES.

than 240 offices in Alabama, Florida, Georgia, Nevada, Tennessee, and Texas.

RAPID GROWTH, HOMETOWN SERVICE

Colonial BancGroup was formed in 1981 with the purchase of Southland Bancorp of Mobile, a multibank holding company with assets of $166 million. Colonial expanded its presence in Alabama before launching a strategic initiative to develop operations in neighboring southeastern states. The BancGroup entered Tennessee in 1993 and Georgia in 1995, before extending its southeastern growth to Florida in 1996 with the acquisition of Southern Bank of Central Florida, which, at the time, was the largest independent bank in Orlando. Since then, Colonial's Florida base has broadened to include South Florida, Southwest Florida and the Bay Area, while also moving west into the fast-growing Texas and Nevada markets.

During 1999, Colonial's deposit operations experienced exponential growth with the creation of a new operations center in Orlando, which brought 50 new jobs to the Central Florida community. The BancGroup continues to place strong emphasis on the Orlando

metropolitan area, as demographic projections place it within the top two or three fastest-growing regions in the nation.

"Central Florida has experienced unprecedented growth, and all the factors are in place to allow the area to take off—the weather, tourism, and an increasingly diverse economy," Sleaford says. "As a result, we look to expand in each market over the next several years and to build new offices throughout our eight-county area."

Currently headquartered in Orlando, Colonial Bank's Central Florida region has offices and ATM locations throughout Greater Orlando including downtown, Winter Park, South Orlando, Lake Mary and Kissimmee. The region's network of 43 offices also expands into cities like Titusville, Melbourne, Daytona, Lakeland, Leesburg, and St. Augustine, among others.

Giving Back to Those It Serves

Colonial Bank believes in giving back to the community. Officers, employees, and board members serve on various committees, hold office and participate on numerous area boards, and actively support local interests. Because the company's reach is so great and its demographic so diverse, Colonial caters to all groups, from singles to young families to retirees—in both commercial and retail areas of the bank. For the growing Central Florida Hispanic population, Colonial Bank provides Spanish-language materials.

Colonial Bank technology allows individual and business customers to do all their banking on the Internet, where they can view their bank statements, make transfers from one

account to another, and see when checks clear. "In today's hectic world, this is a great way to give our valued customers another avenue to handle their financial needs," Sleaford says. "And this is just the beginning. I think there will be a continuing evolution of services to make it easier for our customers to do business."

A defining element in Colonial Bank's continuing success is its commitment at every level of the or-

ganization to develop and provide financial products and services of outstanding quality. The company's winning spirit reflects the total integration of quality into every aspect of Colonial Bank. That, in turn, ensures commitments to profitability and shareholder value, as well as to the highest standards of employee professionalism. And it guarantees that Colonial Bank will exceed the expectations of every one of its customers.

Colonial Bank is an active force in the growth of Orlando and the Central Florida area. Partners in development have included (from left) ChampionsGate, the Florida Urology Center in Ormond Beach, and Pringle Development in Leesburg, Florida.

The region's corporate headquarters, overlooking Lake Eola from East Pine Street in downtown Orlando, is the heart of the regional operation.

CHEP

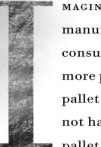

IMAGINE IF EVERY PRODUCT IN EVERY SUPERMARKET, DISCOUNT STORE, OR HOME CENTER HAD TO MOVE FROM THE manufacturer to the retail location one item at a time. It would take years to get all of the goods needed to fill consumer demand, and each product would cost much more because of the added handling. There would be more product damage, and out-of-stock items would be the norm rather than the exception. But thanks to the pallet and the shipping container, shoppers can go to their local supermarket, can find what they need, and do not have to pay an exorbitant amount at the cash register. ⚜ CHEP, a world-class provider of container and pallet systems, operates an equipment-pooling business model in which assets flow from a comprehensive

depot network to the manufacturers and growers that need them to move their products, and then to distributors and retailers for storage or display. CHEP high-quality pallets and reusable containers, operating principles, service organization, and computer tracking systems deliver improved efficiency in product delivery. The company also provides a substantial environmental impact by reducing the demand for timber used in building pallets and the amount of lumber in the waste stream.

At the heart of the CHEP system are the people who develop and implement the latest procedures

and information technology to ensure the company's processes are productive for all trading partners in the supply chain. These professionals work with colleagues in the consumer goods; produce; meat; home improvement, hardware, and housewares; automotive; and durable goods industries.

AN INDUSTRIAL GIANT

CHEP started when the U.S. armed services pulled out of Australia at the end of World War II, leaving behind vast quantities of materials handling equipment such as forklifts, cranes, and pallets. In

1946, the Australian government set up the Commonwealth Handling Equipment Pool (CHEP) to lease this equipment to Australian industry. CHEP was acquired by Brambles of Sydney in 1958, and in 1974, Brambles joined forces with the Industrial Services Division of GKN of London to expand the CHEP business across the globe.

The worldwide CHEP organization now operates in some 36 countries across six continents. CHEP provides equipment-pooling services to many diverse industries, based on five main product categories that include more than 450 products. CHEP originated the concept of materials handling distribution services for industry, based on the pooling of a variety of products, and supported by high-quality services and powerful control systems.

CHEP entered the U. S. market in 1990. Since then, the company has changed the face of material management in the food and consumer goods packaging industries, and is having a great impact on several other industries. The U.S. operation, which started with fewer than 20 people, today employs more than 800 people nationally and more than 4,500 globally. CHEP has grown from zero pallets and containers to more than 44 million in the Americas, and from no revenue to sales of several hundred million dollars. Globally, CHEP owns and controls 134 million pallets and more than 20 million containers.

MAKING A HOME IN ORLANDO

Headquartered in Central Florida since 1996, CHEP has been a supporter of the Boy Scouts of America, American Heart Association, American Breast Cancer Society, United Way, 106.7 FM Baby DJ Fund, Harvest Food

CHEP PROVIDES EQUIPMENT-POOLING SERVICES TO MANY DIVERSE INDUSTRIES, BASED ON FIVE MAIN PRODUCT CATEGORIES THAT INCLUDE MORE THAN 450 PRODUCTS.

Bank, Coalition for the Homeless, Arnold Palmer Hospital, and Central Florida Blood Bank. The company's more than 400 local employees are located in two Orlando offices and at one of the firm's Premium Service centers, inspecting and repairing equipment in nearby Davenport. Of the two Orlando offices, one resides downtown as the CHEP INTERNATIONAL headquarters, overseeing the operations of every CHEP location in some 36 countries around the world. The second Orlando office is headquarters for the U.S. pallet- and container-pooling services.

PERPETRATING EFFICIENCIES FOR INDUSTRY

CHEP is committed to playing a lead role as a provider of integrated solutions for logistics and material handling challenges, and nowhere is that commitment more apparent than in the product and service innovations being developed by the company. From the radio frequency identification (RFID) chips the firm is testing for the plastic container pool so retailers can better control product being delivered, to the offering of plastic pallets that provide shippers with a high-quality and durable platform, to the latest development of Portfolio^sm, which allows customers to easily order pallets and containers on-line, CHEP is dedicating substantial resources to staying on the leading edge of technology in distribution. And all of these new technologies are supported by the latest

information systems that are constantly delivering more and better data to business users so the entire network of suppliers, distributors,

carriers, and retailers can operate at the highest levels of productivity.

Clearly, the importance of efficient logistics and material handling systems to any operation will increase in the future. CHEP is providing the systems to each of the trade channels—served in a way that delivers cost benefits to the entire industry. The company's professionals now look forward to the future when the U.S. CHEP operation will continue to work with its partners to take the next layer of costs out of the supply chain.

CHEP HAS GROWN FROM ZERO PALLETS AND CONTAINERS TO MORE THAN 44 MILLION IN THE AMERICAS, AND FROM NO REVENUE TO SALES OF SEVERAL HUNDRED MILLION DOLLARS.

THE U.S. OPERATION, WHICH STARTED WITH FEWER THAN 20 PEOPLE, TODAY EMPLOYS MORE THAN 800 PEOPLE NATIONALLY AND MORE THAN 4,500 GLOBALLY.

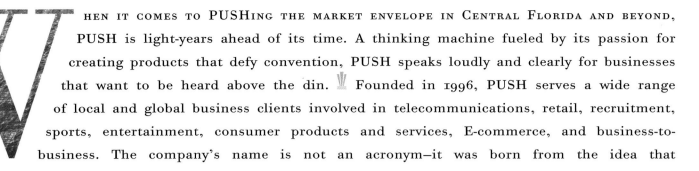

WHEN IT COMES TO PUSHING THE MARKET ENVELOPE IN CENTRAL FLORIDA AND BEYOND, PUSH is light-years ahead of its time. A thinking machine fueled by its passion for creating products that defy convention, PUSH speaks loudly and clearly for businesses that want to be heard above the din. Founded in 1996, PUSH serves a wide range of local and global business clients involved in telecommunications, retail, recruitment, sports, entertainment, consumer products and services, E-commerce, and business-to-business. The company's name is not an acronym—it was born from the idea that

PUSH is in the business of making things happen for its clients. It also reflects the company's philosophy and mission: "To PUSH. Ourselves. Our clients. Our work."

"We are all about providing solutions that exceed our clients' expectations every time," says Richard C. Wahl, president. "To make that happen, we like to get in the trenches to learn everything about the business. It makes for a nontraditional relationship that truly helps the client succeed."

A TEAM OF CREATIVE THINKERS

A key factor in PUSH's success story is its founding team of partners—Wahl, John Ludwig and Julio Lima—all of whom came from major agencies. Since PUSH opened for business on October 31, 1996, the full-service advertising agency has grown from a staff of six to a team of some 30, all of whom are involved in PUSH's creative product. The company now provides account services, creative, production, media strategy, public relations, and Internet programming and development.

Located in thriving downtown Orlando, PUSH recently built its own custom-designed headquarters at 101 Ernestine Street. The one-story, stainless-steel building—which features skylights, brightly colored walls, sweeping windows, high ceilings, and an open-floor design—encourages the kind of creative thinking for which PUSH is known.

"Our team knows how to stay ahead of the curve," Ludwig explains. "We take our clients as close to the edge as they're willing to go, and if they want to jump off, we'll help them."

A COMPANY OF IDEAS

PUSH is known for extraordinary campaigns and for using every medium at its disposal, and earning local and national recognition for its efforts. The PUSH passion for out-of-the-box thinking creates a totally integrated approach to advertising, marketing, promotions, and public relations for each client, each of whom knows to expect the right solution from the agency.

PUSH's approach works well for its growing base of clients, and PUSH's partners are convinced

that Central Florida is an ideal place to grow their business.

"We believe Orlando is on the verge of greatness, and that it provides a solid foundation for our business," Lima says. "Even though some people don't think of Orlando as an advertising mecca, we hope to change that." Since launching the firm, the PUSH team has been active in the Orlando community, contributing to such organizations as the Central Florida Boy Scouts Council, Make-A-Wish Foundation, and American Cancer Society.

PUSH expects future growth to be beyond the radar, but the agency will maintain a midsize staff to guarantee a comfort level with its loyal clients. In a business with traditionally high turnover, PUSH's attrition rate has been minimal among its clients and staff, mainly because the company recognizes talent, nurtures it in a family-type atmosphere, and rewards it.

"PUSH is coming of age, and we now can handle any client from anywhere in the world," Wahl says. "We have the most loyal, passionate team in Orlando, and together we're going to do great things."

PUSH'S CORPORATE HEADQUARTERS STANDS AS AN EXCELLENT REFLECTION OF ITS CULTURE. FROM STINGING CREATIVE, TO PRECISE STRATEGY, THIS DYNAMIC ADVERTISING AGENCY PUSHES EVERY IDEA TO DRIVE RESULTS.

WHEN PHIL COBO-STRELLA SAT DOWN WITH A FRIEND IN A DOWNTOWN ORLANDO EATERY and scribbled his idea for a Hispanic magazine in Florida on the back of a napkin in 1996, *Que Pasa! Hispanic* magazine was born. A native of Puerto Rico of Cuban descent who has lived in Orlando since childhood, Cobo-Strella recognized the dire need for news and advertising geared toward Hispanic business professionals and families who made up a large portion of Central Florida's rapidly growing population. In just a few short months after the idea hit him, the first issue of *Que Pasa! Hispanic* magazine—translated as "What's Happening!"—hit the

market and was welcomed by an enthusiastic readership. Since its first issue hit the newsstands, *Que Pasa! Hispanic* magazine has become the leading Hispanic professional magazine in Florida, reaching well into the heavily Hispanic Miami market.

"We are creating a road map for Central Florida Hispanics to become more active in local government and the overall community, while showcasing our culture, heritage, and language," says Cobo-Strella, the magazine's publisher and CEO of Magellan Media Corporation.

WHAT'S HAPPENING

Central Florida's premier Hispanic publication, *Que Pasa! Hispanic* magazine is published bimonthly by Magellan in both Spanish and English, and reaches thousands of Central Floridians from Orlando to Tampa Bay. Cobo-Strella and business partner Li-Yun Marie Poventud say their main objectives are to help promote minority business opportunities and diversity in business, government, and culture. Since its inception, the magazine has participated in and sponsored many Hispanic professional events. Each year, *Que Pasa! Hispanic* magazine celebrates the contributions of 12 Central Florida Hispanic professionals with the *Que Pasa!* Hispanic Professional Awards Gala.

The *Que Pasa! Hispanic* magazine founders have earned several honors themselves. Cobo-Strella is president of the Orlando chapter of the National Society of Hispanic MBAs and has received several awards for his magazine's outstanding contribution to Hispanic media. Poventud is a member of a number of key Hispanic groups and has been named one of the top 100 Hispanics in Orlando. Recently, the magazine

received the Hispanic Business Initiative Fund (HBIF) Honorary Media Award in Tampa Bay.

More than 250,000 Hispanics now live in Central Florida and, by 2006, the area Hispanic population is expected to reach nearly 420,000. Studies show that Hispanics prefer getting their information from Hispanic media and are more responsive to Spanish-language advertisements. Already representing more than $2 billion of Central Florida's purchasing power, Hispanic professionals and families will yield greater clout each year as their numbers grow.

To channel this growing influence, *Que Pasa! Hispanic* magazine has organized the bimonthly Hispanic Leaders Roundtable, a networking forum for pertinent topics such as education, health care, and Hispanics in politics. In addition, the magazine's founders partner with business powers, such as the

U.S. Hispanic Chamber of Commerce, and with cultural forces, including the Orlando Museum of Art, to present exhibits of particular interest to Hispanics. The publication's principals also work to promote the Hispanic Scholarship Council of Central Florida.

The magazine's Web site, www.quepasahispanic.com, features Hispanic market facts, key editorial pieces, and many resources for its audience. Although based in Orlando, *Que Pasa! Hispanic* magazine keeps its finger on the pulse of Hispanic trends statewide and across the country.

"We can build bridges to other communities like Tampa and Miami, which already have an established Hispanic community, and really draw from their experience to better our community here and deal with the challenges that our growth will bring," Cobo-Strella says.

IN JUST A FEW SHORT YEARS, *Que Pasa! Hispanic* MAGAZINE HAS GROWN FROM AN IDEA ON A NAPKIN TO THE LEADING HISPANIC MAGAZINE IN FLORIDA.

PUBLISHER AND CEO PHIL COBO-STRELLA AND BUSINESS PARTNER LI-YUN MARIE POVENTUD HAVE SEEN THEIR MAGAZINE REPEATEDLY HONORED BY HISPANIC BUSINESS AND CIVIC GROUPS (LEFT).

FOUR DAYS AFTER CENTRAL FLORIDA NEWS 13 DEBUTED AS CENTRAL FLORIDA'S FIRST 24-HOUR ALL news channel in October 1997, a devastating tornado ripped through nearby New Smyrna Beach, destroying homes, businesses, and the landscape. News 13 not only provided complete coverage of the story, but it also teamed with the Orlando Sentinel to organize a relief fund netting more than $15,000 for tornado victims. Since then, Central Florida News 13 has worked around the clock to become the region's most valued television news source and an active community leader. ⚜ Central Florida News 13—from its main studio located in downtown

Orlando—provides award-winning, in-depth local and regional news; continuous weather updates; and complete sports coverage from the pros to the preps. The station launched with a reach of 400,000 households in five counties, and today has an audience of more than 550,000 households in seven counties. Central Florida News 13 is one of only a few dozen 24-hour news operations in the nation.

CENTRAL FLORIDA NEWS 13 FOCUSES ON THOROUGH AND COMPLETE NEWS REPORTING IN STRIVING TO MAINTAIN HIGH CUSTOMER SATISFACTION.

The station is a joint venture of the Tribune Company and Time-Warner Communications. Central Florida News 13's strong editorial partnership with the Orlando Sentinel contributes greatly to its news content and enhances its ability to live up to its slogan, "All Local. All the Time."

A RESPONSIBLE APPROACH TO NEWS COVERAGE

Central Florida News 13 was built with a multifaceted business philosophy focusing on customer satisfaction; ideological and technological innovation; high journalistic standards; credibil-

NEWS 13 CONTINUES TO REIGN AS THE ONLY CENTRAL FLORIDA STATION OFFERING 24-HOUR LOCAL NEWS COVERAGE.

ity; financial strength; employee involvement; and diversity of community culture, ideas, and employees. The station employs more than 70 people in six departments—news, engineering, graphics, production, administration, and promotion—and expects the growth of that number to mirror Central Florida's growth.

News 13 milestones include the January 1998 premiere of Eleven @ 11, which delivers the day's top stories, weather, and sports highlights in just 11 minutes with no commercial interruption. From June to November 1998, the station achieved an

Orlando-area television first by offering two tropical updates hourly throughout the dangerous hurricane season. And in February 2000, News 13 launched a partnership with the Telemundo network to produce Noticiero 40, a Spanish-language local news brief.

Another impressive News 13 success is its popular lineup of featured weekly segments that focus on areas of viewer interest: health, fitness, home, money, future, Florida on a Tankful (travel tips), Expanding Your Mind, and Building Community.

THE CENTRAL FLORIDA NEWS LEADER

News 13 continues to reign as the only Central Florida station offering 24-hour local news coverage. The station debuted as one of the first all-digital, server-based newsrooms in the country. In addition to its East Concord Street headquarters, News 13 has news bureaus in Cocoa Village serving Brevard County, and in Deland serving Volusia and Flagler counties.

In keeping with its commitment to produce first-rate, up-to-the-minute news, Central Florida News 13 provides live team coverage of major local events and breaking news, weather forecasts every 10

minutes, and live reports of every space shuttle launch from Kennedy Space Center. News 13's set sits in the heart of a working newsroom, where information is delivered to a diverse audience ranging from busy professionals and shift workers to students and senior citizens.

In its three-year existence, News 13 has collected several major media awards, including five silver Associated Press (AP) awards for Best Sports Story, Best Short Light Feature, and Best Sports Video.

HELPING TO BUILD COMMUNITY

Since its Central Florida debut, News 13 has stepped forward to provide services and contribute funds in time of need. Together with the Orlando Sentinel and the Robert R. McCormick Tribune Foundation, the station raised more than $2.3 million for local organizations helping tornado victims in 1998, as well as another $450,000 for residents devastated by wildfires. In addition, dedicated News 13 em-

ployees have volunteered hundreds of hours of time to make public appearances to provide information on hurricane preparedness, D.A.R.E., and other topics.

As Central Florida News 13 prepares for the future, the station's management and staff look forward to exciting, new opportunities to be involved in the community and to work toward their primary long-term goal: to become the number one choice for local television news in Central Florida.

IN KEEPING WITH ITS COMMITMENT TO PRODUCE FIRST-RATE, UP-TO-THE MINUTE NEWS, CENTRAL FLORIDA NEWS 13 PROVIDES LIVE TEAM COVERAGE OF MAJOR LOCAL EVENTS AND BREAKING NEWS, WEATHER FORECASTS EVERY 10 MINUTES, AND LIVE REPORTS OF EVERY SPACE SHUTTLE LAUNCH FROM KENNEDY SPACE CENTER.

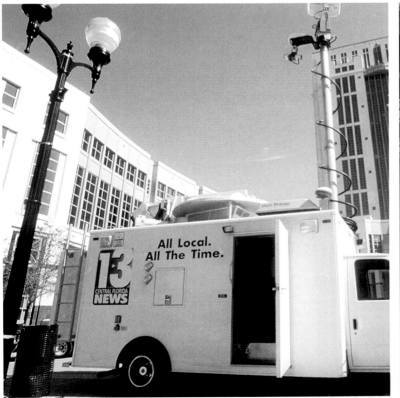

AMERICANS ARE AMONG THE MOST MOBILE PEOPLE IN THE WORLD, AND CENTRAL FLORIDA DRIVERS compose a shining microcosm of the national road-bound trend. With that in mind, Infinity Outdoor, Inc., established in Orlando in 1997, comes in as one of the largest out-of-home media companies in North America, showcasing outdoor advertising for millions locally and millions more nationally who are destined to start their engines and hit the road each day. ▼ From eye-popping billboards of all sizes to mall kiosks, posters, and bulletin displays, Infinity Outdoor provides one-stop shopping for a client's

customized advertising campaign. In the Orlando area, its landmark billboards are precisely targeted and sprouting everywhere—along Interstate 4, on the heavily traveled Beeline Expressway tourist route, and throughout major downtown thoroughfares.

"Outdoor advertising is the last mass medium—we hit everybody," says Art Martinez, Infinity Outdoor general manager. "And we take advantage of that exposure, customizing each campaign to fit the needs of our customers. We can help them reach mass audiences in the least expensive way possible."

Infinity Outdoor was launched in Phoenix in 1980 as Outdoor Systems, Inc., with only 80 billboard displays and the primary objective of being the leading provider of outdoor advertising services in each of its markets. By quickly assembling a first-rate team and providing customers with quality outdoor advertising solutions, Infinity rapidly built a client base throughout North America and earned gross revenues approaching $1 billion.

Infinity Outdoor merged in 1999 with Infinity Broadcasting

Corporation, a subsidiary of CBS Corporation. Infinity Broadcasting owns and operates more than 160 radio stations in 35 of the nation's largest outdoor markets—including the recently acquired Central Florida stations WOMX-FM, WOCL-FM, and WJHM-FM. In April 2000, CBS merged with Viacom, Inc. to form one of the world's largest entertainment and media companies—a leader in the production, promotion, and distribution of entertainment, news, sports, and music.

Infinity Outdoor currently operates more than 115,000 bulletin, poster, mall, and transit advertising displays in 90 metropolitan markets in the United States, as well as in 13 metropolitan markets in Canada and 44 in Mexico. In addition, the company provides sports marketing to professional and collegiate university arenas and stadiums across the country.

Infinity Outdoor is also complemented by its sister outdoor advertising company, TDI Worldwide, Inc., which operates 2,000 billboard and bus displays, 125,000 subway displays, and more than 1 million additional displays around the globe.

A FOCUS ON SERVICE

The company's Orlando headquarters services the Central and North Florida regions. As part of its community outreach, Infinity Outdoor donates display space for public service announcements for Give Kids the World, Altamonte Fire Department, United Way, and other nonprofit organizations.

Broad social trends in the new millennium heavily favor billboard advertising. Americans spend fewer hours at home, where TV, cable, magazines, newspapers, books, and the Internet all clamor for the attention of consumers. Meanwhile, people spend more time than ever in their automobiles. Research shows daily vehicle trips are up 11 percent since 1970, with the number of cars on the road up by 147 percent, leaving only billboards and radio as the reigning media options in traffic jams.

"Starting with that edge, we plan to remain the number one outdoor company in Orlando and in the country by treating our customers in a reliable, service-oriented, timely manner," Martinez says.

FROM EYE-POPPING BILLBOARDS OF ALL SIZES TO MALL KIOSKS, POSTERS, AND BULLETIN DISPLAYS, INFINITY OUTDOOR, INC. PROVIDES ONE-STOP SHOPPING FOR A CLIENT'S CUSTOMIZED ADVERTISING CAMPAIGN.

A CCORDING TO IAN NATHANSON, M.D., CHIEF EXECUTIVE OF NEMOURS CHILDREN'S CLINIC–ORLANDO, "Children are our greatest resource. If we can make the world a healthier place for kids, that's a pretty noble thing to do. When we see a smile on a kid who leaves our office, that's a pretty nice feeling." Nathanson heads a team of more than 70 pediatricians who have completed additional education and training in specific areas such as orthopaedics, otolaryngology, and pulmonology. Together, they treat thousands of infants, children, and adolescents. Nemours Children's Clinic–Orlando is part of a family of nationally recognized centers dedicated to research and educational programs to continuously improve the quality of children's health care.

The Nemours staff takes a team approach to medical care, working in a family-centered environment. Children are referred to Nemours by pediatricians and family physicians who recognize and understand the need for the care of specialists.

The not-for-profit clinic has a threefold mission: clinical care, education, and research, with a high standard of care for all children, regardless of financial status. The Nemours Foundation provides support for research and education programs that enable physicians to participate in teaching, share the latest in medical advances, and develop new and better treatments.

A PHILANTHROPIST'S DREAM

Nemours Children's Clinic is funded in part by the Nemours Foundation, a nonprofit organization that is a beneficiary of the estates of Alfred I. du Pont and Edward Ball. When du Pont, a brilliant industrialist, died in 1935, his will established the Nemours Foundation, named after his hometown in France.

Nemours Children's Clinic–Orlando was created in 1997, providing care in conjunction with Arnold Palmer Hospital for Children & Women. This relationship allows Nemours and Arnold Palmer Hospital to develop and implement joint programs in medical care, education, and research. Nemours staff members also serve as teachers for the Pediatric Residency Program at Arnold Palmer Hospital.

"With Arnold Palmer Hospital, together we are raising the level of care to the top level, comparable with any city in the United States," says Nathanson. He credits Dr. Charles Price, Nemours' surgeon in chief, and Dr. Mark Swanson, pediatrician in chief, as two of the main components of Nemours' exceptional vision. "Our goal is simply to provide the highest-quality care for children in Central Florida and beyond," says Nathanson.

NEMOURS CARDIAC CENTER

Congenital heart disease affects about one in every 100 babies born worldwide. In the United States alone, 25,000 children are born each year who need treatment in the first year of life for an abnormal development of their heart. This is the reason the Nemours Cardiac Center and Arnold Palmer Hospital came together to establish the Children's Heart Institute.

The physicians who work in the institute are a carefully assembled team of highly experienced individuals from around the globe. This world-class team of physicians, nurses, physicians assistants, nurse practitioners, technicians, and support personnel, combined with state-of-the-art technology, provides a facility that is unparalleled anywhere in Central Florida.

KIDSHEALTH

Nemours also reaches out with www.KidsHealth.org, a Web site dedicated to providing appropriate information and advice for parents, children, and teens from the medical experts of the Nemours Foundation. The site is one of the largest providing doctor-approved information about children and adolescents.

"Our goal is to keep seeking better and safer ways to care for children," says Nathanson. In Central Florida, this goal is becoming a reality because of Nemours Children's Clinic.

NEMOURS CHILDREN'S CLINIC HAS A THREEFOLD MISSION: CLINICAL CARE, EDUCATION, AND RESEARCH, WITH A HIGH STANDARD OF CARE FOR ALL CHILDREN, REGARDLESS OF FINANCIAL STATUS.

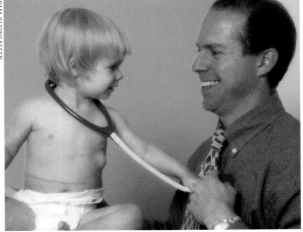

TWO WORLD-CLASS GOLF COURSES DESIGNED BY PROFESSIONAL GOLFER GREG NORMAN—IN TANDEM with an upscale, master-planned community—have put ChampionsGate in the winner's circle as a first-class Central Florida destination resort. After its fall 2000 grand opening, the $750-million ChampionsGate drew high ratings from tourists, business professionals, and golfers from around the world. The resort community features the new international home of the David Leadbetter Golf Academy. When complete, ChampionsGate will also include a four-diamond, luxury resort; a spa; villas; high-end shopping; and exceptional office and R&D sites.

WITH TWO WORLD-CLASS GOLF COURSES DESIGNED BY PROFESSIONAL GOLFER GREG NORMAN AND AN UPSCALE, MASTER-PLANNED COMMUNITY, CHAMPIONSGATE IS MAKING A WELL DESERVED NAME FOR ITSELF AS A FIRST-CLASS CENTRAL FLORIDA DESTINATION RESORT.

As Orlando's premier tourist and commercial development—encompassing some 1,500 acres southwest of Walt Disney World—ChampionsGate welcomes visitors just off its I-4 exit with stately rows of towering palm trees. Sweeping across the ChampionsGate landscape are two 18-hole championship golf courses. The resort also features a 35,000-square-foot clubhouse. David Leadbetter—the instructor of many world-famous professional golfers, including Greg Norman, Ernie Els, and Nick Price—is one of the country's leading golf instructors.

As of 2002, guests will be able to stay at ChampionsGate's 732-room, four-diamond, luxury Omni Orlando Resort. It's a destination ideally suited for meetings and conventions, with 70,000 square feet of meeting space and a 26,000-square-foot ballroom. The development also includes a 10,000-square-foot area devoted to a luxurious spa and six restaurants. A Publix Super Market anchors the development's new, 75,000-square-foot retail center, which will include a wide variety of shops appealing to business and leisure visitors.

ChampionsGate is being developed as a joint venture by Apollo RIDA Development Corp. of Houston and Apollo Real Estate Advisors of New York. RIDA began acquiring tracts of the property as early as 1987; Apollo later added its financial clout to the venture.

The overall project's projected value is estimated at $750 million and is expected to include 4,136 hotel rooms, 1,636 resort villas and apartments, 54 holes of golf, time-share accommodations, and 426,000 square feet of retail space—making ChampionsGate one of the region's largest resort destinations. Ira Mitzner, senior vice president of Apollo RIDA Development, says the resort's location is ideal.

"What we're creating is an upscale destination resort—with all the luxuries of a spa, golf, tennis, and other amenities—that happens to be just minutes from Orlando's tourism epicenter," Mitzner says. "This gateway to Central Florida will be the largest tourist-commercial development outside of Disney World, and its master-planned vision guarantees that the highest standards will be maintained throughout the community."

A TRUE GOLF DESTINATION

To stand out as a golf destination, ChampionsGate has created two golf experiences unlike any others in the Central Florida area. The International Golf Course resembles the traditional links courses of Scotland and Ireland, while the National Golf Course is laid out in the tradition of America's greatest golf destinations.

DESIGNED FOR CHAMPIONSHIP TOURNAMENT PLAY, THE INTERNATIONAL GOLF COURSE AT CHAMPIONSGATE RESEMBLES THE TRADITIONAL LINKS COURSES OF SCOTLAND AND IRELAND.

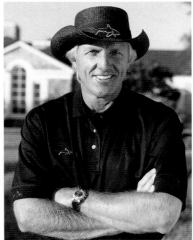

With 18 of the most dramatic and challenging holes in Florida, the International is destined to rank among the top resort courses in the country. The 7,363-yard International course was designed for championship tournament play, and was constructed and seeded to offer a hard, fast-playing surface similar to those found on true links courses. Open and gently rolling like an Irish seaside course, the International has no rough. From fairways edged with dunes, the course continues straight into native grasses. Clusters of pot bunkers, as well as pristine wetlands, complete the course.

ChampionsGate's National Golf Course is a classic layout, with 7,128 yards of play from the tournament tees. Featuring a traditional rough and sweeping white sand bunkers, the National rolls through 200 acres of existing woodlands, wetlands, and orange groves. Unique bunkering, waterways, tree-lined fairways, and intriguing green designs create a challenge for golf enthusiasts. Both courses provide frequent sightings of native birds and wildlife, including herons, ospreys, turtles, and alligators.

Adding further luster to this remarkable golf destination is the David Leadbetter Golf Academy, where Leadbetter and his pro team employ state-of-the-art technology to help analyze guests' golf games and take them to a higher level.

A Public-Private Partnership

RIDA principals David Mitzner and his sons, Ira and Jacob, were able to realize their vision with the backing of Apollo principals William and Richard Mack, Lee Neibart, and John Jacobsson. Key partners include Colonial Bank, Greg Norman, and David Leadbetter. The developers applaud Osceola County and Kissimmee city officials for their part in the public-private partnership that supports ChampionsGate.

The project gives back to the community by creating a tremendous increase in the Osceola County tax base and a special partnership with the Osceola Education Association. The new ChampionsGate Scholarship Invitational golf tournament, which will take place each May, is expected to raise $50,000 each year to support 50 Osceola County high-school students who wish to attend a Central Florida college or trade school.

"It's a win-win situation," Ira Mitzner says. "It's very important that we be part of this community. What better way than to help young people reach their dreams of higher education?"

Uniquely positioned to take advantage of Central Florida's rapid growth, ChampionsGate aims to become one of the world's most exciting and strategically located tourist and commercial developments.

THE SUCCESSFUL DEVELOPMENT OF CHAMPIONSGATE HAS BEEN IN LARGE PART DUE TO PROFESSIONAL GOLFER GREG NORMAN (RIGHT), WHO DESIGNED THE TWO GOLF COURSES, AND DAVID LEADBETTER (LEFT) WHO OPENED THE DAVID LEADBETTER GOLF ACADEMY THERE.

THE NATIONAL GOLF COURSE IS MODELED IN THE TRADITION OF AMERICA'S GREATEST GOLF COURSES.

FOUR POINTS BY SHERATON ORLANDO DOWNTOWN

A LANDMARK WITH A RICH HISTORY, FOUR POINTS BY SHERATON ORLANDO DOWNTOWN IS THE JEWEL OF downtown Orlando. With a spectacular location fronting beautiful Lake Eola, Four Points Sheraton Orlando has been newly renovated in classic Mediterranean style. Combining its prime downtown location with easy access to all of Central Florida's popular attractions makes the hotel the ideal destination for business and pleasure. ❦ With three elegant ballrooms and several smaller breakout rooms totaling 15,000 square feet of meeting space and 250 spacious accommodations, Four Points Sheraton Orlando is the perfect venue for high-level executive board meetings,

WITH A SPECTACULAR LOCATION FRONTING BEAUTIFUL LAKE EOLA, FOUR POINTS BY SHERATON ORLANDO DOWNTOWN HAS BEEN NEWLY RENOVATED IN CLASSIC MEDITERRANEAN STYLE. COMBINING ITS PRIME DOWNTOWN LOCATION WITH EASY ACCESS TO ALL OF CENTRAL FLORIDA'S POPULAR ATTRACTIONS MAKES THE HOTEL THE IDEAL DESTINATION FOR BUSINESS AND PLEASURE.

training seminars, and corporate conferences for up to 400 participants. As it is fast becoming a choice wedding location, the hotel has its own wedding specialist and professional planners charged with helping to make every couple's wedding dreams come true.

The landmark structure was built in 1963 as the Robert Meyer Motor Hotel and was known for many years as downtown Orlando's Harley Hotel. Several expansions later, the hotel had 281 rooms and an exterior that did not do its history or location justice. In 2000, Four Points Sheraton Orlando completed a $10 million redesign that added 44 luxurious executive suites with living rooms and wet bars, striking mosaic designs to the hotel's heated outdoor swimming pool, more banquet space, a state-of-the-art business center, a concierge lounge, and new furnishings and marble countertops in every guest room. The hotel's salmon-colored exterior and arbor gate recall a Mediterranean villa, complete with lush, subtropical landscaping throughout.

"Orlando has been beautifying at such a rapid pace, and we wanted to have the best location in downtown—on Lake Eola," says Javier Callejas, general manager. "We're the most historic hotel in town, and that history is evident here, whether you're in one of the

grand ballrooms or relaxing by the pool with a view of Lake Eola's fountain."

When the Four Points Sheraton Orlando renovation was complete, not only had the structure changed remarkably, but the overall experience, including dining, had transformed as well. The hotel's signature Parkside Restaurant & Lounge earned a stellar review for its breakfast buffet by *Orlando Sentinel* dining critic Scott Joseph. The restaurant also features continental cuisine for lunch and dinner presented by an experienced service staff. Guests can enjoy refreshments in the tropical setting of the hotel's Parkside Terrace and Shades Pool Bar. And, as part of the fastest-growing Sheraton brand in the world, the Four Points hotel's main focus is guest service, and it offers the benefits of the Starwood Preferred Guest Program.

Within walking distance of the hotel are the new Orange County Regional History Center, downtown eateries, nightclubs, and the popular Church Street Station attraction. Also nearby is the Bob Carr Performing Arts Center. Transportation is readily available to nearby golf courses and other area attractions. As a service to the Central Florida community, Four Points Sheraton Orlando provides facilities for the annual Multiple Sclerosis Society of Orlando luncheon.

As the hotel establishes its new identity in one of downtown's most enviable locations, its goal is to attract and retain a well-trained, focused team of hotel professionals who work without fail to exceed guests' expectations. Already, Four Points Sheraton Orlando is establishing a reputation as the Gem of Downtown.

BEGINNING AS A SMALL PUBLISHER OF LOCAL NEWSPAPERS IN THE 1930S, TOWERY PUBLISHING, INC. today produces a wide range of community-oriented materials, including books (Urban Tapestry Series), business directories, magazines, and Internet publications. Building on its long heritage of excellence, the company has become global in scope, with cities from San Diego to Sydney represented by Towery products. In all its endeavors, this Memphis-based company strives to be synonymous with service, utility, and quality. Over the years, Towery has become the largest producer of published materials for North American chambers of commerce.

From membership directories that enhance business-to-business communication to visitor and relocation guides tailored to reflect the unique qualities of the communities they cover, the company's chamber-oriented materials offer comprehensive information on dozens of topics, including housing, education, leisure activities, health care, and local government.

In 1990, Towery launched the Urban Tapestry Series, an award-winning collection of oversized, hardbound photojournals detailing the people, history, culture, environment, and commerce of various metropolitan areas. These coffee-table books highlight a community through three basic ele-

ments: an introductory essay by a noted local individual, an exquisite collection of four-color photographs, and profiles of the companies and organizations that animate the area's business life.

To date, more than 90 Urban Tapestry Series editions have been published in cities around the world, from New York to Vancouver to Sydney. Authors of the books' introductory essays include former U.S. President Gerald Ford (Grand Rapids), former Alberta Premier Peter Lougheed (Calgary), CBS anchor Dan Rather (Austin), ABC anchor Hugh Downs (Phoenix), best-selling mystery author Robert B. Parker (Boston), American Movie Classics host Nick Clooney (Cincinnati),

Senator Richard Lugar (Indianapolis), and Challenger Center founder June Scobee Rodgers (Chattanooga).

To maintain hands-on quality in all of its periodicals and books, Towery has long used the latest production methods available. The company was the first production environment in the United States to combine desktop publishing with color separations and image scanning to produce finished film suitable for burning plates for four-color printing. Today, Towery relies on state-of-the-art digital prepress services to produce more than 8,000 pages each year, containing well over 30,000 high-quality color images.

AN INTERNET PIONEER

By combining its long-standing expertise in community-oriented published materials with advanced production capabilities, a global sales force, and extensive data management capabilities, Towery has emerged as a significant provider of Internet-based city information. In keeping with its overall focus on community resources, the company's Internet efforts represent a natural step in the evolution of the business.

The primary product lines within the Internet division are the introCity™ sites. Towery's introCity sites introduce newcomers, visitors, and longtime residents to every facet of a particular community, while simultaneously placing the local chamber of commerce at the forefront of the city's Internet activity. The sites include newcomer information, calendars, photos, citywide business listings with everything from nightlife to shopping to family fun, and on-line maps pinpointing the exact location of businesses, schools, attractions, and much more.

TOWERY PUBLISHING PRESIDENT AND CEO J. ROBERT TOWERY HAS EXPANDED THE BUSINESS HIS PARENTS STARTED IN THE 1930S TO INCLUDE A GROWING ARRAY OF TRADITIONAL AND ELECTRONIC PUBLISHED MATERIALS, AS WELL AS INTERNET AND MULTIMEDIA SERVICES, THAT ARE MARKETED LOCALLY, NATIONALLY, AND INTERNATIONALLY.

which it continues today, creating community-oriented materials that are often produced in conjunction with chambers of commerce and other business organizations.

Despite the decades of change, Towery himself follows a long-standing family philosophy of unmatched service and unflinching quality. That approach extends throughout the entire organization to include more than 120 employees at the Memphis headquarters and more than 40 sales, marketing, and editorial staff traveling to and working in a growing list of client cities. All of its products, and more information about the company, are featured on the Internet at www.towery.com.

In summing up his company's steady growth, Towery restates the essential formula that has driven the business since its first pages were published: "The creative energies of our staff drive us toward innovation and invention. Our people make the highest possible demands on themselves, so I know that our future is secure if the ingredients for success remain a focus on service and quality."

DECADES OF PUBLISHING EXPERTISE

In 1972, current President and CEO J. Robert Towery succeeded his parents in managing the printing and publishing business they had founded nearly four decades earlier. Soon thereafter, he expanded the scope of the company's published materials to include *Memphis* magazine and other successful regional and national publications. In 1985, after selling its locally focused assets, Towery began the trajectory on

Originally headquartered in London, **Allsport** has expanded to include offices in New York and Los Angeles. Its pictures have appeared in every major publication in the world, and the best of its portfolio has been displayed at elite photographic exhibitions at the Royal Photographic Society and the Olympic Museum in Lausanne.

Voted Photographer of the Year for Asia and Photographer of the Year in the People's Choice Awards, **Bill Bachmann** is a member of the Marquis *Who's Who in the World*, and his travel posters and ads have been published in various countries. He is the author of three books, a screenplay, and numerous magazine articles.

Steve Baker is an international photographer who has contributed to more than 100 publications. With a degree in journalism from Indiana University, he is the proprietor of Highlight Photography, specializing in assignments for clients such as Eastman Kodak, Nike, Budweiser, the U.S. Olympic Committee, and Mobil Oil, which has commissioned seven exhibitions of his work since 1994. Baker is author and photographer of *Racing Is Everything*, and he has contributed to numerous Towery publications.

Specializing in commercial and advertising illustration, **Gary Bender** has photographed for some of the largest corporations in the Central Florida area. He has owned and operated professional photography studios in Ohio, Tennessee, and Kentucky, and was chosen to photograph some of the very first Fairy Tale Weddings for Disney.

Bruce Yuan-Yue Bi has traveled extensively in the United States, Canada, and Central and South America. He is a regular contributor to *Earth Geographic Monthly* in Taiwan and *Photo Pictorial Magazine* in Hong Kong.

A graduate of Southern Illinois University, **Eric Dusenbery**

contributes images regularly to Dimensions Photography.

Owned by Skip Everett and Anne Soulé, **Everett & Soulé** specializes in architectural, residential, commercial, and interior/exterior photography. Everett and Soulé have traveled the country, documenting the professional rodeo circuit and other elements of western culture.

Lee Foster, a veteran travel writer and photographer, has had his work published in major travel magazines and newspapers. He maintains a stock library that features images of more than 250 destinations around the world.

Specializing in photographic and oil portraiture, **Tom Griffin** is the owner and operator of Tom Griffin Studio in Winter Park, and has had prints exhibited at Epcot and other venues around the country.

A freelance photographer, **C. Jordan Harris** specializes in editorial, corporate, and documentary photography. He travels to the Dominican Republic annually to work on a book of photographs documenting his travels.

A contributing editor to *Vacations* and *Cruises & Tours* magazines, and coauthor of the travel guidebook *Hidden Coast of California*, **Dave G. Houser** specializes in cruise/luxury travel, personality, health, and history photography. He has been a runner-up for the Lowell Thomas Travel Journalist of the Year Award and was named the 1984 Society of American Travel Writers' Photographer of the Year.

Owner of Tom Hurst Photography, **Tom Hurst** specializes in commercial/editorial photography for corporate clients. He has contributed images to Nickelodeon, the Kansas City Royals, and AT&T Wireless, and his photos have appeared in *USA Today*, the *New York Times*, and *People* magazine.

Specializing in commercial, stock, travel, sports, and landscape photography, **Alan Knapp** owns Alan

Knapp Photography and has contributed images to AAA, Sprint, Renaissance Cruise Lines, and Rollins College.

Bud Lee studied at the Columbia University School of Fine Arts in New York and the National Academy of Fine Arts. A self-employed photojournalist, he founded the Florida Photographers Workshop and the Iowa Photographers Workshop. His work can be seen in *Esquire, Life, Travel & Leisure, Rolling Stone,* the *Washington Post,* and the *New York Times,* as well as in several Urban Tapestry Series publications.

After studying art in his native Ireland, **James Lemass** moved to Cambridge, Massachusetts, in 1987. His specialties include people and travel photography, and his photographs have appeared in several other Towery publications.

Originally from France, **Raymond Martinot** has contributed images to such books as *Le Louvre, French Castles of Savoy, French Museums, American Art Pottery,* and *In the Oyster Bar.* He specializes in food, museum, architectural, and interior photography, and his work has appeared in *Orlando Magazine.*

Specializing in gallery photography and movie stills, **Anthony Neste** has contributed images to such organizations as HBO, ABC, CBS, NBC, and Hallmark. He has won the New York Professional Photographers of America Best in Show

award and the Art Directors Creativity Award, and has worked for *Sports Illustrated* magazine for 13 years and on HBO's *The Sopranos* for two seasons.

The owner of Silverlake Photo, **James Phillips** has lived in the Orlando area for more than 30 years, contributing images to numerous books, calendars, posters, and magazines. He specializes in nature photojournalism, and won the grand prize in the 32nd Annual Suncoast Photography competition and the 1993 Shelby Gardens Photo competition.

Photophile, established in San Diego in 1967, has more than 1 million color images on file, culled from more than 85 contributing local and international photographers. Subjects range from images of Southern California to adventure, sports, wildlife and underwater scenes, business, industry, people, science and research, health and medicine, and travel photography. Included on Photophile's client list are American Express, *Guest Informant,* and Franklin Stoorza.

Known for her international photography, **Betty Press** has exhibited images from her travels to Africa, Mexico, Central America, and the Caribbean. She was one of 29 artists selected for the 14th Annual Women in the Visual Arts at the Erector Square Gallery in New Haven, Connecticut, in March 2000, and she placed in the top

100 photographers internationally in the 1995 Ernst Haas Awards Competition sponsored by the Maine Photographic Workshops in Rockport.

Having worked in the Orlando area for almost 25 years, **Doug Scaletta** owns Scaletta Photography and specializes in advertising.

Specializing in magazine editorial, advertising, and fine art photography, **Ben Van Hook** has work featured regularly in *Sports Illustrated, Life, Fortune,* and the *New York Times.* He was corecipient of the Pulitzer Prize for photography in 1989, named Kentucky photographer of the year three times, and awarded the 1999 Robert F. Kennedy

Memorial Award in International Photojournalism for a *Life* magazine story.

An editor at the *Orlando Sentinel* for 25 years, **Steve Vaughn** specializes in panoramic photographs of Florida and the tropics. He owns Steve Vaughn Panoramic Photography and has exhibited work at a number of outdoor art shows.

Other organizations that have contributed images include Esquire Photographers Inc., Florida State Archives, and GeoIMAGERY. For further information about the photographers appearing in *Orlando: Sunshine Sonata,* please contact Towery Publishing, Inc.

COPYRIGHT © 2001 BY TOWERY PUBLISHING, INC.

TOWERY PUBLISHING, INC.
THE TOWERY BUILDING, 1835 UNION AVENUE, MEMPHIS, TN 38104

WWW.TOWERY.COM   PRINTED IN CHINA

Orlando : sunshine sonata / introduction by Mike Thomas ; art direction by Enrique Espinosa ; sponsored by the Orlando Regional Chamber of Commerce.
    p. cm. – (Urban tapestry series)
    Includes index.
    ISBN 1-881096-91-2 (alk. paper)
    1. Orlando Region (Fla.)–Civilization. 2. Orlando Region (Fla.)–Pictorial works. 3. Orlando Region (Fla.)–Economic conditions. 4. Business enterprises–Florida–Orlando Region. I. Thomas, Mike, 1954- II. Orlando Regional Chamber of Commerce (Fla.) III. Series.
    F319.07 075 2001
    975.9'234–dc21

                        2001027165

Publisher: J. Robert Towery **Executive Publisher:** Jenny McDowell **National Sales Manager:** Stephen Hung **Marketing Director:** Carol Culpepper **Project Directors:** Lisa McCoy, Tamara Nielson-Pritchard **Executive Editor:** David B. Dawson **Managing Editor:** Lynn Conlee **Senior Editors:** Carlisle Hacker, Brian L. Johnston **Editors:** Rebecca E. Farabough, Danna M. Greenfield, Ginny Reeves, Sabrina Schroeder **Project Editor/Caption Writer:** Stephen M. Deusner **Editor/Profile Manager:** Jay Adkins **Profile Writers:** Pam Brandon, Jennie Hess **Creative Director:** Brian Groppe **Photography Editor:** Jonathan Postal **Photographic Consultant:** Jeanne Euker **Profile Designers:** Rebekah Barnhardt, Laurie Beck, Glen Marshall **Production Manager:** Brenda Pattat **Photography Coordinator:** Robin Lankford **Production Assistants:** Robert Barnett, Loretta Lane, Robert Parrish **Digital Color Supervisor:** Darin Ipema **Digital Color Technicians:** Eric Friedl, Mark Svetz **Digital Scanning Technician:** Brad Long **Production Resources Manager:** Dave Dunlap Jr. **Print Coordinator:** Beverly Timmons

© JONATHAN POSTAL / TOWERY PUBLISHING, INC.

Marilyn Amick   Leroy Manning   Brooke Lundberg   Sarah Carson   RACHEL KUHN

Birgit Delazanos   Karen M. Gratz   Denaé Fluellen   Brianna E. Williams   Melissa Klein

Henry Goode   Sarah Cowen   Leann Hunter   Michael Rozel   Emily Yetzer

INDEX OF PROFILES